THIS STORY of a remarkable woman springs from the memories of scores of people, all of whom have been cooperative in assisting Dorothy Brandon to reconstruct the record of a life. The best source of all has been Mrs. Eisenhower herself, whose memory is exceptionally detailed and accurate. She has given Mrs. Brandon many hours of her time and has been generously helpful in every way, as have Mrs. Eisenhower's mother and sister. Old friends have called back to mind many a half-forgotten scene and episode.

The full-scale biography is informal and casual, in keeping with the winsome personality of its subject, but it has its deeply dramatic moments, and it is warmly alive with stories that will be endearing to every reader.

Mamie Doud Eisenhower: A Portrait of a First Lady is published in Canada by S. J. Reginald Saunders & Co., Ltd. A condensation has been published by newspapers subscribing to the syndicate of the New York *Herald Tribune*.

Mamie Doud Eisenhower

PORTRAIT BY THOMAS E. STEPHENS

Mamie Doud Eisenhower

DOROTHY BRANDON

Mamie
Doud
E*isenhower*

A PORTRAIT OF A FIRST LADY

New York *1954*

CHARLES SCRIBNER'S SONS

IH
McClurg
2.44

FOR

Margaret Thompson Biddle

Contents

CHAPTER ONE — I
WASHINGTON, D. C.
January 20, 1953

CHAPTER TWO — 19
FORT SAM HOUSTON, TEXAS
July 6, 1916

CHAPTER THREE — 44
SAN ANTONIO
1915–1916

CHAPTER FOUR — 73
FORT SAM HOUSTON,
SAN ANTONIO, TEXAS
1917–1918

CHAPTER FIVE — 91
CAMP COLT, GETTYSBURG, PA.
CAMP MEADE, MD.
1918–1919

CHAPTER SIX — III
CAMP MEADE, MD.
1920–1922

CHAPTER SEVEN   126

    CAMP GAILLARD,
    PANAMA CANAL ZONE
    1922–1924

CHAPTER EIGHT   151

    U. S. A. AND FRANCE
    1924–1935

CHAPTER NINE   177

    THE PHILIPPINES
    1936–1939

CHAPTER TEN   202

    FORT SAM HOUSTON, TEXAS
    WASHINGTON, D. C.
    1941–1947

CHAPTER ELEVEN   226

    FLORIDA, WASHINGTON,
    NEW YORK, FRANCE
    1945–1952

CHAPTER TWELVE   245

    WASHINGTON, NEW YORK, PARIS
    1946–1952

CHAPTER THIRTEEN   279

    THE UNITED STATES
    1952

Mamie Doud Eisenhower

Chapter 1

WASHINGTON, D. C.

January 20, 1953

Long after the bright sun of Inauguration Day had set, the occupants of the reviewing stand in front of the White House stayed on to watch the seemingly endless pageantry of the parade that had been winding down from the Capitol since shortly after two o'clock.

The five-hour ordeal wore on the nerves of everyone in the white-pillared pavilion except President Eisenhower and Mamie, his wife. All afternoon the President stood with unwavering erectness at the rail. Even now, in the gloom and chill, his eyes measured every marcher and he waved and smiled with undiminished pleasure. Mamie had scarcely left his side; now and then she would sink down on a chair for five minutes.

It was apparent that this alert woman shared with her husband a sensitive awareness of people as individuals. The marching thousands she seemed to regard with loving intentness as if they were flesh-and-blood kin. Often she recognized a familiar face and would stamp her foot excitedly and call out. A picturesque float, a precise display of close-formation drill, the zip and fervor of a marching tune, and she applauded wildly. Mamie is a woman who releases her emotions. For her the parade was a great and happy adventure, and, since it was in honor of her beloved husband, she let herself go in appreciation.

But the unflagging enthusiasm of the President and his wife was not shared by the million and a half spectators crammed elbow-to-elbow into the last inch of seeing-space along the tree-lined avenues. As night approached, seat-holders and standees became impatient and eyed their watches. All along the line of march—on Constitution Avenue, Fifteenth Street and Pennsylvania Avenue—people started dribbling off to homes and hotels when sunset brought a cutting wind. The first to leave were couples harassed by fretful children, or elderly folk wearied by the excitement and the jostling crowds. The spirits of those who remained ran down-hill in a hurry when the sun vanished. Cheering diminished to token acclaim, and feet were stamped only to thwart numbness. Weary eyes looked beyond the oncoming marchers, hopefully seeking the end of the parade. The public had had enough and wanted to go home.

Most of the dignitaries felt the same way, but if they were in the White House stand, protocol forbade their departure ahead of the President; and so, along with relatives and intimate friends of the Eisenhowers, they had no choice but to endure the long minutes of the raw night. Former President Hoover, who alone was exempt from the enforced waiting, had gone long since. He took himself off while the sun was still high, explaining that he had been warned not to let the pitch of inauguration excitement sap his strength. Mr. Hoover and Mamie had enjoyed a lively time up in the front row; any number of people remarked they had never seen him unbend and laugh so hard.

But that had been Mamie's special brand of magic at work; she carries everyone along in her happy mood. Never has a woman rounded her maturity to more laughter and radiant friendliness. She can wink, make a jest and be "folksy" without losing dignity or a sense of the fitness of the occasion. Spurning conventions, she adapts the amenities to spur-of-the-moment situations. It is the highest form of social grace, and Mamie has

2

it in the highest degree. No one is ever uncomfortable around this dynamic and kindly woman. Rigid etiquette is bent to the physical and mental comfort of individuals, including herself.

After Mr. Hoover bowed himself out of the pavilion, Mamie's great commonsense came to the surface, in such utter disregard for set conventions that next day newspapers across the nation printed pictures of her resting her weary feet. Instead of returning to the front of the pavilion she found a chair in the rear, sat down and slipped out of her shoes. Then she reached down and began rubbing her arches.

The incident would have gone unnoticed except for news photographers prowling around the official stand. They leaped forward when they spied the President's wife half out of her shoes. What a human-interest shot!

Mamie chuckled that of course she didn't mind—every woman in the country would sympathize. Over the click of cameras and the flash of bulbs she made a pun: maybe she shouldn't be caught giving aid and comfort to her arch enemies. There was a craning of official and non-official necks all over the stand. In the hilarity, Mamie winked at her mother, white-haired, dignified, solitary Mrs. John Sheldon Doud, who was braced against a pillar. Mrs. Doud winked back; she understood perfectly that her Mamie, who never had been able to find a comfortable pair of shoes, needed to give her feet a rest.

When the photographers had moved on, Mamie eased back into her black suede pumps and went quickly to the rail, her face impish with amusement. A few seconds later she was gazing with sober eyes at a passing float. It depicted the milestones of her married life: the young years at Fort Sam Houston, Texas; the marking-time years in Panama and the Philippines; the drawn-out, waiting-out years of World War Two; then Columbia University; Paris, and homecoming to the victorious Republican Convention and election in 1952. As the float rolled away she beamed happily at her husband with a devotion that was bride-like.

To observers near her, the moment brought out the special quality of her winsomeness. Mamie Eisenhower is an arrestingly beautiful woman. The vital and mobile loveliness of her fine features and delicate skin eludes the camera. Even color pictures tend to make her appear slightly austere, with the pink-whiteness of a porcelain figurine. Actually, she is a person of warmth and movement and clear, full laughter. Her eyes are a light, bright blue; they gaze with unabashed candor when she speaks or is observing people. In her rare moments of repose they are wide and thoughtful, direct and searching. They never shift from a speaker's face or become clouded with boredom. In compassionate moods, Mamie speaks great understanding through her eyes. But she avoids tears; she almost never cries, even when alone. Slow to anger, but an invariable despiser of gossip, she cloaks her displeasure with blank eyes.

Her full, pleasant mouth never droops or pouts, unless she is grimacing in fun. Then a low chuckle, a ripple of humor rather than a crescendo of laughter, accompanies her mock displeasure. There are times when she pulls out all the stops and shrieks with gusto. Usually these outbursts are in self-ridicule. She cannot abide derision of anyone but herself.

The contours of her broad, firm-jawed face are unmarred by lines, except for fine crinkles that show around her eyes when she laughs. When mildly amused, she wiggles her nose and purses her lips. She shades her favorite exclamation "Goodness" with so many inflections that the word never loses its freshness. In conversation she runs many of her words together and fails to punch her final g's, which overlays her slightly nasal midwest accent with beguiling softness.

In the Presidential stand, Mamie, who is meticulous in her grooming, wore the subdued, monotone clothes in which she had been driven to the Capitol for the ceremony that made her husband President of the United States. A small grey felt hat, with flashes of bright green showing through slashings in the scalloped layers, hid most of her greying hair. Her bangs, outward sign of her personality, rolled like a miniature pompadour at the top of her high forehead, gave her face a touch of austerity. Not much of her grey suit was visible above or below

4

a dark brown mink coat, and the froth of white blouse that filled in the vee of the suit jacket could scarcely be seen. When she raised her slender grey-gloved hands to greet the marchers, a heavily laden charm bracelet tinkled on her right wrist.

Hour after hour the prodigious display had gone on, bigger, noisier and more given to carnival informality than ever before. There were flags, floats, and be-decked automobiles; cowboys and Indians on horseback; prancing drum majorettes; patriotic and fraternal organizations, bravely bright in satin; proud veterans' units, remindful of past wars; mounted police; soldiers, sailors, marines, airmen, West Point cadets, Annapolis midshipmen in close ranks; clattering tanks and field artillery; rubber-tired ambulances, and even padding elephants, symbolic of the victory of the Republican party in the November Presidential election. Bands marched only minutes apart, producing a confusing cacophony of blast and blare. Drums beat and ruffled; cymbals split the air; flags snapped in the breeze.

Above the racket, spectators cheered; children squealed with delight; old men thudded canes and women screamed and waved pennants. In the parade itself the multitude of civilians—men, women and children—who trudged along the pavement or posed on slow-moving floats were also in exuberant spirits. The marchers laughed, sang, chanted and shouted. Some of them broke ranks and cut capers, even to the extreme of a cowboy lassoing the President.

Once an abrupt pall of silence smothered the gaiety. It came when the long muzzle of the 280-m.m. atomic gun swung slowly round the bend of the Avenue at Fifteenth Street. Drawn by a loud-motored vehicle, the great fieldpiece moved at funeral pace over the asphalt, the biggest of big guns ever displayed in public. Spectators with fear-struck eyes spoke in whispers; many shivered and turned away. There was frightened realization on every face; even young children sensed the dreadful portent of the recumbent green-brown hollow shaft of steel, the "long finger of doom". The President's face was inscrutable as he surveyed the tapered length. His wife stared gravely, then pulled her coat closer. Her face did not regain expression until a lively band came by.

When the grey-uniformed West Point cadets executed close-formation drill for the President with scissors-like precision, Mamie Eisenhower's exultation showed her for the wife of a West Point graduate and the mother of another. Her eyes darted over the ranks, seeking Richard Gill, her oldest nephew. Singling out the six-foot-three giant, she made a quick stabbing "o.k." sign with the thumb and third finger of her right hand.

More floats, more bands, more marchers calling "Hi Ike!" "Hi Mamie!" as the sun dropped lower in the west. The next break in the tumult occurred when a decorously robed choral group on a float sang "Mamie," a song popular during the Presidential campaign. With a remembering smile, Mamie stepped forward and waved and called "Thank you," as she had done countless times in the previous autumn from the rear platform of the campaign train, at whistle-stops across the nation.

The tribute had the opposite effect on Mamie's mother. Usually as gay as her daughter, Mrs. Doud's face clouded with sadness. Motioning to her grandson, Major John Eisenhower, Mrs. Doud shook herself free of a lap robe and rose decisively. On the arm of the tall Korean veteran she walked wearily to the rear entrance of the stand and across a boardwalk to the White House.

The President's wife was unaware that her mother had gone until she turned at the conclusion of the singing and saw that Mrs. Doud's chair was empty. Instantly gladness drained from her face and she beckoned to her sister, Mrs. Gordon Moore. Quick consultation shed no light; Mrs. Doud's departure had gone unnoticed also by Mrs. Moore. Repressing a natural impulse to seek out her mother, Mamie asked one of the President's aides to find out quickly if illness had impelled Mrs. Doud to leave. Before the aide was out of sight, John Eisenhower returned to report that his grandmother, jolted by the serenade "Mamie" into full realization of the day's momentous changes, wanted to be left alone in the White House to put her emotions in order

6

and thaw out from the cold. She was not coming back, she said, and asked to be forgotten until the parade was over.

The military phase of the parade was ushered in on a note of high drama by an honor guard of grim, hard men bearing massed colors. As if at a cue, the people in the stands rose. Uniformed spectators snapped to attention, civilian men bared their heads in tribute to the colors and the men. All who bore the flags were fresh from combat in snow-smothered Korea.

For days the press and radio had been reporting that these young warriors, chosen while on active duty with the Army, Navy, Marine Corps and Air Force, were being flown home to represent their comrades in combat at the inaugural. At noon they had flanked the stand at the Capitol while the President took his oath of office. Now they came down the Avenue, shoulders squared, boots crumping in steady cadence, firm hands steadying their wind-swept flags. Abreast of the President, they pivoted with sharp military correctness, yet with a special quality in their bearing, that insouciance of spirit common to men fresh from battle.

The President's tenseness matched the posture of the guard; he seemed inches taller; his firm jaw was resolute. He looked directly at each man, his eyes narrowed with pride and respect. It was a response shared by his wife. She stood drawn very straight, with solemn countenance, a hand over her heart. The cords in her neck twitched, her lower lip trembled, and her eyes glistened with moisture. As the men marched away she regained her composure and joined in the applause.

Now it was night. The hard street lights on the lines of marching men greyed all uniforms to the color of the murk and cast deep and aging shadows on the young faces. Clanking and snorting tanks, motored vehicles grumbling noisily in low gear, somehow added to the eeriness of the spectacle. Only the steady tramp of feet, an occasional service band, the barking commands of officers, dispelled the illusion of wraiths marching.

Mrs. Eisenhower stood beside her husband. Now she was chattering-cold and inwardly distracted by the realization that the hungry and restless children in the stand still could not leave. The original plan had been to provide lunch for the official party at the Capitol after the inaugural ceremony, but a miscarriage had deprived most of the youngsters—and their parents—of even so much as a candy bar since breakfast. Except for one jug of hot coffee, a jug that was not refilled, nothing was served in the stand all afternoon. At five o'clock Mamie's suggestion that more coffee, sandwiches and milk be brought from the White House was put aside by aides who assured her that the parade would be over before the food could be served.

Finally, at ten minutes past seven, the President relaxed. He grinned broadly at his wife and nodded toward a field ambulance. It was followed by two elephants. "Irma" and "Burma" lurched to a standstill in the Avenue precisely abreast of the President. On the signal of their trainer, they wheeled and raised their trunks high in salute; then, bobbing and swaying, they executed a half-turn, dropped their trunks, and padded off into the night, bringing to an end the longest inaugural parade in American history.

Speedily the members of the Presidential party burrowed out of blankets and rose on numbed feet. The President and Mrs. Eisenhower said good-bye to Vice-President Nixon, his wife and their two small daughters, then shook hands with other friends. Calling informally to their relatives to follow them over to the White House for a family reunion, they moved ahead arm-in-arm toward the temporary wooden walk spanning the lawn of the Executive Mansion. The glare of the brightly-lit portico threw their figures into sharp silhouette. Mamie was murmuring confidences, her smiling face turned toward her husband. The President inclined his head to catch his wife's words. Once they paused while he took a firmer grip on her arm.

To those who watched the slow progress of the big man and his moderately tall wife toward their strange new home, the scene held infinite pathos. Behind them were the years of trials and triumphs, culminating in this day's transcending honor. No one could foretell what fresh obligations lay ahead, what self-

8

sacrifice would now be expected of the President and his First Lady.

The ubiquitous Secret Service men stood rooted in the shadows until the Presidential couple crossed the driveway and mounted the steps. There they obligingly faced a covey of news photographers, while the guards closed in at the base of the stairs to keep family and kin, now hurrying over from the reviewing stand, from getting involved in the picture-taking. No one spoke while flash bulbs popped and cameras recorded the high moment. The President, bareheaded and unsmiling, his arm around his wife's waist, seemed withdrawn in mood, and Mamie was serious and without sparkle. Neither attempted to conceal their awareness that they were beginning a grave new cycle.

A photographer called "Thank you, Mr. President," and led the scuttling cameramen away. President Eisenhower, with his arm still around his wife, turned abruptly and guided her past the glass storm doors into the gold and white foyer. It was the first time either of them had crossed the threshold since the White House had automatically become their official home when the President took the oath of his office at noon in the Capitol Plaza.

In the marble and gold hall happiness possessed them at once. While the President took off his coat they smiled and spoke pleasantly to the ushers, as completely at ease as if they were back from a long journey and glad to be among friends once again. The President shrugged out of his overcoat and handed his hat to an usher with a pleasantry. Mrs. Eisenhower was going upstairs, she said, and would not take off her fur coat here. As they moved slowly toward a rear hall they spoke to each man in the line of ushers.

It is amazing how the Eisenhowers charge the air with good will merely by smiling and saying a few words. Individually or as a team, their simple directness never fails to break down barriers of timidity and self-consciousness and to produce a feeling of cordial, mutual interest. Unfailingly they are uncommon-common people, seeking the same uncommon-commonness in others. Commonness, to them, means spiritual unity with all mankind; uncommonness, they believe, is the singular character-istic that makes all personalities interesting. Now the easy, friendly entrance of the President and his wife instantly relaxed the attitude of stiff formality which the White House ushers had assumed as befitting the occasion. Serious faces brightened with pride and respect as the functionaries watched the new heads of the household proceed toward the state dining room.

Mamie, hostess now in her own home, paused briefly in the doorway of the richly ornamented room and ran a practised eye over the appointments of the big tea table. She exclaimed over the beauty of the centerpiece of spring blossoms, then quickly retraced her steps to a nearby elevator. Upstairs, she sought her mother immediately. Mrs. Doud, refreshed from a nap, was having supper in bed, and was eating with appetite. Once more in high spirits, she pointed to her ball dress spread over a chair, saying that she would be up and into the lovely blue garment in no time. Reassured, Mamie became alert to a concern of her own. Had her new ball gown gone astray in its trip down from New York? It was to arrive in a special plywood wardrobe in a motor van transporting other personal effects. The dress and two pairs of gloves and tiny purse were all present and accounted for, said Mrs. Doud—as well they should be after all the fuss and bother that had been going on. Rose Wood, who has looked after Mrs. Eisenhower's clothes for years, had been in earlier and given her a full report, right down to the extra gloves.

Greatly relieved, Mamie hurried across the hall to her small bedroom. There, hanging in breath-taking beauty from a door, was the billowing rose-pink, jewel-spattered dress. Rose, who was waiting, explained that the closet had been too low and cramped to accommodate the regal garment.

Mrs. Eisenhower laid her hat on the narrow bed and hurriedly fluffed her hair and freshened her make-up in the bathroom mirror, there being no dressing table in the cramped little bed-room. Brightly she told Rose not to worry about that; there would be a lot of shifting around once they were settled. Then she went down to get the belated tea party under way.

The party had been one more suppressed worry for Mamie during the parade. Originally planned for five o'clock as an informal reception for cabinet officers and their families and for all the Eisenhower relatives who had come to attend the Inauguration, the affair was threatened with cancellation when word was sent down from the Hill that the Senate was holding up confirmation of Charles E. Wilson as Secretary of Defense. All other cabinet officers had been approved by the Senate and sworn into office; but White House hospitality could not be extended to the President's "official family" while the eligibility of one member was in doubt. Mamie was obliged to send verbal regrets to the other cabinet couples. Loath to visit the same disappointment on relatives, she decided to have the party anyway, for the family.

As the parade went on and on beyond the scheduled ending at five o'clock, it became apparent that the tea would overlap the dinner hour and not everyone would have time to dine and dress for the evening's festivities in reasonable leisure. Since everybody was cold and hungry, Mamie reasoned it would be sensible, no matter what time the parade finished, to fortify the family, the children especially, with plenty of sandwiches and cake before the older people hurried off to get ready for the inaugural parties.

If Mamie was tired she hid it well behind the breeziness of her hospitality. Standing with the President in the doorway of the state dining room, she called to their relatives gathered in small groups in the corridor. The gladness in her voice brought a surge of animation to the tired guests. Weariness forgotten, they quickly formed in line and, laughing and joking, shook hands and offered congratulations. Now Mamie's demonstrative nature really overflowed. She hugged and kissed her kinfolk, made quick asides about a sandwich in the hand being better than two beefsteaks in a restaurant refrigerator, and insisted that the children should detour the receiving line and get something to eat in a hurry.

The President was in gay form too. Right from the start, it was strictly a home-style family party, with cousins, aunts, brothers, uncles, nieces, nephews—each with a husband, wife or parent in tow—all in a mellow mood and all really hungry. They consumed sandwiches and cake, drank coffee, milk, and tea, and didn't turn down the "seconds" offered by waiters weaving in and out of the crowded reception rooms.

The Moores—Frances Doud Moore, Mamie's younger sister, known since infancy as "Mike," and her husband, Colonel Gordon Moore—helped serve their three famished children, Rudolph, Gordon junior and little Mamie, and then retired to the sidelines to drink coffee. Aside from her dark hair worn without bangs and her slightly greater height, "Mike" is a close counterpart of her sister, and is like her also in voice and lively mannerisms. For the moment, however, her bearing showed a worried abstraction, not lost on Mamie. She edged over to her sister, put an arm around her, and assured her there was absolutely nothing to worry about as far as "Mama" was concerned. "Mike's" overcast mood vanished, and in laughing relief she said it was time she gathered up her brood and started for home. The two-mile drive through after-parade traffic congestion might lead to complications, and she did not want fourteen-year-old Gordon to be clock-watching when he outfitted himself in a dress suit for the first time. Since nobody else in the family had to go beyond the downtown hotel district, Mamie agreed that the Moores should not stand on ceremony but should leave at once. The sisters kissed and Mamie released her arm from "Mike's" waist. Then, with a characteristic wave of both hands, she moved into the Red Room, making straight for her son John and his pretty wife Barbara.

John's habitual shyness had dropped away. The grin transfixing his face made him look more like his father. At first glance, father and son seem to resemble each other only faintly, until John's lean face widens in a smile. He is a good three inches taller than the President.

Facing him now under the brilliance of the crystal chandelier in the Red Room, Mamie stood not much more than chest-high to John. At that level her gaze was centered on the narrow bar with a blue rifle pinned on the left breast of his olive-drab blouse, and when she spoke she turned sideways to avoid meeting his eyes. John's combat infantry rifle badge, which she had first seen five days earlier when he arrived for a fortnight's leave from Korea, was still a shock to his mother—and a reminder that in a few days he would be retracing his way across the Pacific for more active duty.

To hide her feelings, she turned to her daughter-in-law, praising Barbara for being, as usual, smart and sensible about the children. Mamie said she was mighty glad that David, Barbara Anne, and Susan had stayed at home near West Point instead of risking colds in the windy pavilion. Barbara blushed with gratification; it was good to know that leaving the children at home had not disappointed her mother-in-law. The young Mrs. Eisenhower is tall, a woman of quiet grace and shyness. Her dark beauty is enhanced by regular features and slightly slanted eyes of deep blue. A Colonel's daughter, Barbara is well-rooted in Army tradition and the hardships of being an Army wife, which may in some measure account for her congenial relationship with her husband's mother. Their affection began at first meeting in 1947, on Barbara's arrival from Europe to be married after a continental courtship during John's tour of duty in Austria, and it has been growing ever since.

Catching sight now of her cousin, James Schaaf, Mamie took quick steps to his side, and with mock concern, peered into his empty coffee cup. Could she get him a refill? Cousin Jim, a bluff, hearty man, was about to accept when a restraining glance from his wife made him change his mind. He took recourse in safe conversation: he and Anna just couldn't get over being asked down for the big doings; it was an honor they would never forget. Cousin Mamie countered with the observation that she was going to be settled in the White House for a space, instead of carting around the world; so she hoped this meeting was the start of closer family ties.

These three had last been together on the hushed occasion of the funeral of Jim Schaaf's mother on a blustery winter day in 1950, just before Mamie and her husband sailed for Paris. This was Aunt Susan, a sister of Mamie's father John Doud. She had married and moved east from Boone, Iowa, along about 1906, when the Doud family had picked up and left Iowa for Colorado. Over the years there has been no visiting back and forth, but birthday presents and Christmas gifts always were exchanged, and occasional letters had kept the family in touch. While Mamie was growing up out West, Jim had graduated from Cornell University with a major in agriculture, had married and settled down in New Jersey, near Bloomsbury.

It was still hard to stand there and realize the White House was Cousin Mamie's home; things like that just didn't happen in a Jersey chicken farmer's family, Jim said. He was glad he had brought Anna down to take in the sights of Washington, but this day strained his credulity; he never figured he'd see the White House even from the sidewalk, much less be asked inside by one of his own family who now called it home. Mamie admitted being a bit baffled too. In spite of all the preparations she had been making since Election Day, standing here right now was like being at someone else's party, she said.

Linking her arm in Anna's, she suggested a quick trip through the first floor, so that her cousin could see all the famous furnishings in the state rooms. Anna demurred: Cousin Mamie had taxed herself enough for one day. But Cousin Mamie would not be dissuaded. Drawing Anna to one of the south windows, she pulled aside the glass-curtains and raised the blind. There was the balcony that former President Truman had built, over a roar of public protest. In Mamie's opinion, the balcony was going to come in mighty handy on hot summer evenings. She had every intention of sitting out there in a rocking chair and enjoying river breezes from the Potomac.

While the two women were studying pictures and gilt mirrors in the Green Room, James Schaaf disappeared; he did not hear his wife gasp with astonishment when she perceived two over-size concert grand pianos, one at each end of the long yellow-and-gold East Room. Never had Anna dreamed pianos were made *that* long. Mamie wrinkled her nose. It would take an athletic musician with extra long arms to get up and down one of the keyboards she said. Personally, much as she liked to play the piano, she thought she could confine her music-making to her own baby grand, which had been moved in upstairs.

Cousin Anna looked the East Room over carefully. The elaborate furniture pushed back against the satin brocaded walls was not her idea of how a room should be arranged. She supposed Cousin Mamie would do a lot of regrouping later on.

Mrs. Eisenhower shook her head. The East Room, in fact all the state rooms on the first floor, must remain as they were; Congressional order barred her from shifting so much as an ash tray. Upstairs, it was different: she could switch furniture to her heart's content, even change room colors if she was displeased with the decorative schemes in any of the family rooms. But all furniture in formal reception rooms and the state dining room was arranged in accordance with historic tradition by the Capital Fine Arts Commission, in order that sightseers who came in droves to the White House would find the rooms just as reproduced on official postcards.

The worst feature of upstairs was the lack of closet space, Mamie said. During her quick look-around with Mrs. Truman in mid-December, the one dark closet in Mrs. Truman's small bedroom made her heart sink. Something was going to happen, and happen fast to that bedroom. Mamie added that she thought she could solve the closet problem by moving out all the furniture and having wardrobes installed to convert the space into a good-sized dressing room. That would mean switching everything in the adjoining sitting room, which offered grand possibilities as a large and comfortable bedroom—once she got the plum-colored rug and mauve draperies out of sight and adopted her favorite pink and green color scheme.

The two strolled back to the dining room to find James Schaaf swapping farm jokes with the President. Farms, Mamie told them, were not in her joke book for the good and sufficient reason that one of these days she was going to get busy and start her long-deferred project of remodeling their farm house at Gettysburg, Pennsylvania, into a permanent family home. It was going to be a big job, requiring the building of additions on each side of the square frame house; but maybe after White House housekeeping got shaken down, she could start doing something about the Gettysburg place, which there never had been time to visit, much less recondition, since she had put the deed of ownership in a safety-deposit box in 1950.

When the Schaafs took their leave, Mamie kissed Anna goodbye, reminding her the latch would always be off at the White House, and the President seconded his wife's invitation with equal affection and interest. Other good-byes came rapidly as the party broke up, and with each of them the Eisenhowers affirmed their desire for continued association with their many relatives. Seeming unwearied by the demands of the last nine hours of successive formalities, and not in the least concerned about the big evening ahead, they talked on with quiet ease to their departing guests.

Inauguration Day brought many instances of Mrs. Eisenhower's consideration for well-wishers. There were unobtrusive gestures of appreciation, such as her choice of the little white hat tipped with brilliants which she wore to early morning services at the National Presbyterian Church. The hat had arrived in the flood of gifts channeled to her hotel room the day before Inauguration. Mamie, who never lets anyone else open her packages, was touched with pleasure the moment she lifted the little white pillbox from its tissue-paper nest. Hats are her weakness. Here was one so bright, so crisp and dainty that she succumbed instantly, knowing instinctively it would become her. A quick try-on, and she announced she would wear it to church next morning instead of a grey model created by a famous New York milliner. The hat, made by a young Virginia housewife, was accompanied by a note that asked her to wear the homemade creation for good luck on Inauguration Day.

Mrs. Eisenhower is extremely fashion-conscious, and pinpoint neat in her dressing. Her choice of becoming clothes has made her the first wife of a President to be included by fashion designers among the "ten best-dressed women" in the nation. If the gift had not been modish, if its lines had been unflattering, she would have put it aside in spite of the good luck involved. But she confesses that she is open to the persuasion of good-luck omens.

There is the story of the "Inauguration handkerchief." It was supposed to be a big secret, and Mrs. Eisenhower was annoyed when the tale leaked out. But she blamed herself; she had confided to too many people, she said, her intention to secrete the lace-frilled, embroidered square in a stocking for good luck on Inauguration Day. The handkerchief's maker, an elderly New York woman, had suggested that it be worn with her ball gown somewhat in the tradition of the "old-new-borrowed-blue" bride's superstition. Since the Inauguration ranked second in importance to her marriage day, the idea caught Mrs. Eisenhower's fancy, and even when women reporters pounced on the prospect she did not change her mind.

Mrs. Eisenhower admits to having several pet superstitions—more habit than anything else—including one that has to do with elephants. She has worn an elephant hair ring since 1929 as a guard between her wedding circlet and diamond solitaire. The original band of hair, purchased in Paris when such rings were the fashionable rage as good-luck talismans, wore out two years ago, but as good luck would have it, she was again living in Paris and was able to get a replacement. She also has several charm bracelets that jangle with a bewildering assortment of bangles, each commemorating an important milestone in her married life. She wears the keepsakes intermittently, choosing occasions when she will not be among strangers who might be distracted by the tinkling mementoes. All during the campaign Mrs. Eisenhower was never without a heavy gold bracelet from which was suspended an "Ike" good-luck cloverleaf, and she tried to display the charm whenever she was photographed. Now it has been put away with other keepsakes in the silver, heart-shaped jewel-box that has been on all of her many dressing tables during the past thirty-nine years.

Mamie thinks that when people talk about "Eisenhower Luck" and mean just her husband, they fail to realize that she's the really lucky member of the family.

"I'm the one who's had all the luck," she explained one day just before the Inauguration. "I married Ike."

Chapter 2

FORT SAM HOUSTON, TEXAS
July 6, 1916

It was a hot, sunny and dusty July morning when the engineer of the huffing locomotive of a travel-stained train from Abilene, Kansas, braked to a grinding standstill beside a landing platform in the Missouri-Kansas-Texas Railroad Station in San Antonio.

There was a mighty sigh of steam. Sleeping car porters handed down valises and suitcases to platform handlers; wilted, baggage-laden passengers straggled from day coaches; waiting friends and relatives surged through the hubbub while trainmen elbowed through the milling crowd toward the station master's office.

A bright welcome of laughter and shrill squeals caused most of the preoccupied throng to pause momentarily and watch a young couple descend the steps of a grimy sleeping car into the outstretched arms of a greeting committee—a boisterous group of young army officers and pretty women.

The shyly-proud, just-married air of the handsome grey-suited man and the slender girl in a white silk dress and floppy hat showed no trace of awkwardness. It was plain that Lieutenant and Mrs. Dwight D. Eisenhower didn't mind in the least that their homecoming was something of a public demonstration. Ever since Ike had sent the wire from Abilene saying they would arrive on the early train, they had suspected they would get this sort of welcome. After all, these friends had missed out on a lot of fun because they had chosen to marry six days before in distant Denver, and had stopped over for a visit with Ike's folks in Kansas. If their own special gang from Fort Sam had been subdued, Ike and Mamie would have felt embarrassed. As it was, they too went overboard with high spirits and joined in the unrestrained whooping and shrieking. Mamie returned hug for hug and kiss for kiss. Her brand-new husband showed he was as good a back-slapper as his infantry officer pals and gallantly accepted the kisses bestowed by their wives.

When the first raucous sallies tapered off to loud chatter, the bride and groom recovered sufficiently to turn their hand luggage over to a bug-eyed porter and tell him to wait at the baggage room until they came and claimed their trunks. The Eisenhower party dawdled on the way to the baggage room, knowing that it would take time to locate their Denver trunks. They could have dallied much longer for that matter, and stopped for coffee in the lunch room too; and so avoided being what Mamie called "the most previous and perspiring bunch of clock-watchers in all San Antonio."

During the half hour they hung around the baggage room, the heat and let-down from the earlier excitement wilted everyone. Mamie and Ike had been natty on arrival, but now the sheer fabric of Mamie's dress clung in damp blobs to her arms and shoulders and the deep dip of hair on her forehead sagged lank and wet and would not stay in place when she touched a gloved finger to the waves. Mamie knew she looked as if she had just left a Fourth of July picnic. Ike was in no better shape. His pin-striped, double-breasted suit was creasing darkly and the starch in his collar oozed in wrinkles. He kept his hat on the back of his head so he could wipe his forehead with a soggy handkerchief.

After the first fifteen minutes of trying vainly to identify their trunks among the stored baggage, Ike began to fear that the railroad had routed the trunks to another city. Instead of keeping his anxiety to himself, he confided his misgivings to his friends, who began thinking of all manner of calamities.

Mamie, in addition to worrying about the baggage, was tortured by her shoes whose tight lacings cut into her insteps. She suggested to her women friends that they either sit in the waiting room or go out to the automobiles that had brought the crowd in from Fort Sam. The automobiles won. In the glare and dust and seething heat outside the station the hooded car crowded with women became a hotbox of discomfort. Mamie, battling a first-class case of the jitters over the missing baggage, tried gamely to divert everyone's thoughts from the heat by holding forth on the details of her wedding. She was well into a description of her bridal grown, when the men charged out of the station, shouting the good news that all baggage was present and accounted for, and was being loaded on a truck. Her feminine audience broke up and was distributed quickly into the three other cars.

Ike jumped in next to Mamie but he kept a sharp eye on the baggage-laden truck that was to bring up the rear of the cavalcade.

The car owners, each armed with a heavy brass starting handle, stepped forward and cranked their well-worn automobiles. After the first whizzbang racket had subsided to a steady grumble, and each chassis had rattled and jounced into a steady tinny beat, each driver withdrew his crank handle, flung it on the floor of the front driving compartment and edged warily behind the shimmying wheel. Then followed the ritual of advancing the spark lever carefully, while listening for the wheezing that would signal expiration of the accelerated motor. But success crowned all efforts that morning. One by one each car jolted fiercely, a signal for the passengers to settle back and prepare for more jolts as the engines were shifted from low gear into top speed.

On that long ago July morning, the caravan of honking and snorting automobiles traveled through the business section of San Antonio at the mad speed of thirty miles an hour. Zigzagging between mule carts and horse-drawn carriages, grazing the ribs of burdened donkeys, choking pedestrians with eddies of dust, the motorcade swayed and bumped over the rutted streets and swooshed on toward suburban Government Hill and the confines of Fort Sam Houston. Affronting the old-world air of Spanish serenity that still dominated the community, the drivers chose to risk a smash-up rather than court engine failure. Shifting to low gear often caused an engine to flutter and die with a finality that no amount of roadside tinkering could overcome. In those days, once you got a motor in high, you kept it there.

Ike and Mamie's friends had planned to cover the seven miles to Fort Sam in time for mid-morning coffee. On they raced through the sparsely settled residential area north of town. *Wham!* into a chuck hole. The passengers bounced like corks. Bumpity-bump, over the washboard surface of the dusty highway. *Whoosh!* around corners, with everyone leaning on the turns.

Mamie clutched her hat and was thankful that Ike's protecting arm prevented her from bouncing too high and possibly hitting one of the ribs in the canvas top. At every turn Ike swiveled his head to glance backward at the baggage truck.

Careening around a final corner, the automobiles went into the straightaway of Grayson Avenue. Without slackening speed they roared past the prison-like stone walls and iron gates of the Fort Sam quadrangle. Klaxon horns going full blast, the procession charged between the gate posts of Infantry Row, sped down the company street, circled the polo field, and clankity-clanked back toward a two-story building some fifty feet inside the main gate. With thrashing gears and whining brakes, each vehicle bucked to a standstill in an orderly line. So ended the epic ride, but not the hilarity.

The clamorous escorts of the bride and groom hustled to the sidewalk and with sweeping courtliness assisted their guests of honor to the pavement. Up and down the street, neighbors spilled out of the long frame buildings and hurried to join in the fun. The handshaking could have gone on indefinitely in the hot sunshine, but several of the motorcade drivers whistled from the porch and announced it was time to start unpacking. The newlyweds backed across the sidewalk, then turned and took the steps two at a time. Ike literally lifted his bride up the shallow stairs. Whirling to call good-bye, they faced head-on into an earsplitting wall of sound. Besides the cheering, the horns were going full blast in a spontaneous "shivaree." The recipients acknowledged the tribute with a few good-natured whoops, then swung gaily into the narrow hall that led to their first home.

What a day! What neighbors! What a ride!

The jammed living room reminded Mamie of a train depot during a holiday rush. Islands of luggage everywhere; more than that, an assortment of droopy humanity slumped down on trunks and suitcases (or on the floor just as they plopped); no laughter or small talk now; just set smiles and half-closed eyes. The fun was over for the members of the morning's motorcade. They were too spent even to grunt. Ike announced he was tackling the luggage, but there was no responsive gesture of aid.

Picking her way around the recumbent forms of her friends, Mamie pushed back one panel of the sliding doors in the rear wall and went into the bedroom. The emptiness was a shock. A chest of drawers, four green walls, two windows, two doors—that was the bedroom. Anyway, it was fresh and clean; the floors shone from a new coat of shellac; the walls had recently been painted pale green; a light cord, with one small bulb, dangled from the ceiling. Mamie peeped around a lowered window shade: only trees and some wooden sheds. Then she tugged at a door. When it yielded, she stepped into the bathroom and was taken aback by the cramped arrangement of the fixtures. At least, she told herself, the tile ran halfway up the walls to meet spotless, cream-colored paint.

Back in the bedroom she looked for the closet. The second of the doors yielded easily, disclosing a small recess. One glance confirmed her fears; they would never be able to wedge their clothes into that space. That would mean cluttering the room up with trunks! Her gay heart banished this first worry.

There was still the living room to inspect. Why, those two lovely, lovely straight mahogany chairs—and that oblong mahogany table! she chirped to Ike. So the Army did start you housekeeping with more than a chest of drawers. Mamie's eyes shifted to built-in bookcases on each side of a gas grate fireplace. Ike, watching her closely, called over to ask if she didn't agree that the bookshelves were extra special. You bet they were, she replied, they'll hold plenty. How about the mirrored mantel and the dusty-rose tile below—home-like set-up, wasn't it? Be cozy on winter evenings—if the gas didn't smell.

The guests stopped playing possum and stood up; could they help unpack or should everybody clear out? One of the wives remembered it was past coffee time and offered to rush a pot over from her quarters, but Mamie said not to bother; she and Ike could wait until lunch. The crowd thinned rapidly. Two bachelor officers stayed to help the bridegroom shove the trunks into the bedroom. Lordy, the trunks weighed a ton; what did they have inside, bricks? No, not bricks, or lead pipe, or books; mostly apartment fixings, said Mamie.

Ike outlined a plan of action. First he would go out with the fellows and find some coffee—sort of felt the need of a mug of brew—then he'd go by his old room upstairs and collect his gear. Might as well get that down and fit it in with the rest of the stuff. Fine idea; fine idea—Mamie had no chance to speak a word, so fast did the men clear out.

With a gasp that could have been the forerunner of tears, she closed herself in the bedroom. Sitting on a trunk, she bent down and impatiently unlaced her high kid shoes. As soon as her toes were free, she calmed down. It was good to get out of that armor. Wiggling her toes, she stood up, unpinned her hat and hopped across the slick floor. Up on the closet shelf went the hat. Off came her dress. She hung it on a peg and darted into the living room to drag back a suitcase.

Her husband and his friends were absent long enough for her to slip into a blouse and skirt and low-cut shoes, and to unpack and arrange toilet articles in the bathroom. She was baffled not to find soap-dishes, and the doll's-size medicine cabinet would not hold half of the jars and bottles she tried to jam on the shelves.

When the men thumped in laden down with Ike's gear, Mamie gazed at the strange assortment of articles with the fascinated intensity of a little girl before a Christmas tree. In addition to uniforms, boots and shoes, a service revolver, dress sword, hats, caps, underwear, knickknacks and books, Ike's possessions included a ponderous camp bedding roll. Everything was dumped in a heap on the floor, except the uniforms which Ike carried to the bedroom with loving care.

Mamie sized up the sausage-shaped bedding roll and said she was glad there was a musician in the family if she had to live with *that*.

Ike's friends looked bewildered. Was she about to trot out a bugle or drums? Goodness, no! The piano was her specialty. The piano? Yes, the piano. Well, what on earth did a piano have to do—? Mamie wrinkled her nose and sauntered into the bedroom to see what Ike was doing with his uniforms. Ike was doing all right; he had squeezed all the well-filled hangers on to the clothes bar in the closet. Mamie asked just where would she hang her dresses. He looked blank, then worried; they hadn't counted on buying a wardrobe, but he said he supposed they'd have to get something—she couldn't keep her clothes in a trunk.

It would have to be a something, not a wardrobe, she replied, their furniture budget could not be stretched to include such an expensive extra. Moist and mussed as he was, Ike perked up. He didn't want to rush things, but wouldn't it be a good idea to call quits on the unpacking and get along downtown to a furniture store before lunch? His bride's eyes gleamed happily. Yes, they'd better get along to Stower's if they expected to have a bed to sleep on by night.

Two couples who each owned an automobile turned up again in time to provide transportation and their company. Ike balked at another motorcade, so they promised to drive the cars business-like as all-get-out; no speeding, no Klaxons. How was that?

The two automobiles containing eight young people—the bachelors insisted on being included—left Fort Sam without fanfare and thrashed and bounced toward San Antonio in the blinding mid-day heat at a pace that was more in harmony with the city's slow-moving traffic.

Indian-file, the group snaked slowly into the gloom of the big store. Ike, in the lead, braced a salesman, then fell back with Mamie for a promenade down long aisles of furniture spaced as neatly as soldiers on parade. Ike and Mamie knew by heart exactly what they were going to buy; more important, they knew exactly how much they could spend. They kept their eyes forward, so as not to be tempted by large, expensive items.

With grave formality they examined over-stuffed easy chairs offered at reduced prices. Those green ones looked all right. Was the armchair roomy enough for Ike's big frame? Yep, perfect. How—how much? *Ouch*, kind of steep. The salesman guaranteed the mohair as being best quality; the hardwood frames built to last a lifetime. Mamie chose a rocker with green cushions.

Now a bed. The salesman suggested that brass was richer looking; it didn't cost much more than wood. Brass it would be. Next, a spring and mattress. One of the wives cautioned against inferior quality; nothing worse than a caved-in mattress and springs, she said. The salesman prodded and drove his fist hard into mattresses, praised coil-spring construction and strong steel frames. Ike decided to do his own testing. He sat down hard on several models, then beckoned to his friends. Let everybody get in on the testing! The men needed no urging, but the women stood off to one side trying to decide whether to wait out the horseplay or retreat in dignified silence. Up and down; creak, wham! The more the men bounced, the louder they laughed. The salesman became uneasy. United States Army officers shouldn't carry on like small boys, the girls said. Boys nothing, serious testing was in progress. Whang! That's the best one; didn't sag under all of us!

The wives said enough was enough, they weren't going to be party to this nonsense another second. What if a colonel's wife happened along? Besides, Mamie wanted to pick out a dressing table. All right—you girls go ahead—we just want to be s-u-r-e.

Mamie was in stitches. She would never have believed Ike would let go like that. He was a riot! Funny, but all along she had thought of him—West Pointer that he was—as a duty-and-die character. Just showed you never knew a man until you married him. Ike was the most wonderful—She pulled her thoughts back and hurried after her women friends. By then they were cooing over a Circassian walnut table with triple mirrors. Wasn't it divine? Mamie suppressed her delight for fear it would be priced beyond her reach. Plenty of drawer space, fine finish, well matched wood, the salesman said. A table fit for a queen, but not queenlike in price. Mamie read the moderate figure on the tag and nodded happily.

Yes, that was all for now. If the men were through "testing" the bill could be added up.

Ike said he thought any spring and mattress that failed to sag under a four-man bounce would probably give lifetime service, and offered a final demonstration.

Any chance of getting the purchases out to Fort Sam before night? Sure, sure; take the stuff right off the floor; we'll get the horse van started right after lunch, promised the salesman. Then let's have the bill. Mamie took the itemized statement, added it at a glance and opened her purse. She counted out the exact change in wedding gold pieces and some greenbacks from her bridegroom's savings.

Ike did not interfere. A good business woman, Mamie; believed in budgeting everything. She had figured out what it would cost to set up housekeeping when they were first engaged. See how she put the receipt away. Hard to believe she wouldn't be twenty until November; here she was, a veteran householder already. Beautiful, sensible, smart, a dollar watcher. Ike came out of the clouds, cupped one of his wife's elbows in the palm of his big hand and led the procession out of the store.

A sidewalk conclave developed at once. Some problems had to be solved. Everybody was hungry—you bet! Was it past mealtime at the Fort Sam officer's mess? Yes. Restaurant food came too high? Sure did. All right! How do we eat? Simple. Stop at a grocery store on the way out; buy bread, sandwich fixings—maybe some cake.

The picnic lunch served in the Eisenhower living room was a big success. One wife brought over her electric percolator; so coffee flowed all afternoon. Great gadget that percolator; made coffee as quick as plugging in an electric iron. Ike thought they should get one. Mamie wrinkled her nose. Gadgets cost plenty, she said, and didn't always work—still, Ike and his coffee-at-all-hours—maybe it was a good idea.

Eating and talking were secondary to work that afternoon. At the start of full-scale unpacking, the bride and groom were showered with free advice that made little sense, so they told their friends to stop butting in and to help get the rugs down and the drapes and curtains hung. Ike dug down in a trunk and came up with the red Khiva oriental for the front room and a silky pale green broadloom carpet for the bedroom.

The luxurious floor coverings were not wedding presents, Mamie explained; they'd been used in her home for years. Her mother let her "rescue" them from attic storage. Mrs. Doud had also passed on the four pairs of Brussels net curtains. They looked brand new, like something straight from the Ritz, don't tell us different, declared one of the girls, bunching a panel on her head like a bridal veil. Ritz, nothing, retorted Mamie; the curtains had been in the Doud hall and parlor as long as she could remember. Besides, nobody with an ounce of sense would want hotel curtains. All right, all right; we were kidding. All the same they were better than anything covering windows up on Generals' Row.

Ike proved he was a good man on a ladder. He fussed over evening up the gathers as if he had hung curtains all his life. The new dark red drapes, chosen to pick up the red in the Khiva rug, were badly wrinkled from packing but he hung them anyway.

The living room bookshelves were life-savers. Family pictures on the top row; below, Ike's books and alarm clock; Mamie's desk set; some porcelain bowls and vases and a few fancy boxes. Also lumpy packages wrapped in newspaper. Household linens were stacked on the table. Here's a rose-colored counterpane. A classy touch with the green carpet, observed one of the bachelors. Pity it would hide those lace pillow shams—or would it? Yes, it would. The shams were wedding gifts, might get turned into table covers.

Five o'clock, and no sign of the furniture. Everyone was watching the clock and glad of an extra cup of coffee. Ike kept dodging out to the porch and craning his neck up the street. Mamie stocked up the dresser, refused to become edgy, and put the overflow of bathroom and toilet articles on windowsills. Still things to put away! Now if the dressing table would only come; but *goodness*, it wouldn't be any real help so far as all those clothes hooked over the doors on hangers were concerned. The men got around to disposing of the empty trunks in the entrance hall. The women chattered. Still no furniture!

Ike said the bedding roll would do for him, but Mamie would have to have a cot—if one could be wangled. Before a decision was reached on the most likely source of a cot, Ike held up his hand for silence.

Whoa! What was that? Horses! The van? He tore out on the porch, and yelled back. It sure was the van. And the driver had a helper!

Easy with those springs around the door! No use chipping the paint before we have to. Yes, the bed goes in there. Mamie took command; her clear blue eyes caressed each proud new possession. The bed was a space-eater in the room; it crowded the dressing table by the windows. Wasn't the table beautiful! she demanded over and over. Her husband strode in and out, telling her everything was great. He praised the chairs, remarking on the rightness of the green mohair. Amateur furniture-shoppers, they beamed over their first purchases.

Somebody reminded the happy couple that it was getting near time for chow. In a flutter of farewells their friends hurried away.

Alone for the first time since they stepped off the train, the bride and groom sat back in their chairs and sighed contentedly. It was wonderful to be so well on the way to being settled. Plenty of odds and ends left undone, but by tomorrow when Mamie had a chance to work unimpeded by visitors, the disarray of clothing in the bedroom and the cluttered bookcases would be less confusing. She felt there was no use broaching the subject of more storage space when they were both tired and hungry.

Dinner was a typical Army menu served in the small, very hot dining room of the makeshift Officers' Club just up the street. Meat and potatoes, plenty of greasy gravy; a sad grey-green vegetable; a "gloppy" pudding smothered in a pale yellow sauce. Mamie barely touched the meal. Her husband ate mechanically. This was the day-in-day-out food he had warned her about; the food that would cost them sixty dollars a month. Sixty dollars! Mamie did rapid subtraction. A big chunk of Ike's $166.67 paycheck would be wasted on this offensive food. Besides, if she was unable to eat, she'd get sick—but bother the problem! This wasn't the time to worry. Maybe she would be able to fall into her husband's pattern and eat to satisfy hunger.

In the late twilight, Lieutenant Eisenhower and his bride, shoulders touching, walked slowly toward the low frame building —so very like a barracks—that was to be their home for many months. Pausing in front of the steps, they looked for the first star. There it was, low in the west, between the gateposts. Bright and beautiful as an altar candle. Their star! Mamie made a wish. Her rich, low voice repeated, whisper-soft: *Star-light, star bright. First star I've seen tonight. I wish* —— At the jingle's end, she pressed her eyelids tight shut, then told herself wishing on a star was childish.

"It was silly of me to wish. I had Ike and I knew I could never wish for anything greater than his love."

Next morning, at the sound of reveille, Mamie stirred, dimly aware that her husband was already cat-footing around, dressing by easy stages. He told her to rest a while longer, but just remember to wander over to breakfast before the mess closed at eight. He was reporting back on duty, so he was making an early start.

A fellow could never tell. With all those rumors floating around about America being drawn into the European war, new orders might have come.

Orders! Leave! Ike in suntans, "a spiffy soldier if there ever was one." Her husband, but a soldier, subject to duty. Mamie sat up. Army wife, wasn't she? Well, lying in bed was not for her.

After breakfast, she began her housekeeping in earnest. First there was the bed to make. Oh, dear, that was going to be a tussle. Last night Ike had pulled the sheet drum-tight in a jiffy. With his training, he wasn't going to approve of her bed-making. Still, it looked pretty smooth once she had the pink cover on top. A few more lessons and she'd have the West Point system down pat, but now there were other more important matters, chiefly identified with shopping for bookcase curtains. She laid plans to go to San Antonio in a jitney bus.

What a ride for five cents. What a ride! Stop and start; pick up and deliver. Soldiers, shoppers with small children, old folks, everyone polite and sorry about the tight squeeze.

Now let's see, where should she get out? Better make it the St. Anthony Hotel, that would be near the music shop, and only a short walk from Joske's department store.

Mamie knew San Antonio well. Every winter for the past six years, she had been a seasonal visitor with her family. The big white house they rented annually, out McCullough Street near Fort Sam, was her second home. Bigger than the house her parents owned in Denver, it had the added delight of a sweep of porch around both sides and the front. Almost like the deck of a ship, that porch, and much more secluded. Ike had done most of his courting on the porch; no wonder she was thinking about it now.

This was Mamie's first excursion alone in a jitney. Most times in the past when she went into town, it had been with Mrs. Doud and the girls, with Papa Doud at the wheel of the family Packard. Last season Mama freighted her electric brougham from Denver. It wasn't speedy or noisy, and the springs, covered with plum-shaded broadcloth, cushioned every bump—just like sitting in a porch rocker. Mama didn't mind San Antonio traffic a bit, and enjoyed weaving silently around the busy shopping district "smooth as duck's feathers." She would press a bell in the end of the steering bar, waiting with a smile for pedestrians to recover from their bewilderment. Women almost never drove, and the brougham, quiet as a bicycle, was the town's curiosity. Now, in the jitney that must have been the worst rattletrap in Texas, Mamie longed for the easy-riding brougham. But at least the jitney didn't stall during the forty-five minutes required to reach the St. Anthony Hotel.

Mamie went rapidly up the street, turned into a piano store, and plunged into the business of renting a piano. She tried several shiny-cased pianos before deciding on one with mahogany woodwork. The rental was five dollars a month, quite a dent in the family budget, but Ike had insisted on the extravagance. In fact, he didn't consider it an extravagance at all, even suggesting how useful it could be if the piano was slung cater-corner in the living room. Chances were, he said, they could hide enough stuff behind the piano to offset buying a wardrobe. Mamie knew this was impossible, but she went ahead and rented the piano.

In those days, Joske's was San Antonio's best-stocked department store. Mamie made straight for the drapery section and had the salesman drag down bolts of curtain material. No, red was out, she said. Enough red in the living room. Patterns or brocades wouldn't do either. How about dark green poplin? inquired the clerk. Nice and serviceable, easy to sew. Dark green poplin it was. About eight yards would do nicely. Did she need matching thread and needles? She nodded solemnly, veiling the worried look in her eyes. The little man behind the counter must not discover she was buying her first case of needles and spool of thread.

"I can't cook, I can't make a decent bed, I can't sew; I might as well be back in kindergarten," Mamie told herself. "But I will. You bet I will!"

Her mood quickly changed as she took the parcel and went

32

out to hail a jitney. If it took her the rest of the year, she was going to make those curtains single-handed!

Hot and dusty, Mamie fitted the key in the lock of her door. She was tired and hungry and there wouldn't be a crumb in the apartment. Oh, wouldn't there! A package of doughnuts, several bottles of soda pop and a hand of golden bananas lay on the table. Ike had been home. Thoughtful, mind-reading Ike. Why, there was even a bottle-opener. She ate hurriedly, her mind busy with the problem of getting the curtain material cut into lengths.

A heavy knock on the door announced the arrival of the man with the piano. Yes, it went over there, out from the corner. Thanks.

The piano hid the bedding roll all right—and quite a few other things, like Ike's boots, rain poncho, old football uniforms and canvas carryalls. Thank goodness that stuff was out of the way!

Late in the afternoon the bridegroom breezed in. He beamed approval of the piano. Swell, just swell! Now we're really settled. The curtains would be fine, just fine. Might as well get the rods up. Rods? Yes, rods. A pause. "Forgotten," confessed Mamie.

She steered the conversation to her husband's day. How had things gone? Fine. No change in orders. Going back to night duty with a military police detail in town; same old grind, keeping an eye on spreeing soldiers. Not too bad, all things considered; be around home all day, help get the apartment orderly. Mamie's face went blank.

"Whoa, brighten up, take a look at this Denver mail!" her husband said briskly.

A letter from Mama. Papa had written too. Mamie rushed through the pages, handing them over to Ike. Then a penciled up-hill, down-hill page. Bless nine-year-old "Mike" for such a fine outburst of sisterly affection. "Buster" had tacked on a postscript, more young-ladyish—it should be; "Buster" was twelve. Both sisters missed her.

Mamie's thoughts enfolded her family. Was ever a girl blessed

33

with such a dear, wonderful family. Now they loved Ike just as much. Lucky, lucky, lucky!

At day's end, the bride and groom ate an early and unappetizing meal at the officer's mess and returned to their quarters to sit around until it was time for Ike to go on duty. Wasn't the food downright awful? Let's have some music and forget it. Mamie played a few rippling melodies, only to stop short in the middle of a measure. Her husband had come out of the bedroom dressed for duty. Goodness, that pistol and cartridge belt! Mamie tightened. Was it show, or protection? Not a thing in the world to worry about; just that regulations required side-arms. She should go to bed early, he advised. Sometimes it was almost daylight before the patrol wagon brought him back to Fort Sam.

Mamie took small comfort in Ike's parting suggestion. She'd write letters, she told herself; rearrange the book shelves; maybe start sewing the curtains. Bunched in a chair, her hand shading her eyes from the bright, ceiling light, she toed the rug as her mind clicked.

Why did aloneness have to be stood up to right away? Night aloneness. Empty chairs; silent rooms; the black, still out-of-doors; creaking floor boards. There seemed to be nothing to give a young heart courage except the piano. For over an hour she played, softly, musingly—the well-loved popular melodies that Papa, Mama, the girls and Ike (after he started coming around regularly) had sung so many times. What a voice Papa had; how he ripped through gay tunes. And Mama, playing the mouth organ—and "Buster" bowing the violin.

Mamie played by ear. She'd never taken a lesson in her life, and was proud of it. Her tempo was good, and she was snap-fast at picking up new ballads and ragtime. She'd learned Army songs too, because Ike liked them. A self-styled parlor performer, she found roaming over the keys as much fun as dancing. Well, almost as much fun; for Mamie would rather dance than eat. Ike was a superb dancer too.

Mustn't play too long—might disturb the neighbors; besides, Ike said get to bed early. Time had flown as fast as her fingers.

She stood up and closed the piano. The lid hit sharply, causing the strings to wail ever so slightly. Mamie jerked her head with annoyance, this was no time for a wail in the night. She turned away and moved blindly into the bedroom and undressed with nervous haste. Turning back the counterpane in orderly folds, she lifted it carefully and put it on the living room table. Then she carried one of the straight chairs back and placed it in front of her dressing table.

Seated before the three little mirrors, she fumbled through her hair, seeking the pins that held the light brown coil low on her neck. Five minutes, ten, fifteen; a crackle of static as she plied a silver-backed brush through the brown strands that reached nearly to her waist. Then, a few flicks of the comb and her high forehead was hidden by a swirl of hair and her ears disappeared under soft fluffs. Tidily, she braided the thick hank, combed loose strands from the brush and twisted them around the tapered ends of the plait.

Goodness, a yawn! That was a hopeful sign. No one was ever lonely in sleep.

Mamie took the chair back to its living room station, pulled one panel of the sliding doors over far enough to divert the glare of the front room ceiling light from the bed, then reached up and gave the cord of the single bedroom bulb a tug. She stretched out slowly, her eyes fast shut.

Bed without saying goodnight! Why, this was the first time she remembered ever ending a day without Mama, Papa, the girls—or Ike—wishing her goodnight. Just one week ago she had married so she could have her beloved always—and here she was alone.

Across her thoughts, the thin clear bugle spoke taps. Oh, no, not *that,* the saddest melody on earth—the soldier's farewell. The finality of each sobbing note cut deep into her heart. She wouldn't cry; only the unloved and the cowardly cried. Papa had taught her that. She was loved, she wasn't afraid. It was just the newness of being alone. If only Ike would come home—if only . . . Then she slept.

Where? What? Mamie thrashed over, perked to an elbow and stared at the shaft of light until her senses sharpened. A faint, tinny tick—the alarm clock. Two o'clock. Only two o'clock? Slap, slap, slap—that confounded shade; it had awakened her. She dropped back and catalogued the shadows. No, those weren't boring eyes, just the knobs on the dresser. The blotches on the floor near the closet—silly, just shoes. Was Ike all right? Surely he'd be coming soon.

Boot sounds on the porch—in the hall. The door-hinge creaked. Mamie flashed out of bed and peered around the sliding door. "Honey," she called softly to her husband, who was bent over locking the outer door.

Except on Ike's off-duty nights, the cycle of waiting changed but little. Sometimes she sewed. First, the curtains; later, aprons, potholders and hems on dish towels. Seated in a pool of light cast by a chairside lamp, bought as "a downright household necessity," Mamie taught herself to sew. At first her seams and hems were wavy, but once her thimbled finger gained dexterity, she did fairly well. At last the curtains were hung; best of all they were straight and true. This gave her the courage to go on and make things for the hide-and-seek kitchen that was now providing apartment-cooked meals.

Ike and his improvised kitchen! What a blessing his cooking magic had visited upon them. After two weeks of the dispirited food at the officers' mess Ike had jutted his jaw and said it was mighty silly to go on wasting two dollars a day when he could turn out better meals for less money right in the family living room. Would Mamie consent to the fuss and bother of an electric plate and some other things?

The quicker we shop for the plate, the better, she told him. Otherwise we might not have any stomachs left. They made a deal. Ike would cook; Mamie would wash up and put away.

The term "things" soon came to cover a lot of culinary terri-tory. In addition to the plate with two grids, they bought a chafing dish, an electric percolator, a toaster and sundry pots and pans. There was also a pine table for meal preparation. Morning, noon and night, out came the utensils from behind the bookcase curtains and the family chef turned to.

What wonderful, glorious meals! Ike's fried eggs—crisp and crunchy around the edges, soft and smiling in the center—were the best fried eggs in the whole world. Everything, just everything he cooked, was perfect. Of course, manlike, he was a bit messy and scorned potholders in favor of towels, but who cared? Mrs. Eisenhower has never changed her opinion; she says she is married to "the world's best cook!"

While engaged to Ike, Mamie had made one stab at learning to convert recipes into food, a course of cooking lessons at the San Antonio Y.W.C.A., but had absorbed only enough of the abracadabra of instructions to beat up mayonnaise. She was a fudge-maker of long experience, she'd picked up that art from her mother.

Ike didn't offer to add to his bride's slender culinary skill. Better let well enough alone; at least until they had an honest-to-goodness kitchen. They planned the meals together. Mamie shopped at the post commissary, openly boasting to her friends that Ike, not she, did the cooking. It was a tidy and economical arrangement, all the more so when they wedged a small refrigerator into the bathroom.

Social life was practically at zero for the young junior officer and his bride. Once in a while, on evenings when he was off duty, there might be a card game with neighbors, or a songfest. But, as for going into town for dinner, the theatre and dancing afterwards on the St. Anthony Hotel roof—it couldn't be managed on a lieutenant's pay. There were no movies on the post and it took a change in command or a major holiday to spark a post dance. Social life was grim all right; even the two-by-four Officers' Club barred women before sundown, which meant that even if Mamie could have afforded luncheon with her women friends, they had no place to hold forth.

Throughout those first summer months, she gave no sign of loneliness, even though the solitary night hours invariably filled

37

her with fear—not for herself, but for her husband. Just once, she rebelled against his night duty. That was the time he came back and told her he'd been ambushed in an alley, but had ducked in time to miss a bullet. He said he saw her point; he was sorry that all the nights to follow would be breath-takers for her, but that was just too bad. A change in duty could not be requested by a junior officer. And she must please understand once and for all that she was not to interfere with his career; that was strictly his department. Her department was running the home and he would respect her rights in it. He would never question her judgment on how she spent his pay or handled household matters. He wouldn't butt in, but neither must she.

Inflexible Ike. Mamie accepted his dictum without rancor. In her childhood she had observed how Papa Doud was boss; yet look how happy Papa and Mama were. Ike was right, and though she couldn't banish fears for his safety, she abided by his decisions without further complaint.

Mamie could not cook, but she possessed a special degree of magic when it came to dispelling the clutter of the two small rooms. Her orderliness gave a feeling of luxury and well-being to their meager belongings. A bowl of flowers on a small table; several good landscapes on the walls; the ceiling glare shaded; pillows for the easy chairs. She kept to her budget, even though pennies loomed large as dollars just before payday, and managed to have the weekly services of a "tidier-upper" for the heavy work.

Then came October. Oh, happy day! Mr. and Mrs. Doud and her sisters wrote that preparations were being made for their arrival down South.

John Sheldon Doud and his wife waited for the fall equinox before undertaking the annual motor pilgrimage to San Antonio. Mrs. Doud's last letter said Papa was counting on a new Packard touring car which would clip days off the usual three-week's running time; so would Ike and Mamie get set about October 10 for a telegram from Bandera, the last overnight stop before the family reached San Antonio.

Sure enough, right on time, came the message. The new car was a road-eater all right; or maybe the weather in the Texas Panhandle had held, and there had been less need for Alfred Landers, the houseman, to unstrap a shovel from the running board and go around and dig the rear wheels out of chuck holes. Mamie knew the thousand miles between Denver and San Antonio almost by heart. Papa had been shuttling the family back and forth every year since 1910. Never a dull moment on that trip. Mighty, mighty rough at times, and made them all feel like trail-blazing pioneers in a Conestoga wagon—especially when the motor went dead, and there was nothing but sand and scrub growth to the horizon. But Papa never wavered. On the first trip, when most people were queasy about driving an automobile to the city limits, Papa packed up the family, put Marian Dawson, the cook, and Landers on the jump seats, and headed his touring car for Texas with no more fuss and bother than if he'd been going for a Sunday afternoon drive. Mama was as stout-hearted as Papa. She'd laugh and sing with the rest of them, but she never forgot to keep a weather eye on the gasoline and water supply. The rip-snorting wind of the Panhandle might blow; the rain leak through the side curtains; or the dust powder everything and everybody; but Mama never fretted. Not even when an unseasonal snow froze her nearly blue. All she'd do was snug the girls in blankets and start asking silly conundrums and put everybody in stitches. Even Landers and Dawson let up being scared.

Nobody ever fussed around Mama, not even during long waits while a tire was changed, or Landers was off hustling up a span of horses to tow the car to the nearest town. Often, when they marked time like that, Mama fished down in her handbag and came up with her harmonica. *Bluep, bluep, bluep,* she'd lilt away, then nod to the girls to sing louder.

Filled with these happy memories, Mamie worked over her little apartment so her mother's eagle eye would see enough proof of housewifely zeal. All evening she bustled, her mind alight with bright thoughts for the morrow. Near sundown, she and Ike would go over and plant themselves on the porch of the McCullough Street house and keep their fingers crossed, hoping that the family would get there before Ike had to go on duty. It was going to be just like old times—wonderful old times—everybody together again at McCullough Street. Meanwhile, the piano and the mahogany table in the Fort Sam apartment could do with another rub-down; and what about a final going-over of the dressing table mirrors. Mamie worked steadily until midnight. A faint aroma of furniture polish still hung on the air when Ike came in near dawn.

Ike and Mamie were just coming up the block toward the house when *whoosh*—Papa brought the Packard to the curb. Look how easy it stopped! The engine just purred.

Papa followed Mama out of the front seat; the girls cried to Dawson and Landers to get the jump seats down fast so they could open the rear door. Such hugging and kissing and goings-on; a person'd think they'd been apart a lifetime instead of three months. Let's get on inside before the neighbors think the girls've come off an Indian reservation, suggested Mrs. Doud. Fine! fine; but hold on a minute. Ike must see Mama's hat box fitted "slick as a whistle" within the spare tire. Papa figured out how to use that center space. My, but Papa was proud of that hat box. Dawson bounced out of sight toward the kitchen door; Landers had the running-board luggage compartment open and was lifting out suitcases. This Packard had everything, even a self-starter.

Mamie and Mrs. Doud shooed "Buster" and "Mike" up the front steps and followed the girls into the wide hall. What a homecoming—what a day! Mamie and her mother chuckled in unison and held each other close.

Days went by, but nobody showed signs of being talked out. What a mutual admiration society! Mr. and Mrs. Doud were wonderful, wanting Mamie and Ike over for dinner every single night, and even for lunch. Papa Doud would not hear of them wasting money on cab fare, or trying to walk the two miles to McCullough Street. Night or day, he was glad to start up the Packard and shuttle them back and forth. Ike, who knew every

gully and rock up and down Dewey and Josephine from courtship days when he'd hiked the streets night after night, would
have liked the exercise, but Mamie, who was never a walker,
had to be considered. Mrs. Doud's matter-of-fact approval of the
apartment had the bride and groom aglow with pride. They knew
their first attempts at housekeeping were a success, otherwise she
would have indulged in outspoken sallies. Mrs. Doud is not a
woman who represses her feelings. The improvised kitchen arrangements were evidence of dollar-saving sense, she said.

On October 14 the family staged a gala dinner to celebrate
Ike's birthday. "Buster" and "Mike" had labored feverishly creating paper favors; Papa Doud indulged his love of flowers and
arranged a colorful centerpiece; Mama Doud kept a watchful
eye on the kitchen to see that Dawson, the cook, prepared a near
banquet. One more happy birthday in the family was all the
Douds needed to whip themselves into a frenzy of excitement.
When Landers, the houseman-butler, came out of the kitchen
bearing a big cake with twenty-seven candles, Mamie slipped
away to the living room and struck the opening chords of "Happy
Birthday" on the piano.

"Ike said we had one too many candles, but I told him the
extra one was for luck; that an Army man needed a little luck
and a lot of brains to become a general," remarked Mrs. Eisenhower a few weeks after her husband had been elected President
of the United States.

Always nostalgic about her youth, the First Lady likes to dwell
on the small gay happenings, such as her husband's twenty-sixth
birthday party, that have always enlivened and brought into
closer affection the tight family circle. You get the feeling that
making ornaments for birthdays, Christmas, Fourth of July and
Thanksgiving meant much more to her than paper symbols of
celebration. From her little-girl days, Mamie Eisenhower has
done her share to make such celebrations bind closer family ties.
So much younger in heart—and face and figure—than most
women in mid-life, it has been her lively love and interest in
family solidarity that has kept her youthful and unchanged. The

President has always shared this viewpoint and carried it over into his genuine concern for people as individuals. There isn't a pompous, domineering or rank-conscious bone in the bodies of this singular couple. The stern right-mindedness and devotion of their parents molded these characteristics in each at an early age, but their parents contributed also a warm light-heartedness and rousing humor.

Several days after Lieutenant Eisenhower's birthday party, his father-in-law took to disappearing for hours on end into San Antonio. Mrs. Doud, who usually enjoyed her husband's confidence, was a bit nonplussed at being on the receiving end of vague remarks about "odds and ends of business" when she asked the reason for his unusual absences. He had then been retired nearly ten years from active business though he still had a finger in many private financial deals, but it was not like him to behave in a mysterious fashion. After almost a week of sorties, Mr. Doud confided to his wife that he had been visiting every second-hand automobile dealer in town, searching for a runabout for Ike and Mamie. At last he had found exactly the right car; a black Pullman "Cloverleaf" roadster, with a jump seat, that gave every indication of having a lot more service in its five-year-old chassis. Mr. Doud, whose hobby since 1906 had been the buying and repairing of a series of automobiles, knew a four-wheeled bargain when he saw it. He said he had taken the Pullman out on the road and was satisfied the motor would stand up. It was a 1912 model and not equipped with a self-starter, but Ike was young and strong and wouldn't mind cranking it.

Mrs. Doud, surprised and happy that the newly-weds would be free to go and come as they pleased, still couldn't quite believe her ears. Mr. Doud, a man of firm convictions, had made a great point of telling Mamie and Ike that once they were married they must never look to him for help except in a great emergency. Under no stretch of the imagination could lack of an automobile be construed as an emergency in 1916; therefore Mrs. Doud wondered what had caused her husband, a man who never retreated from a firm position, especially where money was concerned, now suddenly to be willing to underwrite a car. She never did find out his reason, but suspected that he'd cast aside his resolution because he liked the way both Ike and Mamie were pinching every penny. Financial self-restraint, in his estimation, was the key to a happy marriage.

Chapter 3

At the conclusion of Sunday morning worship at the First Presbyterian Church in downtown San Antonio, John Doud and his son-in-law Dwight D. Eisenhower moved quickly through the front door and, politely but firmly edging past the throng of chattering parishioners massed on the steps and sidewalks, stalked up the street to their automobiles.

Both were men of deep religious convictions, but both had little patience with the social aspect of church attendance. Mr. Doud, who limited his church-going to Easter and one or two other Sundays spaced over the year, was in no mood to stand around in the bright November sunlight while his wife and daughters made trivial conversation. Impeccably dressed as always in a navy blue suit, with a spotless band of white piqué edging his vest, Mr. Doud settled his black fedora hat more firmly on his head and opened the front and rear doors of his Packard. Lieutenant Eisenhower, resplendent in a grey-striped double-breasted suit (secretly detested by his wife), retrieved the crank handle from the floor of his Pullman roadster. The older man eyed the crowd with set lips, but Ike moved forward and fitted

44

the handle into the notch under the brass radiator. Then he went back and stood beside his father-in-law.

Mr. Doud's temper was always something to be kept in mind; he thrashed about when kept waiting. But this time it was only a matter of seconds before Mamie, as pretty and as well preened as a robin, came tripping down the walk. She was followed by her two sisters, breaking trail for Mrs. Doud, who looked quickly at her husband to sense any storm cloud that might be gathering behind his snapping blue eyes; the way he twiddled the black ribbon attached to his nose glasses could also portend anger. Mrs. Doud, then as always the family peace-maker, asked innocently for a report on the organ-pipe situation. An inveterate organ-pipe counter, Mr. Doud roared his laughter and handed his wife and young daughters, "Mike" and "Buster," into the car. Flipping the self-starter, he said it had been a very high tally; in fact he was about out of pipes when the preacher stopped talking.

The family had gone to church that morning to please Mamie, who wanted an excuse to ride in the Pullman. Her father, deeply touched by her wish for an outing in the little black car that had been his gift, offered no objection to getting out the Packard for the rest of the family. Willingness to subject himself to a preachment on salvation was a great concession on Mr. Doud's part. He was a nimble-minded man who fumed under long-winded expositions of religion. Stern, perhaps sometimes too demanding, he was a sensitive person who resented any form of dictation. Scrupulously honest but a respecter of fine-line bargaining, he preferred, when in need of spiritual counsel, to read his Bible in solitude rather than worship in public. First, last and always, he lived to love and protect his family.

Mrs. Doud has said that her husband had many acquaintances but was wary of forming close friendships. This exclusion of outsiders promoted overemphasis of family ties. "We were always at the beck and call of each other," she asserted. "Now, looking back over the years I think we were too self-contained, too clannish—but Mr. Doud wanted it that way; none of us ever stood up to him, we loved him too much."

For Elvira Doud, these Sunday morning happenings of more than a third of a century ago are still bright prisms of remembrance. One by one, she can draw out the mental filing-cards of her long life—she is now seventy-five—and relate her experiences with crisp, unflagging wit. She even recalls, after the conversation about organ-pipes, how Mamie, reed-slim and lovely in a billowy dress covered by a flowing coat with a small wrapped turban framing her laughing eyes, gave a deft swish to her skirts and popped into the Pullman in one quick movement.

Then Ike gave the crank an upward snap that sent the motor rip-roaring; the Pullman shook. Mamie smiled with satisfaction. What could life hold that was finer than the sleek black car that had liberated her from months of humdrum living at Fort Sam? Now she and Ike went places: in and out of San Antonio, over to McCullough Street to be with the family. Best of all were those sunset drives around the edge of town—glorious, never-to-be-forgotten. Mamie still laughs to herself over the way Ike lavished care on the Pullman. Twenty times a day it seemed, at the slightest excuse, he polished every inch of its gleaming black surface. And what a shiner of brass! He had learned that knack at West Point. Under the supervision of her father, who was never done emphasizing that every man should know car repair if he expected his car to run, Ike had already learned the rudiments of cleaning spark plugs, timing tappets and changing a tire. Smooth-running automobiles were a hobby with Papa Doud, who liked to shed his sprucely conventional clothing, don overalls and pull down the engine of his Packard. He had much more know-how than most mechanics of that era. Ike for his part didn't mind getting grease on his hands. The Pullman was to be the first of many cars he cared for during his years as a junior officer.

Mamie's mother, always an accomplished housekeeper, had synchronized preparation of the Sunday meal with the family sortie to church. That meant Landers was ready to serve dinner as soon as the Packard (nobody ever out-drove Papa Doud) and after it the Pullman drew curbside in McCullough Street. Sight of the well-laden table put Mr. Doud in fine humor. Meals on-the-dot always made him happy. He carved the roast with a flourish.

Later, when after-meal drowsiness overtook Ike and Mr. Doud, who were buried behind newspapers on the front porch, Mamie and her mother quietly disappeared upstairs. "Mike" had scooted down the block to give high cry to her uninhibited feelings, but "Buster" was already settled down for an afternoon nap, made necessary by her diabetic condition. Christened Edna Mae, "Buster" had acquired her nickname during her robust infancy. Now, at fourteen, she was a wan semi-invalid, the tragic antithesis of her pet name and a constant source of suppressed worry to her family. There had been an older sister, Eleanor, Mamie's senior by three years, who had died of heart disease in 1912. Last born was "Mike," so-called by her father when she was only hours old. Mr. Doud had hoped for a son, and ever afterwards he protested that his nickname for Mabel Frances was inspired by her belligerent countenance, a veritable "map of Ireland," he said. From babyhood, "Mike's" hoydenish behavior delighted her father, and he spoiled her outrageously. She became the out-and-out family terror; being Papa's favorite, she was rarely punished, and insists today that she was known as "that obnoxious Doud child."

Mamie—and incidentally it is her given name, formally entered in her christening record—was a tactful, orderly child, shy about being the beauty of the family. She has always been called "Baby" by her mother, who says she was "handable" at home and in school. An average student who would much rather play jacks or the piano than do homework, Mamie knew how to placate teachers. She squeezed through the lower grades each year in public school, then went on to Miss Wolcott's Classes, the educational summit for the daughters of Denver's prosperous families. From her dancing-class days, Mamie had a swarm of beaux. She has remarked that it took her years to discover that it was the billiard room in the basement of the Lafayette Street house, rather than her personality, that accounted for her popularity. Grudgingly she admits that her ability to play ragtime by ear on the billiard room piano and stir up a pot of cold fudge without

47

fuss and bother may also have been added attractions. At any rate, when she reached young ladyhood and put her hair up and lengthened her skirts, Mamie was dated up weeks in advance for dances, theatres and picnics. Denver or San Antonio made no difference—she always had plenty of admirers. But until Lieutenant Eisenhower started calling, just after she turned nineteen, she had not been involved in a serious romance.

As they exchanged confidences that quiet Sunday afternoon, Mrs. Doud was aware that four months of married responsibility had tamed her social butterfly to a serious housewife, one who was perhaps too worried about household matters. They are certain their talk had to do with wifely economy. Mamie had started keeping monthly account books, patterned after her mother's accurate columns, but she says she was looking for pointers on how to "squeeze a dollar until the eagle screamed."

Mrs. Doud's disciplined spending did not rest on the rock-bottom base on which her daughter was forced to operate. "Mama had to make ends meet on her personal allowance, which meant there was always Papa to draw on in a time of emergency," explains Mrs. Eisenhower. "But I had nothing but Ike's $166.67 a month to cover everything. Many a time we were down to our last twenty-five cents when payday dawned."

The two women were half alert to hear the pleasant voices of Judge and Mrs. Robert P. Ingrum echoing from the front porch. The Ingrums, next-door neighbors and congenial friends, were frequent Sunday afternoon callers. Mrs. Doud and Aunt Belle, as she was known to the Doud girls, behaved almost like sisters. Marketing for week-end supplies in Mrs. Doud's electric brougham was one of their established habits. Mrs. Ingrum says she never had the faintest idea how to keep house until the Douds moved next door; then Mrs. Doud showed her how to set up a household budget that accounted for everything, right down to the last nickel's worth of onions.

This businesslike spending floored Texas-born Aunt Belle, who had never counted pennies or nickels. When Mrs. Doud bought a crate of oranges, at a saving, she shared them with Aunt Belle.

Share-and-share-alike was Mrs. Doud's creed, so long as you kept tabs in the book. It was the same with potatoes and dried stores; with coffee, sugar and flour. No hit-or-miss purchases for Mrs. Doud, who learned buying and bookkeeping from Papa when she married him before she'd turned sixteen. Papa gave Mama a bicycle the first Christmas after they married back in Boone, Iowa, so that she could shop more easily. Mr. Doud was easy-going about everything but wasteful spending for necessities, and he figured food the hardest-come-by necessity in married life; that's why he raised a rumpus if his wife's books failed to balance, sometimes going on the warpath for days if she had lost track of only a few cents. He taught her to be as exacting a money taskmaster as he was, which was saying something. After he retired in 1904—with what was rumored to be a good million in sound investments—Mr. Doud was his own bookkeeper.

Mr. Doud liked luxuries too, even for himself. He was never without a box of his favorite cigars, San Felice or Robert Burns, and he spent lavishly on flowers. His wife and daughters never lacked fine clothes, but everything, even house furnishings and a new automobile every year or so, had to be bought within the annual budget that governed all expenditures.

When he died in 1951, just over the eighty mark, his books were as concise and accurate as any mariner's log. There is a strong possibility that his business sense, transferred to Mamie by her mother, has had a lot more to do with the much-publicized "Eisenhower luck" than most people realize.

While Mamie was a girl at home her father gave her $3 a week spending-money. If she ran short, that was just too bad; not even Mama Doud dared help her out. Papa Doud was strict about the finality of a given word. If you promised, you fulfilled or you took the consequences. Mamie has never gone back on her word, not even in a minor matter. She's punctual too, another of her father's inflexible "musts."

That November Sunday afternoon brought the expected visit from John and Belle Ingrum. John Ingrum and John Doud had a great deal in common. Both were up on automobiles, real estate values and politics. They played an equally stiff game of poker, but had never been beaten by their wives, who knew the value of cards. Judge Ingrum's legal mind and John Doud's sharp business sense meshed in keen analysis of current problems as they sat and drew on long cigars and wondered if President Wilson's friendliness toward France and England was going to draw the United States into the European war, already two years old.

Was war coming? Would the Mexico border trouble stiffen, or was Woodrow Wilson more concerned about German aggression? The Judge's brother-in-law Hunter Harris, an Army captain, had been chasing Mexican bandits over the border for a year; there had been enough shooting for full-scale war, but it was all shots and excited talk, so far. Papa probed Ike with "What-about-it?" in his eyes. Lieutenant Eisenhower predicted that the United States would get into war in Europe. That was why he and Mamie hadn't waited until November to be married.

The women were close to shuddering. Mrs. Doud switched the subject, suggesting it was a fine sundown for a ride. Where would they go? A circuit of the missions, over to Fort Sam, or down and around the Alamo? Belle Ingrum was for cancelling Fort Sam, unless "Buster" and "Mike" wanted to feed the deer and peacocks in the quadrangle. Winking, she said, if her sister, Lulu Harris, were living in Infantry Row, like last year . . .

Laughter pealed. It had been just a year ago, on a Sunday too, when the Ingrums drove the Douds over to Fort Sam to see Lulu and chatted comfortably on the front steps of her quarters. Who had come out of bachelors' quarters across the street but that brand-new West Point Second Lieutenant, Dwight Eisenhower. Remember how he came over and got himself introduced to Mamie and her folks? Remember? What a lucky, lucky day that had been for everybody.

Mamie blushed, as well she might; it had been a merry-go-round afternoon for her all right. It all came back cameo-clear; the routine Sunday ride with the Ingrums, that wound up changing her whole life.

There stood Ike on the sidewalk below the steps where she was sitting next to Lulu Harris, "the spiffiest-looking man she'd ever talked to in all her born life." Pressed and polished, that was Ike. How his uniform fitted! He was Officer of the Day and wore sidearms and a campaign hat squared forward like a Rough Rider. Tough and businesslike, but what a smooth talker! Big, blond, masterful, but laughing easily, he neatly separated her from the crowd—including several bachelor officers—and, before she could protest, had her by the arm walking up the street.

Pebbles, dust, and ditches, that was the difficult under-foot path of their trip around the post. Goodness, every step was murder in those tightly-laced beige kid shoes. Worse still, Mamie was kept busy trying to hold on to a big chip-straw sailor hat and keep her flowered cretonne skirt from snagging on underbrush. Once Ike had her sit down, not because he realized that she was about spent, but merely to broach a supper invitation! Of all the nerve, knowing a girl half an hour and thinking he could make a date with her. Supper indeed! Mamie remembers herself as a sputtering firecracker of indignation. She was busy that evening. Was it a supper date, Ike wanted to know. No, it wasn't, but she had to be home in plenty of time to dress. Ike asked what was wrong about staying at the Fort for supper, she'd be back in plenty of time. Yes, what *was* wrong? When he looked at her that way, her heart went *ping;* so they ate at the infantry officers' mess, after her family and the Ingrums drove off. Before Mama left, Mamie spoke right up, making it clear that she intended to keep her evening date. And keep it she most certainly did, taxiing back under the escort of Lieutenant Eisenhower, who for all his smooth talk didn't succeed in getting so much as a foot in the front door.

For three weeks, the "louie from Fort Sam" kept the Doud phone tied up two and three times a day trying to convince Mamie that she should change her date-book in his favor. Finally Papa Doud stepped in and told her to stop her flighty nonsense, or "the Army boy" would give up in disgust. Papa really gave her such a talking to, it dawned on her that her father admired the young lieutenant from Kansas, and anybody Papa liked was in her book.

Mrs. Eisenhower draws great delight from recalling her romantic courtship. Next time Ike phoned, she said she would give him a date the following Monday night; he proposed dinner at the St. Anthony Hotel, then the "society night" vaudeville show at the Majestic Theatre.

That's how the romance started. Week after week, they went to Monday dinner, to the show, and danced afterward on the St. Anthony roof. Spendthrift Ike didn't care how he tossed around his $141.67 second lieutenant's pay, even though it meant skimping the rest of the month. In midweek, or at the week end he'd hike over from Fort Sam after duty, hopeful for a few words. If Mamie was out, he'd sit around and chin with Mr. and Mrs. Doud. He waited out many an evening that way, just to say good-night to his beloved.

Mr. and Mrs. Doud didn't think it made much sense having him coming over after dinner, and invited him to eat with the family even though Mamie was out—or going out. Fine business that was, having her dates always running into Ike. But Ike's strategy began to have the desired effect, Mamie stayed home more and more and wound up refusing invitations from other admirers.

Papa and Mama were delighted, but Mamie's sisters, sniffing a serious rival for her affections, grew jealous. "Buster" remained quiet and withdrawn, but "Mike," a fiery, pell-mell eight-year-old, broke into open warfare. When her parents weren't looking, she bit, kicked and scratched her big sister's caller. Mamie and Ike gave her as wide a berth as possible, but "Mike," even in her less violent moods, would thunder up and down the north porch, screeching insults. Mrs. Doud, always a mild disciplinarian, was forced now to call a halt; "Mike" could racket on the south porch, or out in front, but she must avoid the north porch, on penalty of being put to bed.

"Mike" and Ike really tangled one Sunday when he was sent down the block by Mrs. Doud to round up the tomboy for supper.

Ike, braced for the fray, found her hop-scotching with a couple of other gangly-legged girls and delivered her mother's message. She ignored him with studied insolence. All right, so she wanted to be flippity! He closed a big hand over one of her arms; she was coming, and coming fast. Oh, was she! "Mike" screamed defiance and insults, this big, fresh guy who thought he could order everybody around because he'd gone to West Point—she'd show him he couldn't boss her! Her body sagged to the pavement. A sit-downer, eh! Ike blazed. Scooping her up, he slung her across a hip and marched back to the house in triumph. "Mike" was sent to bed supperless. From then until the day he married her sister, "Mike" was a fireball of resentment toward Ike.

Perhaps it was a good thing that lean finances compelled Ike to do most of his courting on that wide, unroofed north porch of the McCullough Street house. Except for the deck of a ship—and the porch gave that illusion—there couldn't have been a more romantic and isolated environment. The three-story white mansion on the brow of terraced lawn at the corner of Josephine Street was a show place in the new district of fine residences. Constructed entirely of wood, it was basically Deep South classical plantation style, with white columns rising three stories from the front steps. However, a more modern curve, accented by the horseshoe porch and big rounded windows in the upper stories, gave the structure a bulging bigness. The house was situated on a lot far too small for its bulk, which caused the north porch almost to overhang Josephine Street. On the south side, a driveway to the garage at the rear marked the boundary of the Ingrum place. Josephine Street was rutted and hilly and rarely used, which gave seclusion to the north porch.

Under a mellow moon, or on crisp, indigo nights when the stars seemed ready to shower down, the wide expanse of sky was a mysterious canopy of sheen and sparkle above Mamie and Ike, rocking to and fro on the north porch. On Friday and Saturday along about ten, strolling troubadours made slow rounds of the neighborhood. Their soft Spanish voices, rising and falling above the twang of guitars, came through the night with haunting unreality. Gradually the volume of the voices would swell to a loud serenade at the corner; then, if unrewarded by a dime, the group would move on to weave in and out of other byways. Tamale vendors would hawk their wares, and then tiny tinkling cymbals sounded through the darkness with unhurried, agreeable insistence. M-m-m-, those tamales were divine, not a tummy ache in a bushel, regardless of Mrs. Doud's fears. The imminent sweethearts would connive in whispers and suppressed giggles, and Ike would rush out and buy the forbidden treat.

Mama vowed over and over again that she would not permit Mamie to risk a stomach upset from corn-husk bundles of spiced meat. Goodness only knew what sort of meat it was, and in what dirty kitchens it had been cooked. Mrs. Doud had a habit of hovering inside the screen door until the vendor had passed, but if she and Papa were over visiting the Ingrums, Ike and Mamie were sure to have a forbidden feast. Many a night Ike started back to Fort Sam with a newspaper packet of greasy corn husks to be disposed of in the open country, far beyond Mrs. Doud's range of vision.

Mamie tried to whittle down "Mike's" hostility with bribes: a new hair ribbon, pennies for candy, a Sunday-best handkerchief. But nothing seemed to dull "Mike's" belligerency. She was determined to hack away at Ike and force him to leave her sister alone. But Ike paid her no mind, though he was often obviously irritated. "Mike" eventually leveled defiance at her family. One Saturday afternoon, when Mamie was away rooting for the football team which Ike was coaching at the Peacock Military Academy, "Mike" returned from playing down the block with a new companion. This, she proclaimed, was going to be dearer than any sister ever born. For once, her "pain-in-the-neck," small-sister rebellion had the aspect of high comedy.

The companion that was to replace Mamie in her affections was a small, docile, very ragged burro, dragged on a frayed piece of rope. The runty animal's long ears were no higher than "Mike's" narrow shoulders, and one of its tiny hoofs would have fitted into her hand. Mr. and Mrs. Doud, who had been raising girls for going on twenty years, weren't quite prepared for this braying object of juvenile devotion. W-h-a-t on earth! Take it back this very moment! The house isn't a zoo! Mama Doud gave way to unaccustomed wrath, only to discover that her husband and "Buster" were holding on to each other to keep from falling down with laughter. "Mike" screamed back that it was her donkey, her very, very own, bought with her very, very own dollar saved from her allowance.

A dollar for that! Mama Doud scanned the pint-size donkey. It was so thin that every flea, tick and burr on the little animal was as conspicuous as a thumb. No! No! A puppy, a cat, even a parrot—but not that motheaten, vermin-ridden beast!

Papa Doud moved in as truce-maker, suggesting that for the night the animal could be bedded down in the garage. His angry wife countered that it would probably have to stay over tomorrow too—there was no way to dispose of a donkey on the Sabbath. Come Monday, he promised, no donkey would be stabled at 1214 McCullough Street. "Mike" was mute. She knew better than to argue with Papa. Papa was boss; besides, Mama might be won over during the week end. It took "Mike" the next half hour to lure the burro into the garage even though her father gave the beast an occasional wallop with a rake handle. On Sunday morning the burro cropped weeds in his narrow tethered area in the backyard and heed-and-hawed. "Mike" had to go off to Sunday school after staking out her pet, but during the afternoon she rounded up playmates and offered free rides, only to discover that the burro would not serve as a beast of burden. Lone guardian of the skittering animal, "Mike" obstinately refused to budge from the kitchen steps until darkness forced her to beat and shove the protesting grey-hided fury over the garage threshold. What with sniggers from neighbors, it was a week end the family would long remember. A good spanking might have brought "Mike" to her senses, but Papa and Mama never went that far with their children.

Monday, and "Mike" out of the way at school, Mr. Doud took Landers into the backyard for consultation. Before mid-morning, the houseman set out in the general direction of Fort Sam with "Mike's" pet. It was never learned what sort of a deal he made. "Mike" has often wondered if Landers sold or gave away the donkey. What, if any, profit derived from the animal's departure was all in Landers' or Papa's pocket. "Mike" never recovered any part of the dollar she spent for her pet.

Almost overnight it was Christmas, the happiest time of the year for the Douds. Ornaments came out of wrappings, the tree was set up, popcorn strung and new candles stuck in every holder. Caches of gifts; hot and cold guessing; blank faces; parents and children pitting their wits against each other in breathless mystery.

Christmas Eve—and Papa Doud high on the ladder. "Mike's" fortress of aloof disdain was swept away by the strong current of holiday good will and the prospect of gifts next morning. She didn't think it politic to overreach herself with tantrums; after all Mama and Papa, much as they loved holidays, and especially Christmas, were not above putting presents away unopened as a penalty for misdemeanors. In an about-turn, "Mike" made herself busy and helpful, handing up ornaments to Papa, traipsing up and down stairs to accomplish small chores for Mama, and hovering over "Buster," who was stringing the last of the popcorn.

Christmas carols had to be sung, not alone by the wandering Mexican troubadours (who were businesslike enough to come off the sidewalk and ring doorbells), but also by "Buster" and "Mike," up and down the block, accompanied by Papa, and by Mama with her harmonica.

Ike came late, after the younger girls were in bed. He put several parcels under the tree, then drank coffee and joined in the singing around the piano. Mamie noted with a start how casually he entered into the family festivities; her heart galloped and did somersaults. Then she crashed chords, refusing to let her mind race ahead into romantic conjecturing.

Next morning while Papa and Mama and the girls opened

packages, Mamie tried to unwrap Ike's gift with a casualness her heart did not feel. It was a big box; it was heavy; it was wrapped as if it came from a jeweler's—what on earth? Her hand plunged through tissue paper and drew the gift halfway out. It was a large silver heart for jewelry, with her initials scrolled on the lid. Right back into its wrappings it went. *Phew!* What would Papa and Mama say? There was no mistaking the implications of the lavish gift. A heart! Expensive silver! While Mamie had never been cross-examined by her parents about Ike's intentions, she knew now that she was in for a third degree. How could a girl who hadn't been asked the big serious question explain such a gift? What to do? Maybe sit tight and keep the gift under cover until Ike came, then let him do the explaining? That wouldn't work, he wasn't due until dinner. Her mother was sure to ask about his gift—she was asking right now. With a gulp, Mamie handed over the pasteboard box. One dig and Mama uprooted the gleaming object. Before anyone could speak, Mamie fled upstairs. Mama's sharp "Well!" sounded like a hammer stroke splintering her dreams.

From her bedroom Mamie heard the monotone of voices, then the positive tap of her mother's feet coming upstairs. Mama walked in looking very grim; she didn't pry or probe, merely laid the jewel-box on the dresser with cold finality. The box was to be returned the instant Ike walked in the front door, she declared. Mamie must understand that only engaged girls accepted expensive presents. Mama presumed (and here her voice reached up for thin, darting words) Mamie was not engaged to the young man! He was either ignorant or presumptuous to think a well-brought-up girl like Mamie would welcome such a gift.

But Mamie *did* welcome the gift. She said so. Giving it back was unthinkable; she would not only look foolish, but Ike might be driven away forever. Further than that, the box was the loveliest present she'd ever received. No indeed, it was going to stay right there on her dresser. Mrs. Doud was stunned by the pitch of Mamie's voice. This wasn't like Mamie at all. She picked up the box and stalked out, saying that she would return it to Ike. Oh no, never that! Mamie started to scheme. She would gamble wildly and speak to her father. If Papa backed Mama, that was the end of everything; but maybe, just maybe, Papa could be argued with.

Mr. Doud was in the den. He told her to sit down and listen: No well-brought-up girl. . . . No, no, not all that again; Mamie's mind shut out his words and she kept her temper down. She knew that if she bided her time, maybe she would find a chink in Papa's wrath. Ah, there it came. Papa was saying that his "Poody" was now a young lady. "Young ladies don't . . ." "Poody" was her father's "just-between-them" nickname, a term he used only in moments of great endearment. Mamie surmised Papa was willing to be wheedled. She dropped to her father's lap and snuggled close, patting the white hair that fringed the back of his bald head. Gradually her fingers slid upward over the shiny pate, tweaking stray, upstanding hairs. "Papa," she said with positive inspiration, "Papa, you're not really bald, I feel an awful lot of new hairs." That did it! Mr. Doud kissed her and said gruffly that she could keep Ike's present. With a fine show of sternness he grumbled that he had been swayed in his decision by consideration for the young man's financial predicament. He was sure Mama Doud would relent when she realized that return of the jewel-case would amount to waste, sheer waste. There wasn't a chance that Hertzberg's jewelry store would make a refund on an object scrolled with a monogram— and just what earthly use would such a personalized, feminine trinket be to a soldier? Mamie snuggled closer. Wonderful, wonderful Papa; my, but he loved her!

Mrs. Doud, learning that the jewel-box was not to be returned, began a restatement of her position, but her husband cut her short with a brisk explanation why this situation was an exception to the rule—adding that he would be pleased if there were no more arguments on Christmas Day.

Tactful, artful Mamie thanked Ike profusely, interweaving her mother's objection and her father's exception. Ike got the impression that Mamie and Mr. Doud were distressed about his bank account, a personal consideration that showed he was being taken seriously. He had not expected this carefree girl to worry her pretty head about his finances, much less enlist her father's interest. Already deeply in love, Lieutenant Eisenhower wasted no more time dallying on the outer fringes of courtship.

Admitting that the jewel-box episode speeded romance, Mrs. Eisenhower exhibits justifiable reticence regarding the circumstances under which she agreed to become the wife of Second Lieutenant Dwight David Eisenhower. "He proposed, and I accepted—right after Christmas," she says. "Of course it was romantic, aren't all proposals romantic? But I was luckier than other women, I agreed to marry the most wonderful man in the world."

New Year's celebration over, Ike braced himself for a session with Mr. Doud, half expecting to be told that Mamie could not be expected to live on a second lieutenant's pay. Instead, Mr. Doud was reassuring; he said there was no reason why scrimping and saving at the start would not lay a foundation for an enduring marriage. Assuming next the unfamiliar role of stern parent, Mr. Doud made his position clear: he would not give Mamie a penny of allowance, she would have to live on what her husband made. If Ike wanted to risk having her learn to keep their bodies and souls together on less than $150 a month, they could become engaged. Second Lieutenant Eisenhower (stipend $141.67 a month) said confidently that he expected promotion— and more pay. Mr. Doud supposed that was "possible, not probable." They shook hands, Ike solemn as a preacher.

But the solemn mood was short-lived. Leaving the den of his future father-in-law, Ike almost stumbled over Mamie, who did not exactly have her ear glued to the keyhole, but had been flattened against the wall, catching the drift of the wind. Papa Doud, overhearing her weak excuse, joined Ike in teasing her, then called to his wife to come downstairs and hear some good news. Mrs. Doud showed no surprise. She said, with a sly twinkle, that all along she had expected this would happen; she couldn't conceive of a young man as smart as Ike hazarding investment in a Christmas present that would be left on his hands.

On the news of the engagement, "Mike" adopted new tactics; she was still glowering, but less rambunctious. Her silence made no dent in Ike's armor of devotion, but it was a relief to the rest of the family.

The engagement ring finally arrived from Bailey, Banks and Biddle in Philadelphia, and nested in Ike's pocket in time for presentation on Valentine's Day. He gave her the golden circlet that evening, when the McCullough Street house was garlanded and bedecked with appropriate hearts-and-flowers decorations. Mamie was delighted; the ring was precisely what she wanted, an exact duplicate of her fiancé's West Point class ring—a large amethyst sunk in the heavy carved gold insignia of the Military Academy, instead of the miniature replica most West Pointers bestowed. Weeks before, Mamie had asserted that unless she had the big ring she would never feel truly linked with her dearly-beloved if duty took him away from her, and Ike, convinced that the war in Europe would soon engulf the United States—and the Army—was ready to indulge her.

March came on, and it was time for the Douds to climb into the family Packard and head back to Denver. Ike and Mamie were forlorn, wondering how they would bridge the gap between March and the mid-November date set for their wedding. To be over a thousand miles apart—the prospect was sheer agony. Ike had wanted to marry on the spot, but Mr. and Mrs. Doud would not hear of it. Papa Doud cautioned his daughter over and over that as a junior officer's wife she would have to practise rigid economy, if her marriage was to be free of the suspicion of debt. More marriages "drowned in debt," he said, than any other way; so let her become a budget probationer during the months of waiting.

The Douds were still en route to Denver in the Packard when President Wilson called out the National Guard to back up General John J. Pershing, who had been ordered across the Mexican border with 6000 men to pursue the bandit Pancho

Villa, after the Mexican leader had swooped in and out of Columbus, New Mexico, in a bloody and defiant raid. Villa was believed to be hiding in the rugged mountains of Chihuahua with some 2000 followers and it was up to "Black Jack" Pershing to track him down.

So here it came: a bigger Army, with National Guard divisions moving into border posts. Fort Sam mushroomed with tent cantonments, and there was talk of new permanent barracks and warehouses. Young Eisenhower, as a regular Army officer, had high hopes of being assigned to a training command with the newly-arrived guardsmen; instead he was given duty with the Provost Marshal's office as a nocturnal law-and-order officer, with a military police detail that patrolled San Antonio's red-light district.

Word began spreading over the military grapevine that the strong stand of the Wilson Administration against the Mexican bandit might result in a stiffening of over-all international policy. The grey-heads at the Infantry Officers' Club said it would not surprise them if Germany's mailed fist overreached itself and dragged the United States into the European conflict. "Watchful waiting," Woodrow Wilson's policy so far, was not expected to exceed notes of protest until the November election determined whether he was to be in the White House another four years. If Mr. Wilson was re-elected then there might be no more marking time with the Kaiser.

Wars and rumors of war. Lieutenant Eisenhower listened carefully, weighing how the threat of hostilities would affect his marriage plans and military career. Why should he and Mamie wait until November to be married? His name was on the promotion list; if war came, he would almost certainly be sent overseas; so the sooner he married the more time he would have with his wife before combat duty. If she would consent to marrying late in June or early in July, and if Papa and Mama Doud could be won over . . . He would write and find out.

Mamie said she was "really thrown for a loop and Papa and Mama climbed on the anxious seat," when Ike's letter arrived.

What to do? Yes, what to do? Wonder of wonders, Mrs. Doud approved, and Papa was nodding! The wedding would have to be in Denver! Did Mamie suppose Ike could get away? Her parents said to phone and find out. *Goodness*, this was all so sudden! A war bride—how dramatic; only there really wasn't going to be a war, she told herself. Besides, if war came, maybe Ike wouldn't be sent into the shooting. But her mind was all made up. Somewhat dizzily she asked a long-distance operator for Fort Sam Houston.

On the phone Mamie blurred her words with excitement, finally gave up and let her parents, talking by turns and only a shade more calm than herself, make the arrangements. Fine, Ike, fine, you put in for leave, then let us know and we'll set up the wedding. It was ridiculously simple—and frightening. Mamie was not the swooning kind, but she saw red stars before a black curtain of oblivion, and her mother administered a dose of aromatic spirits of ammonia.

Soon Ike wired that he had obtained ten days' leave beginning June twenty-seventh. So, allowing two days for the train trip, how would July first do for the wedding?

July first it would be!

Mamie decided to keep her home wedding a family affair, since it was obvious that the Doud house was too small to accommodate many guests. Her parents brought up the possibility of a more pretentious wedding at the First Presbyterian Church, but she vetoed the idea. For sentimental reasons she wanted to be married in the familiar environment of her happy childhood.

The Lafayette Street house, now termed "The Summer White House" because the President and Mrs. Eisenhower prefer to vacation there as guests of Mrs. Doud, remains much as it was at the time Lieutenant Eisenhower claimed his bride. The formal furnishings of the compact parlor include an upright piano and three carved chairs, upholstered with petit-point; several marquetry tables rest on a fine oriental rug. The largest painting in the room, a portrait of Mrs. Eisenhower in a heavy gold frame, hangs over the mantel of a small fireplace. Glass-paneled doors give access to the dining room, where large glass cabinets, filled with silver, crystal and china, and a carved sideboard leave only minimum space for the round dining table. An electric chandelier of multicolored glass hangs above the table. The wood-paneled entrance hall, separated from the parlor by a wide, uncurtained opening, has leather chairs and a sofa facing the brick fireplace. One corner of the hall is cut off by an open staircase that turns at a square landing four steps up. None of these rooms exceeds fifteen by eighteen feet in dimensions.

The four bedrooms and one bath on the second floor are even smaller. Under the roof, besides an old-fashioned attic, there is another bedroom, with a dormer window which faces on the street. This was Mrs. Eisenhower's girlhood room. On their visits she and the President occupy a second-floor room over the parlor. The one-time billiard room in the basement has the piano given Mr. and Mrs. Doud when they married in 1893. A host of family pictures, sheet music, knickknacks and even a 1910 victrola are there.

During the summer, wicker furniture is used on the front porch, and the red-and-green carpet is bolted to the steps just as it has been every season since Mamie and her sisters played jacks and hop-scotch on the short stone walk leading to a second flight of steps that lead in turn to the sidewalk. The iron hitching post, cast like a tree stump, is still at the curb. The terraced lawn and shrubs are still tended by Timothy Guiney who has been Mrs. Doud's gardener since 1912.

In 1916, bridal consultants and ready-made wedding finery were not available in department stores. Mrs. Doud and Mamie selected a pattern, shopped for material and findings, and hunted up a dressmaker who agreed, as a special concession, to put aside her other work and finish the bridal dress in less than two weeks. Fine chantilly lace was used for the full, floor-length dress and tight-sleeved bolero jacket. A wide, pale pink satin cummerbund encircled Mamie's hand-span waist. She had decided on this touch of color to accent the pink baby roses she intended to have combined with white sprays of lilies-of-the-valley in her wedding bouquet.

While Mamie whirled through the days, standing for hours to be fitted and refitted, and packing her trunks with everything from rugs to chair tidies, her husband-to-be went on with his night patrol duty in the more unsavory areas of San Antonio. He did not get around to buying a diamond solitaire and wedding band until about ninety minutes before he caught the midnight train for Denver. It was well after ten o'clock when he succeeded in locating Frank Stone, manager of Hertzberg's, and induced the good-natured jeweler to go down and open the store. Even though Lieutenant Eisenhower's financial reserve was as lean as his waistline, he selected a fine blue-white diamond weighing well over a carat, and a platinum and diamond wedding ring.

Perhaps by an accident, Army red tape came unrolled at the right time and the nervous bridegroom found a telegram confirming his promotion to first lieutenant when he returned to the Doud house from a mid-morning foray on the florist to get a bridal bouquet for his future wife. He had known his promotion was coming through—but to have confirmation arrive on his wedding day! Mamie has often wondered if some benevolent senior officer at Fort Sam didn't plot it that way.

Ike had no time to exult, no time to rush downtown before the noon ceremony and locate the silver insignia of his new rank. Landers had pressed Ike's white dress uniform and was standing by to lend a hand so that First Lieutenant Eisenhower could be eased into the starched garments without a wrinkle.

Five minutes to twelve. The harpist was seated at the turn in the stairway. Ike, in creaseless uniform, was behind the pantry door, waiting for a signal from Dr. William Williamson, the minister. Mrs. Doud, "Buster," and "Mike" stood alone in the parlor. There came a deep chord from the harp. The girls broke from their mother and shrank close to the muted piano; they were suddenly very frightened. More chords, eddying into the wedding march, and with a swish, Mamie joined Papa at the foot of the stairs. Ike walked lightly and silently—there was his West Point drill-training—through the dining room and up to the mass of flowers that hid the parlor mantel. The last thrummings of the harp mellowed into the hot air of noon, and Dr. Williamson began speaking. . . .

The alchemy was at work in "Mike"; she was sure she was going to cry—it was all so beautiful, so wonderful. To her Ike looked like a white knight, Mamie a fairy princess. During the simple ceremony, a great new love was born in her turbulent heart. She clutched "Buster" and found her sister icy-cold and wracked with sobs. As the bride and groom embraced after the short ceremony, the little girls cried openly, then rushed to cling to the big man. "That day I found a brother," says "Mike" Doud Moore.

There was no rice-throwing or pell-mell honeymoon departure. After the flurry of hugs and kisses and handshakes, it was time to move into the dining room for a "Sunday-style" dinner. There was champagne, good luck toasts, a cake to be cut with the groom's sword—all the happy traditions of an Army wedding. It was dinner at the big round table—the table Mr. Doud insisted on keeping because its pedestal bore the gouges and scuffs of the little-girl shoes of his daughters. Here again was that streak of sentiment which was forever battling his stern sense of material values. A man rich in worldly goods, he was richer still in dedication to family unity.

For John Sheldon Doud as well, this was a day of significant change. Since his twenty-first birthday, he had centered his life in his wife and daughters. Until he acquired Ike as a son-in-law, no man had been really close to him, and now he was happy in the prospect of a father-son relationship. He had the conviction of confidence in Mamie's husband; he reached the age of eighty and saw Dwight Eisenhower rise to wear the circle of five stars of a General of the Armies, the world's foremost soldier. He did not live to witness the ultimate honor. Death came to him quickly and painlessly in 1951 while he was sitting pen-in-hand in a dressing gown in the small upstairs nook of his Denver house. His wife was far away in France with Mamie and Ike. Months before, he had become privately aware that the end was approaching, and chose to retire to Denver and set his affairs in final order.

"Mike," the youngest, was first in her father's affections, whereas Mamie, the second-born of Mrs. Doud's four girls, was plainly her mother's favorite. But there was never a cleavage. The two surviving sisters loved each other with mounting understanding as the years passed. "Mike" has been married twice, but the transitions of her personal life have in no way affected her ties with her own family—and that includes her brother-in-law, the man she took to her childish heart on his wedding day.

Before anyone realized it, the time had come for Mamie to go upstairs and change into a white silk traveling dress. Ike put his white uniform aside and reappeared in a grey suit; then he took "Mike" into a corner and asked her, in their first head-together conversation, to be guardian of the bride's bouquet. Ike wanted the Cecile Brunner roses and lilies-of-the-valley to be held overnight in the refrigerator until he could return and experiment with dipping the flowers in wax. Then he sat on the front porch with his father-in-law and tried to talk casually until Mamie was ready.

The thirty-two-mile wedding trip began at the interurban station when the electric trolley departed for Eldorado Springs. The leave-taking was sprightly. The bridal couple would be back in Denver the following afternoon to catch an eastbound train for Kansas, to stop over a few days in Abilene with Ike's father, mother, and brothers. Time enough tomorrow for a real good-bye. Ike had not been too disappointed when his original idea of a five-day honeymoon at the stylish resort hotel in secluded Eldorado canyon dwindled to overnight because the popular retreat was booked solidly for the Fourth of July week end. Eager to have Mamie know his family, he was glad to divert the extra days of his leave to visiting his home.

Next morning, however, almost from sun-up, the Doud household was buzzing with preparations for an early start to Eldorado

66

Springs. It was to be a surprise trip, voted by Mr. and Mrs. Doud after a prolonged discussion of the bleakness of the trolley as a conveyance for newlyweds. The bride and groom could at least return in comfort in the Packard, though it would take three times longer than the half-hour trolley ride.

By mid-morning the Packard was lurching over the rough road that wound through the foothills, with "Buster" and "Mike" curled up asleep on the back seat. By noon they arrived at the big yellow-and-white wooden hotel that towered with incongruous civilized elegance against a rock wall of the deep canyon. There was a long front porch, with the inevitable battery of red rocking chairs. There were curlicue railings, and elaborate fretwork framing doors and windows, for the Eldorado was one typical, huge gimcrack of neo-Twentieth-Century architecture. The Douds found Ike and Mamie in the dining room and lunch turned into a celebration.

Mrs. Eisenhower's sharp memory recalls the trip back to Denver only as a quick blur of going somewhere in a hurry. Her sister "Mike" remembers distinctly sitting on Ike's lap part of the way, and recalls too that everyone sang foolish songs, with Papa's voice roaring over the others.

Ike's attempt to preserve Mamie's wedding bouquet was a fiasco. Back at Lafayette Street, he went into the kitchen and melted down a batch of paraffin, then plunged the blossoms—still icy from their night in the refrigerator—into the hot liquid. "Poor Ike," says Mrs. Eisenhower, "he French-fried the flowers to a shrivelled brown mass." There was a general moan all through the house, with "Mike" in pitiful tears. If he had only let her take a few blossoms for pressing in the family Bible!

Dinner was served; then the newlyweds collected and packed the last of their belongings. Landers had checked the bride's trunks earlier in the day, but several suitcases remained to be filled with Mamie's things. By nine o'clock the last lock was snapped. A good two hours would pass before it was time to leave for the Union Pacific Station to take the eastbound midnight train. "Buster" and "Mike" had catnapped, so they were

67

in reasonably good shape for the late farewell. Wearing fresh dresses, with faces washed, hair combed, they sat primly on the red-and-green carpet on the porch steps and listened to the hum of conversation inside the house. Finally their parents emerged and Landers elbowed through the screen door with a tray of lemonade and sandwiches. It was going to be a party! The girls squealed with excitement. Mamie and Ike came out and joined the girls on the steps. It all turned into wonderful fun. "Our family has always liked to laugh," Mrs. Doud reflects back on that evening. "We have also known times of great sorrow, but somehow our ability to laugh together made our tears less bitter."

The break in the fun came when Mr. Doud said he would go back to the garage and get the car. That was the signal to go in and scramble for hats; when Papa Doud was ready to go, you went. The Packard backed humming to the side steps of the porch, and the bride and groom, Mrs. Doud and the girls, followed by Landers, hurried to the porch. Dawson, the cook, brought up the rear and stood quietly waiting to say good-bye. Blinking back tears, she managed a cheerful "Luck, lots of luck, Miss Mamie," and vanished indoors. Mamie and Ike bolted after her. In the pantry they tried to console her; in only a few months, they said, they would all be together in San Antonio. But Dawson could not bring her workworn hands down from her ebony face.

Even now, when the President is with intimates, he often calls his wife "Miss Mamie." Neither of them remembers how it began, but Mrs. Eisenhower likes to believe it stems from that night when Dawson said her tearful good-bye. Dawson has long since died, but Landers, who served Mr. and Mrs. Doud continuously except when he was a soldier during World War One, is now in a California veterans' home. Feebleness alone prevented him from accepting the formal invitation to witness the inauguration of the President, whom he still respectfully regards as "Miss Mamie's husband."

The train out of Denver for Chicago, by way of Kansas, was

68

late. It was nearly one in the morning before Landers was able to put the bridal baggage aboard the Pullman sleeping car and duck back to the platform to wait while Lieutenant Eisenhower and "Miss Mamie" said good-byes at the porter's white-matted stool. Here was the real parting, the real going away to start a new life, and it was tearless, a matter of seconds. Mr. and Mrs. Doud watched with broad smiles as their first-married daughter gathered her skirts over her arm, like a half-opened fan, and climbed lightly into the Pullman car ahead of her broad-shouldered husband. Mrs. Doud says, "We were truly happy, Ike was such a fine young man."

The train did not cover the four-hundred-odd miles to Abilene with lightning speed; it took all night, all next day, and into the small hours of another endless cycle of blackness. There were agonizing spells of sidetracking and prolonged station waits. In 1916, crossing into Kansas in midsummer, even by Pullman, was pretty much a slice of perdition. Whether the train made scheduled stops or pulled into isolated sidings to take on water, every car became an inferno from the fierce blasts of heat off the sun-scorched flatness of the countryside. When the train's motion generated a breeze, cinders and soot even sifted through the window screens to coat with grit and grime the green plush elegance of the Pullmans. Passengers in the red plush seats in the day-coaches up ahead fared little worse, except for a heavier shower of cinders.

It was well after two o'clock of the second night of travel when the train ground to the stop at Abilene. Mamie, who had an immense distaste for dining car menus, had fought car-sickness as well as dust and cinders; she barely had strength to stagger down the aisle and out on to the platform. Tired Ike made a fine show of brightness when he presented his bride to his parents, and Mamie remembers that David and Ida Eisenhower, wearied though they must have been by their night-long wait, beamed on her as devotedly as her own parents.

The trunks had been checked straight through to San Antonio. Ike stowed the hand luggage in the back of the buggy, and away they went on a fifteen-minute jog-trot to South Fourth Street. Alighting from the carriage with groping stiffness, Mamie could still feel the rock and sway of the train's motion, and her stomach was tight with queasiness. Clinging to her husband, she walked slowly into the snug hall of the square wooden house that had been his home since his fifth year. She remembers her first reaction in the shaft of light from an overhead gas jet; it was wonderment that the neat furnishings, and especially the stair carpet, showed no signs of wear and tear from the impetuous boyhood of Ike and his five brothers. Hearing a blithe greeting from overhead, she looked up and smiled at a sleep-rumpled boy of near-man stature standing in a nightshirt in the upper hall. "Milton!" said his mother in mild reproof, and with another smile Ike's seventeen-year-old "baby" brother faded from sight. Fond as she became of Edgar, Arthur, Earl and Roy, her other brothers-in-law, Mamie says the glint of affectionate understanding in that first stairway meeting so warmed her heart that Milton has ever since been her favorite.

The square frame house of the Eisenhowers, over the tracks on a lot big enough for the boys to do truck gardening during the summer, was similar to Mamie's Denver home. The front parlor, though furnished less elaborately, was a model of conservative formality; the upstairs rooms fitted just as tightly around a small hall that gave access to the bathroom at the rear. Mamie's home was buff brick; the Abilene house was of wooden clapboards, painted yellow. The Eisenhowers' long, combined living-dining room, shut off by a door on the left of the downstairs hall, was the center of family life. Summer and winter kitchens were in the rear. During cold weather, the Eisenhower boys took turns rising before dawn and shaking down the coal stove, but in summer, cooking was done on a gas range in the outside kitchen.

Fourth of July picnic celebrations were over, but the visit of the bride and groom called for hospitality that would bring neighbors from blocks around to pay their respects with a lunch-basket supper. Ike knew this Kansas custom, but his bride was not prepared for the fried chicken, potato salad, cakes, pies and jams and jellies that were dumped by guests in bewildering profusion on the long Eisenhower table. There were pickled pigs' feet, sauerkraut, baked beans, freezers of ice cream, and five-gallon cans of coffee. A feast!

Never in her born days had Mamie dreamed people could get together like this. After the first few minutes of constrained introductions, she was at ease and having as much fun as everybody else. Names and faces might be strange, but here beside her husband, who acted as if he had been out of town for only a week, she was bubblingly happy. What pleased her most were the flowers the women brought from their gardens. Their small bouquets seemed to her the sweetest tribute any bride could hope to have. Mamie's great capacity for enjoying people and parties perhaps can be traced to that long-ago Kansas evening. It was the first time she had been on her own with a large group of strangers. She had grown up in close contact with her neighbors in Denver and San Antonio, but Mr. and Mrs. Doud had never held open house, nor were they much for church socials and picnics.

It was also her first taste of true small-town life. In contrast to Denver and San Antonio, Abilene was a very small town with one main street, uncrowded except on Saturdays when the farmers drove in to market. Ike had grown up in the rural center, a typical small town boy who would perhaps have married and settled there if he had not been appointed to West Point. Mamie knew that the root of the strong bond she felt with the laughing, happy visitors was shared pride in Ike's achievement.

During the three-day visit there was no further excitement for Mamie. She stayed close to the house, learning to know the quiet purposeful strength of her husband's mother. His young brothers, Earl, Roy and Milton made much of her; the two older boys, Arthur and Edgar, were working in Kansas City, and it was years before she met them. David Eisenhower, her husband's father, a man of gentle nature, talked with her shyly. She recalls that she felt perfectly at home, although it was the first time she had ever been a guest under another family's roof.

71

Honeymoon notwithstanding, Mamie remembers that she and Ike bogged down in a first-class argument during their Abilene visit when Ike overstayed the supper-hour to play cards in a downtown rendezvous with cronies from his high-school days. When he wandered in well after midnight, his bride's wrath was high. She might as well have saved her breath; her brand-new husband was too sleepy to answer back. During the flurry and hurry of packing next day, Mamie's temper cooled, and they started on the last leg of their journey to Fort Sam in high spirits.

Chapter 4

FORT SAM HOUSTON,
SAN ANTONIO, TEXAS
1917–1918

As July first, the anniversary of her year-old marriage, loomed on the calendar, Mamie Eisenhower faced up to the fact that she and her husband would soon cease sharing their honeymoon apartment at Fort Sam Houston. Ever since Congress had declared war against Germany on April 6, 1917, Mamie had been living with a leaden heart, knowing full well that her husband, as an officer in the regular Army, was going to be ordered out of Texas for combat training that would fit him for trench warfare in France.

Almost immediately after the formal declaration of hostilities, Ike had been transferred to Camp Stanley, a small military outpost some twenty-three miles from San Antonio, where he was on duty as an Infantry supply officer. This shift brought him back to the apartment only on scattered week ends, so Mamie had plenty of time for fitful conjectures about the future. No married quarters were available at Camp Stanley and Ike knew better than to attempt commuting with the Pullman over the adobe-caked hollows of a sand-swept wagon trail that was hard enough going for military vehicles. When he had enough of his desk work cleared up for a week-end leave, he would hop whatever was moving in the direction of Fort Sam, which meant he rolled into Infantry Row in anything from a motorcycle side-car to a truck. The trips were always through a tunnel of dust, and he was usually one of the dirtiest men on duty with Uncle Sam's Army by the time he embraced his wife. Not that Mamie minded the dust; he could have come in crusted with mud and she would have been delighted.

On these brief get-togethers, there was no cranking up the Pullman in the lean-to behind the apartment and driving over to McCullough Street for fun with the family. The Douds had headed back to Denver months ago. Instead, Infantry Row friends came by for crullers and coffee, and maybe a few hands of poker or a songfest. But mostly, it was "war talk." Mamie says she and the rest of the wives smiled so hard they were about to crack their faces, but it was the only thing to do while you listened to your husband chafe about "marking time in Texas" and speculate when the War Department would "get wise" and start transferring regular Army officers to overseas combat training.

At other times Mamie screened her anxiety and loneliness behind smiles and laughter. At whist games, in the commissary, mailing letters to her family at the post office; wherever she met up with other wives, she tried to match their light chatter. Scarcely a day passed without one of the women reporting that her husband had been assigned to a distant camp for stepped-up combat training. A wave of congratulations always followed; Lieutenant So-and-So, Captain Brown, Smith or White; lucky, lucky men. Lucky? Oh, no they weren't; not where their wives were concerned. It might be military glory for the men in khaki to move in the direction of the trenches of France—the mire, the blood, the frostbite, snow and sleet of winter warfare; but for their women who must wait—and hope—what could be greater torture?

Often Mamie, dazed with disbelief, would rush back to the

solitude of her living room (she suspects that other wives shut themselves in bedrooms, baths, kitchens . . . any place to be alone) and cast off all self-deception. At those times she felt trapped in a pit, sealed off with her sorrow—and dreadfully alone. But she dared not risk losing her calm for long; she had to consider the well-being of the baby she expected in September. Ike had warned her about the threat to the unborn child if she allowed herself to be fearful.

September? Where would Ike be in September? Where would she be? The baby: would it be a boy, with his father's big fine hands? She must act and *be* a soldier's wife, even when alone.

Mamie had many kind neighbors, and a few who were not so kind; a normal ratio in any small community and especially an Army post where, if you didn't know all about your neighbors (and the wives on Artillery Row), somebody was bound to supply the missing information. Having promised Ike to shun gossip, Mamie curbed the spitfire in her nature and treated friend and foe alike. It wasn't always easy, when she learned that behind her back some of them termed her "a callow kid" who should "go home and let her mother take care of her." Not for worlds would she have gone home; she was an Army wife and she was going to have her baby at the station hospital, even if her husband was thousands of miles away. What was more, her mother would be on hand in plenty of time to welcome her first grandchild.

Mrs. Eisenhower's proudest footnote on the months she was a "lady-in-waiting" at Fort Sam concerns making a complete layette for her baby, even to a christening dress. She rarely cooked more than eggs for herself, but when a Dutch lunch was in prospect, she spent hours preparing Mexican food from recipes supplied by her cleaning woman. These share-and-share-alike parties were the mainstay of the social life of the penny-counting junior married set who could not dig in their pockets for elaborate entertaining. Whist and poker, usually played for matches, followed the food; or Mamie played the piano for singing and dancing. She refers to those good times as her "potato salad days, with frankfurters and mustard on the side." Undoubtedly the wife who knew the least about cooking, she remembers that she was the only one in her crowd who varied party menus with *chile con carne* or *chicken la estancia*.

Because she was lively and never complained, she had few lonely evenings until it was time to prepare for bed in her empty apartment. One night, after hours of tossing, she was startled out of hard-won sleep by the crackle of splinters on one of the bedroom screens. Too frightened to move, but in full possession of her vocal chords, she screamed loud and long. When the commotion of neighbors in the hall made her realize that aid was just beyond the door, she suddenly recalled that her husband's service pistol was in the dresser instead of under her pillow. Weeks before, he had left it for her protection, but she had never been able to summon up the courage to touch the weapon. Now she is certain that if it had been within reach, she would have squeezed the trigger.

After a search party reported back that the would-be intruder had almost wrenched the screen from the window frame, Mamie said would everyone please go back to bed; she had a pistol in the apartment and felt quite safe. With all the windows latched, the door bolted and the lights on, she sat up the rest of the night. Occasionally she glanced at the drawer where the pistol reposed, but was blessed if she could bring herself to lay a hand on the cold steel. Next morning word came from headquarters that she was being moved across the street to an upstairs apartment.

Right in the middle of the disorder of moving a letter came from her father in which he tried to tell her gently that her mother was in the hospital under observation for a possible major operation. Under no circumstances, he said, was Mamie to travel to Denver; family life was upset enough without risking further trouble. Even if the operation took place, Mrs. Doud was convinced she could be up and well enough to keep her promise to be in San Antonio by mid-September; so Mamie must be sensible and stay in her comfortable apartment near Ike.

"Comfortable apartment!" Mamie gave her jumbled belongings a frenzied look. "Near Ike!" He might as well be deep in deepest Texas, for Camp Stanley was as inaccessible as a border station. What about Ike's new orders? It was almost the end of July; he was bound to be gone before September. Mamie felt an impulse to walk out the door and catch a train for Denver. Confusion and loneliness she could stand up to, but uncertainty about her mother's condition could not be borne at a distance. Ike would understand; Ike would want her to go—or would he? Mamie closed herself in the bathroom and for a wonder gave way to tears. When her emotional storm was over she began to be ashamed. Her mother and father were right—they were always right. She splashed water on her face, grinned sheepishly as she patted the moisture with a towel, and went out to reduce the chaos of the apartment. She must not worry her husband. He had a war to fight.

"I knew almost from the day I married Ike that he would be a great soldier," she said. "He was always dedicated, serious and purposeful about his job. Nothing came before his duty. I was forced to match his spirit of personal sacrifice as best I could. Being his wife meant I must leave him free from personal worries to conduct his career as he saw fit."

Parching August, a sun that burned unmercifully on the roof of the long grey building and glared all day against the drawn blinds of Mamie's top-floor apartment, made the small rooms hard to bear. Day by day, the stairs seemed to grow longer and steeper, but the twenty-year-old girl who was soon to become a mother never complained. Her husband was still coming in from Camp Stanley when he could; her mother had withstood a long and difficult operation and was on the mend. Mamie spent a lot of time writing her family—and it was always cheerful news. Luckily, her pregnancy was without complication; still she hated putting aside pretty clothes for sack-like maternity garments.

Months before, her husband, who was a handy man with a needle, had spent an evening letting out the middle sections of several dresses. She remembers the repairs he made on the white silk dress, the one she wore first a few hours after her marriage—how his big hands contrived to cut and hem casings for tapes in the blouse and skirt; and pride of achievement, when she adjusted the top and bottom and covered the join with a wide band of bright ribbon.

On the few hot August nights when her husband was with her, Mamie tied black velvet bows at her wrist—just as she had done since girlhood—and wore her biggest and floppiest hats, if they decided to go for a spin in the Pullman.

There is a story about that automobile that has been told so many times in recent years that it can almost be considered an "Eisenhower Classic." However, unless you have seen Mrs. Eisenhower wiggle her nose and give you her personal and private views on just how far and how fast a Pullman, vintage 1912, will run under supernatural guidance, you haven't heard the story in its entirety.

You must bear in mind that Mamie Eisenhower is as full of fun as she was thirty-seven years ago. (So is her mother, but that is another story.) She likes nothing better than to settle back and tell breathlessly the stories that background her life. We tried one time, out in Denver, shortly after her husband had been named the Republican candidate for President, to do a tape recording of her fast-moving voice; but she took one look at the machine—it was on the porch of the Lafayette Street house—and said: "That whirling disk makes me selfconscious. You write, I'll talk."

The story of the Pullman begins on a peaceful Sunday morning, one of the Sundays when Lieutenant Eisenhower could not make it to Infantry Row. For no reason at all (which is reason enough for most wives to toss caution aside), Mamie was beset with an impish urge to try her luck at steering the Pullman out to Camp Stanley at Leon Springs. She went down to the lean-to, removed the dust cover, rejoiced in the beauty of the brass-bonneted radiator, and, after dusting off the front seat, climbed up and experimented with the foot pedals. What followed is best described in her own colorful speech.

78

"I'd never driven, so what! Papa let me steer the Packard plenty of times, and while Ike wouldn't allow any monkeying with the precious Pullman, I knew just what he did to get it into high gear. How he loved that car! When he first had it, he polished it so much I thought he'd work through the lumpy repainting and get right down to the metal.

"I said to myself, 'It's now or never,' and fumbled around with the ignition, which was fine as far as it went. But who was going to crank it up? I went out and looked up and down the street. Sure enough, I was lucky; a sergeant was in sight. He looked kind of funny when I asked him to help get the car started (few women drove in those days), but he gave the handle a tug, and *bang!* the motor caught. I backed out slowly, but must have had stage fright. The engine died, but the young man gave the crank another yank and the engine whanged away. I started forward, steering slowly until I was off the post, then I went into high gear and kept going, ruts and all—it was as much fun as a roller-coaster—until I reached Leon Springs."

Mrs. Eisenhower says it is not true that she honked around Stanley, yelling to her husband to come out and stop the car.

"That's pure fiction," she declared. "When I got there I just reached over and turned off the ignition, then yelled for Ike. He was surprised and very angry, but after he took me to lunch he got permission to drive me back to Fort Sam."

Early morning pedestrians in the Katy (Missouri-Kansas-Texas) Station in San Antonio must have been amused on September 17 when they saw a dignified woman of middle age riding on a baggage truck. She was balanced precariously on two upturned suitcases, her hands grasping the forward metal bars and her feet well grounded on the floor of the truck. As you can guess, it was Mrs. Doud; and she was making all manner of jokes with her serious-faced son-in-law, who had an arm flung out to catch her if she teetered. Unable to walk after her recent surgery, Mrs. Doud was using the truck as a substitute for a wheel-chair, something the station was unable to provide. She had just arrived from Denver to make good her promise to be on hand when her first grandchild arrived. Neither the doctors nor her husband had been able to alter her determination to pack up and go to Texas, even if she couldn't walk. Aside from wanting to comfort her daughter when Mamie's time of physical travail occurred, Mrs. Doud had learned during a telephone conversation that orders had come through transferring Ike within the week to Camp Oglethorpe, Georgia. That settled everything, and away she went.

Mrs. Doud went from the station to the St. Anthony Hotel and for several days concentrated on regaining her strength. Then it was time for Ike to leave for Georgia. She was carried up the stairs to the Infantry Row apartment by her son-in-law and one of his friends, seated on a chair lashed to a yoke.

Mamie's first wartime parting from her husband was unclouded by tears. Though she might never see him again, she bade him good-bye with smiling eyes and promised to write every detail of the baby's birth—right from the moment she felt her first labor pang. As the car carrying Ike receded, Mamie and her mother waved mutely from the upper gallery. Mrs. Doud remembers that Mamie clasped her left hand over the heavy gold and amethyst ring that weighted the slim fourth finger of her right hand, and blinked hard at the blurred brightness of the trees.

Four nights later, Mamie woke her mother shortly before twelve to report labor pains. Without a telephone, and not wishing to disturb the family across the hall unless a serious emergency developed, mother and daughter waited out the hours until daylight. Scorning a return to bed, Mamie had resolutely begun her promised letter and it was not until morning that she put her pen aside. Then she bathed and dressed and added toilet necessities to her well-filled suitcase. It is noteworthy that she arranged her hair carefully, gave her nails an extra buffing, powdered her face and rouged her lips—all before the sun was up. Just as reveille sounded, she added a final paragraph to her letter, then tip-toed across the hall and tapped quietly on a door. Response was instant—she learned afterward that her neighbors had heard her run the bath and suspected they would be needed. While the young officer thumped downstairs to race to headquarters to summon a mule ambulance, his wife collected Mamie's suitcase and offered to go along to the hospital. Mrs. Doud, quite as serene and unhurried as her daughter, said it would not be necessary to trouble an extra person; as soon as the ambulace came, she and Mamie would be off.

Weren't the stairs going to be too much? Not at all, replied Mrs. Doud, and to prove she felt strong she began a crab-wise descent. Knowing her mother would resent assistance, Mamie gave a final tug to the counterpane of the neatly-made bed, kissed her hand to Ike's picture atop the piano, pulled down all the shades and shut and locked the outside door. Just as she started down the stairs, she heard jangling harness and the clop-clop of mules; the ambulance had arrived.

Mrs. Doud and Mamie were helped up the high rear steps of the van-like vehicle by orderlies. The men slammed and bolted the doors before their passengers were firmly seated on the lengthwise benches. In spite of its solid rubber tires, the wagon lurched violently and banged in and out of the road's many ruts. After each jar or wide swing, Mrs. Doud eyed her daughter apprehensively. But Mamie seemed to be taking the twenty-minute ride as a lark. Her comments were whimsical; she was sure they were in a patrol wagon, not an ambulance. She sat with her feet braced against the bench opposite, otherwise she easily could have been thrown to the floor. After the trotting mules made an abrupt turn that kimboed the rear wheels, Mrs. Doud called testily through a small wire-covered square, instructing the driver to rein the animals to a walk.

The "whoaing" of the team in front of the hospital ended Mamie's levity. Without a word, she solemnly extended the letter she had been holding so tightly throughout the uncomfortable ride. Mrs. Doud took the sealed envelope and tucked it in her handbag.

Re-living the tense minutes and hours of that day, Mrs. Doud said, "When Mamie handed me Ike's letter, I knew what she was really made of. There hadn't been a whimper out of her—she wouldn't even tell me when she had a pain. She was all woman, and fit to be a mother; she was all wife too, keeping her word to write."

Admittance to the hospital was by Army form—and more forms. Mrs. Eisenhower was in labor, but the nurse at the desk made her answer a string of questions so that a card could be filled out. It was all in slow-motion, exasperating to Mrs. Doud whose experience in bearing children told her there was no time to waste. Finally the nurse murmured a room number and pointed down a high-ceilinged corridor. As Mrs. Doud started to go with Mamie, who was bravely picking up her suitcase, the nurse announced in bitten-off words that in *military* hospitals, the relatives of patients were permitted in rooms only during stated visiting hours.

Mrs. Doud gave the nurse a withering look and stalked down the hall after her daughter. They entered the designated room, to find a great gritting and groaning coming from the general direction of a woman tossing in one of the beds. Mrs. Doud stared in disbelief; surely Mamie, an officer's wife, would have privacy! Mamie was beyond caring; she put down her suitcase and fumbled with buttons on her blouse. Starch rustled in the doorway and another nurse gave a quick smile, pointed at a vacant bed and concentrated her attention on the pain-wracked patient in the far corner of the room. While her daughter disrobed, Mrs. Doud yanked open a dresser drawer, unsnapped the locks on Mamie's suitcase and quickly dumped its contents into the dresser, except for a nightgown and slippers. Meanwhile, the nurse swished out, which added more pressure to Mrs. Doud's pounding arteries. She did not speak until her daughter was prone, then announced she was going to find a doctor—fast. At the door she almost collided with a young man in white, who started to give her a bit of his mind for her infraction of the rule: "No relatives are—" Fiddlesticks on Army regulations, cried outraged Mrs. Doud; what kind of regulations forced a patient to find her own room and put herself to bed—when the baby might be coming any minute? Just then Mamie's room-mate shrieked. The doctor, thinking it was Mamie, ducked inside.

Still scrapping mad, but knowing her place was in the waiting room, now that the doctor had taken charge, Mrs. Doud retraced her steps down the corridor and sank with great weariness into a chair. The glare of the newly risen sun hurt her eyes, so she lowered her lids and turned her mind inward! Her daughter was durable as granite, as self-contained as a judge. But this time of waiting would not be easy; Mamie had not fooled her mother one bit in the ambulance. Dim as it was, Mrs. Doud had noted that Mamie was breathing like a frightened bird. In the hospital room, Mamie had turned away, her eyes closed in pain. Just as she herself had borne her children in agony, Mrs. Doud knew that her daughter must pass through her time of torture. Alone. It has been that way since the time of Eve. Mamie was young and strong; all would be right.

The doctor's voice broke Mrs. Doud's reverie. He said with professional dispassion that Mrs. Eisenhower was coming along just fine. There was no reason to expect the baby before noon, so there was plenty of time for breakfast—and a walk. Then he vanished. A new nurse at the desk, who could not help but hear the doctor's soothing words, smiled woodenly. As if coming up with a happy coincidence, she suggested the school bus; it was about to leave and would go by the Infantry Officers' Mess. Mrs. Doud consulted a watch pinned to her dress: half-past seven, high time for breakfast. She rode in a high wagon, also pulled by mules. Unlike the ambulance, it was a springless vehicle with no suspicion of rubber tires. She jounced over the mile-long road while the long-eared beasts alternately raced and wobbled.

Ike's officer friends needed no great power of deduction to realize why his mother-in-law was having breakfast alone in the mess. Word flew up and down the long tables, and all too late Mrs. Doud was told she and Mamie could have avoided the "medieval torture" of the ambulance. If only someone had "yipped" for a driver, they could have come in the Pullman. "Fine, fine; *now* they tell me," was Mrs. Doud's reaction as she toyed with her meal. It was heartening though, when one of the men, who owned a car, spoke up and said that "an automobile, and nothing but an automobile," would be her means of conveyance the rest of the day. It was nearly half past eight when she was whisked back to the hospital. As she stepped out of the car she remembered Mamie's letter, and handed it over for mailing. Prepared to spend the rest of the morning in the lounge, Mrs. Doud crossed the lobby toward a comfortable chair. Three steps, and she was confronted by a radiant nurse. Wasn't it wonderful to be the grandmother of a fine boy!

Grandmother! Boy! Mrs. Doud was fit to be tied. Her normally rosy complexion glowed like a well-stoked grate; she glowered at the nurse.

"I was insensible," she says. "I had been cheated out of the greatest moment of my life, I've never gotten over it."

Mrs. Doud's strong pride had been dealt a heavy blow. She wanted to cry, so towering was her self-recrimination for having left the hospital. But this was no time for self-pity; Ike had to be notified. Borrowing a phone, she called infantry headquarters, located one of her son-in-law's friends and asked about dispatching a telegram. The voice on the wire offered to send the message, so she dictated a few brief words. That was that; Ike would know in a matter of hours that he had a son! It would be time enough later in the day, after she had seen the baby and talked with Mamie, to call Denver.

Humor has always been a great balance-wheel for Mrs. Doud; it altered her mood quickly that morning as she sat waiting to see her daughter. Someone gave her a newspaper. She read it, right down to the last want-ad. Perhaps the everyday local happenings, or even the bargains offered for sale recorded in print dispelled her anger. When she put it aside she was a grinning good loser; nature, unbeatable nature, had won this round. She was in a joking mood when she left the nursery and entered her daughter's room; she had just looked on a red and wrathful replica of her son-in-law. Mrs. Doud's soothing words of praise about Little Ike howling in the nursery were brief. Mamie, tired

84

and bewildered, was barely able to summon a proud smile. Satisfied that a wire was on the way to Ike, she closed her eyes.

Knowing that sleep would claim Mamie all afternoon, Mrs. Doud left the hospital as soon as possible, talked long distance with her husband, then quite willingly permitted herself to be carried upstairs to her daughter's apartment. She went to bed immediately. September 24 was only half over, but she had had about all she could take.

It had also been quite a morning for Mamie. Left unattended after the doctor's hurried first visit, she soon began to suffer critical birth pangs. Luckily, her room-mate, a sergeant's wife and already the mother of two, realized what was happening and punched and repunched a bedside bell. The nurse who answered the summons went into a whirl of activity, which is why Mamie was able to reach the delivery room five minutes ahead of her son's first cry. Gossip later revealed that the demands for constant attention by a major's wife in a private room up the corridor had brought about a neglect of other patients. Years later, when her own husband had attained the rank of major, Mrs. Eisenhower, who had never forgotten what she had suffered because of one woman's selfishness, helped organize a hospital for women and children on a small Army post in Panama. Prior to World War Two, when the Army established adequate medical facilities for the families of the millions of men in uniform, hospitalization of Army dependents, except at big military installations, was often on a hit-or-miss basis.

During the first days of her recuperation, Mamie looked in vain for word from her husband. On the fourth morning, Ike's jubilant reply was delivered. Field duty had taken him away from Camp Oglethorpe, so he did not learn for three days that Little Ike had been born. Nicknames being a tradition in the Doud family, Mrs. Doud ruled out "Little Ike" as much too long, and said it could result in his father answering to "Big Ike," which would never do. She suggested "Icky" as a pet diminutive of Ike—and "Icky" he became.

Mamie went home from the hospital wondering just how long

85

it would be before "Icky" and his father became acquainted. She was able to remain at Fort Sam through the kindness of the commanding officer who, knowing that there would be no family quarters at Camp Oglethorpe for many months, permitted her to go on occupying the apartment until Ike was ordered overseas, or transferred to a post with permanent housing. The Georgia training center was a mishmash of tents and wooden barracks. Ike wrote that he expected to be a tent-dweller for some time, as work on the barracks was hampered by a shortage of lumber, to say nothing of the lack of fittings, carpenters and plumbers to assemble the material.

Mamie took the disappointment calmly, telling herself she should be grateful Ike was still in the country. In a few weeks her father arrived with her sisters and Duncan (Landers had gone off to war), and soon she and "Icky" made daily visits to the McCullough Street house. Her parents could not convince her to give up the quarters and live with them. In the back of her mind was always a faint hope that the Army might send Ike back, or at least grant him Christmas leave. She wanted him to find his son in his own home.

Captain Eisenhower (promotion had come in November) received almost daily reports on the progress of his son. Snapshots by the dozen as well as studio portraits reached him. Night after night, with "Icky" slumbering in his crib, Mamie's large firm script filled pages with the day's events. She wrote with the breeze and gusto of her everyday conversational style; sometimes slangy, always endearing, with never a hint of her difficulties. Bedtime was still a bad time. She was always sleepless until "Icky's" one o'clock feeding, which consumed over half an hour. If lucky, she then fell into exhausted slumber until six, when her hungry son bawled for another bottle. Mrs. Doud knew what was going on. Daily, she drove over around noon in her brougham, collected Mamie and "Icky" and glided them back to McCullough Street for lunch. "Icky" was the center of family attention during his wakeful periods in the afternoon, while his mother napped in her old upstairs bedroom.

86

In spite of daytime relief from baby care, the young mother stayed tense. She ate only a token amount of food. Her pretty trousseau clothes were oversize; worst of all, her eyes had put away their laughter. The agony of waiting for word on her husband's future was drawing her fine. Sometimes she played the piano with a show of her oldtime fervor, always ending with a heavy crash of chords and tightshut eyes. So long as the days brought letters from Ike, Mamie felt reprieved. Ike made no attempt when writing to hide his discontent with his job of molding civilians into officers. As an Army regular he felt entitled to combat service and was sure it would come very soon. He would wire if ordered for European embarkation.

Thanksgiving had passed; December was heading toward Christmas and still no telegram. Mamie was building hopes on a reunion during the holidays and lived for each day's mail, but midway through the month came a letter—Ike could not get leave. In a matter of hours her chest constricted with pain and a heavy cold set in. Her fever mounted. So strong was the threat of pneumonia that she went back to the hospital two days later on a stretcher. The infection spread to both lungs and it was not thought she would survive. Her husband was granted emergency leave, but a blizzard snarled his train and he was held in a coach for four days and nights. He arrived on Christmas Eve, to find his wife in what might be a fatal coma. Prayerfully he sat through the night.

In the morning she stirred, and he knew she sensed his presence. Wishing to be within call if she rallied enough to ask for him, Ike stayed all day at the hospital. By night she was more rational, but he made no attempt to leave until the following dawn. Long before breakfast was served at McCullough Street, Ike was watching Mrs. Doud give "Icky" a six o'clock bottle.

For weeks after Ike returned to Oglethorpe Mamie was kept at her parents' home. Logic born of desperation took hold of her. Though "combat duty" was still written in black letters on her heart, an enfolding responsiblity toward "Icky" left her less and less time for introspection. She went back to Infantry Row, resolved to worry no longer about mail or telegrams. It was almost with disbelief that she read a letter in March filled with glad news that Ike was being sent to Camp Colt, Gettysburg, Pennsylvania, to command the tank training corps center.

Whose lucky star was ascendant this time, Mamie asked herself. Maybe it was twin stars; Ike, three years out of West Point, was young to be given a command. Wonderful, very wonderful. Of course he would make good; but it was more wonderful having him still in the country. His words conveyed that he was proud to merit the confidence of his superiors, but he still harped on wanting to get to France.

Mamie fell to wondering about tanks. Vaguely she remembered seeing a picture of a steel monster. Weren't tanks a British invention—armor-plated versions of the Trojan Horse? An unexpected nightmare for the German High Command? She began asking her friends for more details, but found she was not alone in her ignorance; nobody around Fort Sam was beyond the picture stage in tanks.

Mamie's star was overhead all right. Ike had been transferred almost no time when he wrote that he had found quarters. The house was off the post, in Gettysburg; a barn of a place and partially furnished. He suggested that Mamie look into the matter of storing their household effects. Freight shipments would probably be shunted around for months due to wartime railroad congestion, or might be lost altogether. Far better to put their things in a warehouse and live with makeshifts; he did not expect to be at Colt too long. Ike mentioned that he had picked up a second-hand Ford with the proceeds from the sale of the Pullman. He had disposed of the old car before leaving San Antonio. All in all, it was a good prospect; they had a house and transportation. All that remained was for her to pack up and come North with "Icky."

Word of Mamie's impending departure spread up and down Infantry Row. Before she had time to arrange for warehouse space, a neighbor made a morning call and appeared surprised to learn Mamie was going to wear herself out packing the furnishings of the apartment. No experienced Army wife ever thought of moving anything but antiques from post to post; they sold and bought as they went—it was as simple as all that. Mamie showed only mild interest at first, but the older woman pressed home her argument. New people coming in to Fort Sam would snap up the whole kit-and-kaboodle, and Mamie would have a lump sum to buy second-hand things either at Camp Colt, or some later post. Out of one pocket, into another. Just a good, sound custom among Army wives. Mamie wavered and said she would sleep over the idea.

If Mr. and Mrs. Doud had been around to exert their shrewd trading instincts and experience, Mamie would have avoided the pitfall of selling under pressure. Relying on her own judgment, however, Mamie decided to accept her neighbor's advice and convert the furnishings into cash. She knew nothing of second-hand values, which was why she accepted $90 for all the furniture, plus such incidentals as lamps, dishes, glassware; even the broom, dustpan and mop were included. She kept only the red Khiva rug, linens, some cutlery, and odds and ends.

When she thinks back on the transaction, Mrs. Eisenhower shows unusual indignation. "How could I have been so gullible?" she says regretfully. "I know I was young, but not *that* young; surely I could have applied simple arithmetic and figured out that $90 would never replace another apartment. What I exchanged for nine $10 bills cost originally over $900. It's a wonder Ike didn't wring my neck."

Forever angry over having been "hoodwinked by an older woman," Mrs. Eisenhower does not feel she was cheated in another second-hand deal she consummated on the same "give away" principle before leaving Fort Sam. This was the sale to an old clothes' man of two of her husband's suits for $10. She had formed an instant dislike for the garments when she first saw them during their courting days. His evident pride in his taste forced her to suppress criticism of the "horrid eyesores." Just after graduating from West Point, while visiting his older brothers in Kansas City, Ike had paid a tailor the astronomical sum (for

1915) of $150 each for two custom-made double-breasted suits. One was grey, the other navy blue. Both were made of striped material and far too "natty and nifty" for Mamie's satisfaction. Since the Army's wartime ban on civilian clothing in off-duty hours, they had reposed in a packing trunk; and Mamie was ready to take the calculated risk that they would not be missed until war's end and *Goodness*—when would that be? If she was called to account for their absence, she was prepared to point out the wisdom of realizing money on the garments before they became moth bait.

Chapter 5

CAMP COLT, GETTYSBURG, PA.

CAMP MEADE, MD.

1918–1919

The spring of 1918 was still young when Mamie Eisenhower reached Gettysburg, Pennsylvania, to set up what was to be the third home in her twenty-one months of married life.

Never in the thirty-eight years of their marriage, have the President and Mrs. Eisenhower lived in a home of their own. Mention has already been made of their purchase in 1950 of a small farmhouse set in 189 acres of the historic rolling countryside of Gettysburg. They had every intention of renovating and enlarging the box-like wooden house into a spacious country seat. General Eisenhower planned to improve the breed of the dairy herd, and his wife was looking forward to decorating the house for easy country living and informal entertaining. Before an architect could be consulted, the cold-war crisis in Europe resulted in the formation of the North Atlantic Treaty Organization, and General Eisenhower was asked to take leave of absence from the presidency of Columbia University and become head of NATO. In a matter of weeks after he was back in uniform, General and

Mrs. Eisenhower sailed for France, to become tenants of still another strange house. In the spring of 1952, his mind made up to be a candidate for President of the United States on the Republican ticket, General Eisenhower resigned his NATO command and flew back to New York with his wife. If the Presidential election had ended in defeat, the Eisenhowers planned to go ahead at once and make their Gettysburg farmhouse into the home of their dreams. Now, as occupants of the White House, they have finally begun renovation of the farmhouse to meet the needs of the future.

Why, after thirty-two years and with the whole United States to choose from, had they decided to buy their first home in Gettysburg? Mrs. Eisenhower said happy past associations had always endeared them to the community.

"We went there as strangers in 1918 and the townspeople took us in and made us their friends," she said, explaining that there had been no sharp demarcation between civilian and military families in the little Pennsylvania town, such as commonly exists in most communities where Army posts are situated.

Mamie Eisenhower was an exhausted and travel-stained mother when she first arrived by train in Gettysburg with her small son "Icky." The April journey up from San Antonio had stretched over half a week. Keeping her seven-months-old son fed and reasonably clean would have been too much for her ingenuity had it not been for the considerate sleeping car porter. "Icky" was almost entirely bottle-fed, and this posed the problem of fresh milk, not always obtainable from the dining-car refrigerator. At more than one station stop, the porter would rush into a lunch room, buy several bottles of milk and turn them over to the dining-car chef for safe keeping. As "Icky's" feeding time approached, the porter would appear with a warmed feeding bottle of milk. He also provided cans of hot water so she could bathe the child in a dressing-room wash basin. After Washington, however, where she changed trains for a five-hour run in an express-local over the circuitous route to Gettysburg, Mamie was entirely on her own in a day coach. Ike met her at the little railroad station and lifted "Icky" from her weary arms. While they waited for the trunks to be unloaded—once again Mamie was traveling with the big black cases—she sat transfixed watching her small boy in his father's arms. Suddenly she felt light and young again, and burst into laughter. "Icky" and his father were such "look-alikes"!

In the months ahead, while "Icky" grew and learned to walk in the big white-pillared brick house overlooking the campus of Gettysburg College, he became more than ever a diminutive blueprint of his father: a wide grin, the promise of fine broad shoulders and sturdy arms and legs. Here was a second-generation football player coming along, perhaps even a second-generation soldier, Mamie told herself. Her husband loved the child with consuming passion. Though a high-school girl helped care for the energetic youngster, Ike often relieved her of her duties, bathing and feeding "Icky" with surprising ease.

During her first week in the rambling two-story Colonial house on Spring Avenue, Mamie rattled around in complete bewilderment; then she figured out how she was going to make the huge establishment homelike. The upstairs presented no great problem. The bathroom was old but workable; a large sleeping porch would be good for summer nights; two of the four big bedrooms could be closed off. But just how she would manage the kitchen-less lower floor had her baffled. All original room partitions had been knocked out when the house had been rented by the Sigma Alpha Epsilon Fraternity, making the downstairs area as big as a ballroom. Fortunately, Mamie had brought along the electric appliances and two-grid plate; so a kitchen of sorts was rigged up behind a screen.

The scuffed and worn furniture was none too plentiful; there were no window curtains, and the red Khiva rug was a lonely island on an ocean of bare flooring. The few other things that had been packed in with the rug, such as linens, knickknacks and a meager assortment of plated knives and forks, were mere drops in the bucket if the house was to be outfitted for the most funda-mental living. A crib for "Icky", pots and pans, dishes and glass-

ware, broom, dustpan and mop, were purchased straight off—
and not second-hand. They made heavy inroads into Mamie's
$90 nest-egg from her "give-away sale" at Fort Sam. She hoped,
once she was more settled, she could hunt up used bargains in
lamps, bookcases and the like.

Ike was still blissfully unaware of her "give-away" of the apartment furnishings and she hoped to keep him that way; she'd
been blasted enough already for selling his suits. That misdeed
had been discovered almost at once. Before the trunks had been
emptied, Ike started looking for his suits; so she blurted out the
truth. The explosion that followed rocked the high beams of the
old house. Like most people who are even-tempered except under
great provocation—and Mrs. Eisenhower says candidly, "The suit
episode was enough to unsettle a saint"—her husband raged
briefly, then cooled off and canceled the whole matter. Sadly, he
told her he hoped she'd grow up and learn a true sense of values,
a remark which hurt more than his anger.

In her sense of values, Mamie matured much faster than her
husband suspected she would. Only, it was an undercover operation, since she did not dare let him know how little of the nest-
egg money was left. He had never asked her directly how much
she was paid for the Fort Sam furnishings, and so long as she
did not have to tell him all would be serene. It took only one or
two shopping excursions for her to realize, from the fancy prices
asked for inferior used furniture, that she had been bilked. The
knowledge rankled all the more when he bragged about the
bargain he had found in the second-hand Ford.

It was years before she told him her secret. By that time he
thought it very funny, because in the meanwhile, having learned
values the hard way, she had never parted with so much as a
wornout frying pan. Her hoarding holds to this day. There is a
warehouse in Washington where every purchase of Mamie's,
from a potholder to a bedstead, along with the plethora of gifts
received since her husband became world-famous, is crated,
boxed, or barreled against the day they can be unpacked in the
Gettysburg farmhouse now being remodeled.

Under the pressure of his World War One training command, Ike spent most of his off-duty hours in study. It was not very long before other Army couples who were living around town became friendly and they were welcomed also by oldtime residents. On evenings when Ike felt he could put his books and papers aside, there was usually a game of poker. Bridge, the new game just becoming popular, was the center of Mamie's daytime social life with other Army wives. According to the Gettysburg-born Mrs. Dorothy Lynch, who was then married to Major John B. Duckstad, a West Point classmate of Ike's, the group was known as "the inner circle of the headquarters crowd." Until October 1918, when her husband was killed in combat, Mrs. Duckstad and Mamie were together constantly, either playing cards or sitting in each other's homes, minding their young sons.

Dorothy Duckstad lived with her mother, Mrs. E. B. Zane, in Gettysburg's finest mansion. The steep-roofed, brown brick house was as formidable as a castle. Turret-like cupolas, numerous balconies as stout as ramparts, and eighty narrow windows recessed in the thick walls helped to create a medieval atmosphere. Indoors, in spite of the many windows, the rooms were gloomy even on the brightest day. Massive furniture from the ball-fringe and horsehair era of the previous century stood in dim outline against the fancifully carved black-brown woodwork. And yet it was a friendly house, and Mamie spent many an afternoon and evening there. On summer days the dim main hall offered a cool and spacious retreat from the heat. Mrs. Duckstad would set out lamps and tables and invite the "headquarters crowd" over for bridge and whist. Many of the women backed away from learning bridge, but Mamie and Dorothy Duckstad were natural bridge partners. When they won—the stakes were twenty-five cents a corner—they pooled their winnings and bought war-savings stamps for their sons.

During the summer Mamie had the company of her sister "Buster", who came overland alone from Denver rather than go on a West Coast motor trip with her parents and "Mike." She seemed to be overcoming her invalidism, so there seemed to be no reason why she should not make the visit. She stayed several months, and though "just learning," sometimes made a fourth at bridge. At the penny-ante poker sessions, she often proved her Doud kinship by coming out the winner. Men were still scornful of bridge, calling it a "woman's game" and an outgrowth of "Old Maid" and whist—which was why poker was still the most popular game when men and women decided to spend an evening at cards.

When it came her turn to entertain Mamie fell back on her Mexican recipes. Her sketchy kitchen, always a subject for con- dolence from her friends, was adequate for a one-pot meal, such as frijoles or a tongue-burning dish of chicken and rice, and her Mexican suppers and luncheons had the added virtue of being cheap. Pennies still loomed as large as dollars in Mamie's monthly budget, bent and battered from new expenditures for household necessities.

The bright side of the picture was Ike's rapid advancement. He was promoted to major in June, and became a lieutenant- colonel in October. Both were temporary wartime ranks, but sure yardsticks of his leadership in the new and untried field of armored warfare. How he was able to develop a successful Tank Corps training program, without tanks for the use of trainees in simulated battle maneuvers, was for many years a little known marvel of World War One. The War Department finally recog- nized his achievement and in 1922 officially awarded him the Distinguished Service Medal. The citation accompanying the decoration said that as commanding officer of the Tank Corps Training Center he "displayed unusual zeal, foresight and marked ability in the organization and preparations for overseas service of the technical troops . . ."

In the early days of the training program, someone had the foresight to ship in from France a beat-up Renault tank that had obviously outlived its combat usefulness. Though it ran, and served as an experimental vehicle for Ike and his instructors, the tank remained a curiosity so far as the trainees were concerned. The situation was comparable to trying to teach infantrymen to shoot without rifles, and ranks as one of the most extreme cases of military procurement "bejizzlement" ever to threaten a war-time training program. All Ike and his staff knew about tanks was what they absorbed from studying reports, manuals and blue-prints—and from clanking and snorting over the training area of Camp Colt in the obsolete Renault.

Tanks were a British invention. Constructed in Britain with such phenomenal secrecy as to earn the appellation "best-kept secret of World War One," they created a nightmare of surprise and confusion for the enemy when they first advanced over German trenches in 1916. The French promptly started manu-facturing an adaptation of the British tank and used it with equal success. When the United States entered the war, French and British tank production was still limited; so the U. S. Army decided to start a rush job of tank production by tooling up auto-mobile factories in Dayton, Ohio. Instead of diverting tanks for the Camp Colt training program, the War Department ruled that because of the critical shortage of tanks in combat, all armored vehicles coming off Dayton assembly lines would be shipped directly to Europe. That is why American soldiers trained in the highly technical duties of tank warfare did not come face to face with an American tank until they reached France. The instruc-tion they received at Camp Colt, however, was so thorough that the trainees needed no further training in France, but were immediately integrated into combat units and sent into battle.

In this atmosphere of training responsibility, it can readily be understood why there was always plenty of "tank talk" at the Eisenhower dinner table, especially in the first few months of Ike's command, when the success of the program still had to be tested in battle. His tension was eased after favorable reports began coming in from France, and along about then Mamie came out with the daring suggestion that maybe some afternoon he might take her for a ride in the Renault. She says it was a spur-of-the-moment whim, put forward jestingly with no expectation that her husband, a strict military disciplinarian, would take it seriously. He replied that if she wouldn't complain afterward about the physical discomfort, he would be glad to give her the ride of her life; tanks, he said, out-bucked broncos.

Until Saturday afternoon, Mamie was in a dither. She kept the plan secret from her friends, not wanting the expedition to become "ladies' day." What to wear was a problem; it must be nothing tight, nothing frilly, and certainly nothing even second-best. She knew the driving platform was approached by climbing in through the front—there would probably be plenty of grease. Learning of her worries, her husband said she could wear anything she liked; inside and out, the tank was as tidy as a limousine.

After supper they drove in the Ford to a back road. There was the Renault, as painted and polished as a museum piece, but growling and coughing like an irritable old giant. At their approach a sergeant crawled out of the nose of the vehicle and gave a snappy salute. Ike stooped down and pulled himself up into the tank, worming his way to the driving platform. Popping his head through the open circular conning section, he yelled to his wife to get aboard. With an assist from the sergeant, Mamie got her feet off the ground, then scrambled through, steadied by Ike, who reached forward and grasped her hands. The motor raced, then rose to a roaring bark as the heavy gear caught in first. The cleats slapped and clopped in the dust, giving the tank a hunching motion; then came top gear and greater speed, and the hunch became a rock and buck. Mamie shook like jelly. She hit a wall and bounced back when the tank made a sharp turn into a lane. She remembers that all was pandemonium, that her cries were drowned out. It was as if a boiler factory were going full tilt in a two-by-four room. Ike couldn't have driven more than a quarter of a mile at top speed when he slammed on the brakes, threw the motor into reverse, backed deliberately into and over a gully, then pivoted the long tail around with a *zing* and started forward in the general direction of the waiting sergeant.

It is Mamie's considered opinion that no boy at Christmas was ever more blissful with a tricycle. The Commander of the Tank Training Corps had great fun putting the Renault through its paces. Mamie, with ears ringing, eyes smarting from gasoline fumes, drenching wet from the hot interior, knew that she was a sight (and Mamie doesn't like to be a sight); but when the run was over she laughed gamely and slid out through the raised front to solid ground.

"Checked out in tanks," that was Mamie. She felt most privileged; but once was enough, thank you. She was proud and pleased to be the first woman in the country, if not the world, to ride in a tank under, well, *almost* combat conditions. She speaks of the experience as her biggest excitement of World War One.

Summer moved into autumn with little or no change in the daily pattern of living. "Buster" returned to Denver, and housekeeping was less complicated. Casualties were mounting in Europe; troop-ships were reported every day as leaving with replacements—including officers and men trained at Camp Colt. The draft was taking men from farms, offices, colleges, factories, and off city streets. Army wives and mothers talked constantly of the war as being "a great opportunity" for their men, but their hearts hurt them. In October, time ran out for Dorothy Duckstad; her husband was killed in France. She stayed on with her mother in the big brown castle-like house that now was a fortress for grief. Mamie and the Army wives of the bridge and poker crowd were numbed. They knew all too well that if the war kept on— and there was every likelihood that it would continue for years— more husbands would go to France, fight brilliantly and never return. The hills around Gettysburg were russet and gold now; suddenly one could not forget that their soil had been red with the blood of Union and Confederate troops in the tide-turning battle of 1863.

Ike's promotion to lieutenant-colonel came through on orders a few days after he heard of his classmate's death. Her husband's new rank set Mamie to wondering if his value at Camp Colt would not root him in that command all through hostilities; but she dared not express her conjecture. Ike was as determined as ever to be sent into combat.

In the first days of November, there was shut-in suspense in the Eisenhower household. Ike came home one grey afternoon looking happier than at any time since the start of World War One. Mamie heard his light step, saw his wide grin, and her guard went up. Ike could be *that* happy for one reason only. He handed her a sheaf of papers—his orders to report to Camp Dix, New Jersey, for embarkation to France on November 18. Two weeks and he would be gone! She froze, fumbling inside herself for the ability to act, to match his gladness, share his happiness. All the time her heart was pushing against her ribs, starting to climb to her throat.

She dropped her eyes, slowly reread the orders, dotting every i, crossing the t's. Then she looked up, studying the wall behind her husband. To gain time—and composure—she weighed a sentence, something about "destiny" and "his lucky star" but the words were erased when he spoke her name and forced her to meet his appraising gaze. She was on trial as a wife, an Army wife—and she knew it. Looking back at the orders she said carefully that since they represented his heart's desire, she would try to abolish her fears for his safety and make his rejoicing the keystone of her happiness. When she finished he kissed her gently on the cheek. It was his way of saluting the staunchness of her spirit.

After this brief time of disciplined emotion they began to plan for the future. Mamie could not stay in Gettysburg—or could she? Normally, her family was now in San Antonio, but recently there had been disquieting news from Denver. "Buster's" condition had worsened and Mr. and Mrs. Doud thought it best to spend the winter in Colorado. Mamie did not want to live in the far West while Ike was in France; perhaps through the many friends she had now made around town, she might be lucky in finding a small apartment. Occupied with apartment hunting in the next few days, she mustered new courage.

Then Papa Doud telephoned. Certain that he was calling in response to Ike's wire about overseas duty, Mamie greeted her father lightly. She did not want her husband, who was within earshot, to guess the true weight of fears over the separation. As Papa Doud spoke, his quiet voice strained by emotion, Mamie's head dropped as if from a hammer blow. Calling to Ike to take the receiver she wavered across the room and sat at the dining table with her head on her outstretched arms.

"Buster" dead. Fragile, patient, pain-burdened "Buster." The sister, who in all their eighteen years together had been the essence of loyal devotion. As Ike talked her grief reached out to Papa and Mama and young "Mike." They needed her and she needed them—immediately, not ten days later, when Ike was gone. Tearless, in control now of her feelings, Mamie went back to the telephone and told her father she and "Icky", somehow, in some way, would leave for Denver next day. Yes, she was going to stay with them until Ike returned from France.

Ike went to the station to arrange transportation for his wife and son, and Mamie started sorting and packing trunks and suitcases. With energy born of emergency she worked far into the night. Forced to be a bystander, except when there were heavy things to be lifted, Ike worried to see her crowding her endurance.

At least he could cook the evening meal. But Mamie ate only in snatches, between stooping or reaching and running up and down stairs. Her feet ached as always when subjected to unusual activity, but all she did was kick off her shoes and keep going.

Ike rode with her on the morning train for the fifty-odd miles to Harrisburg, where she was to catch an overnight express to Chicago; from there, after a layover of several hours, she would begin the two-day ride to Denver. For the sake of "Icky", who wiggled on his father's lap and resented not being able to stagger in the aisle, the saddened parents made a show of lightness. In the midst of strangers in the Harrisburg station, their parting gave no outward sign of inner tragedy. The farewell was harder for Ike; he would return to an empty apartment, and would have no loved ones near him until the end of the war. Mamie had "Icky" to mother, and would be living with her family.

She arrived in Chicago November 9, just after noon, to find the city in an uproar of celebration. Sirens screeched, bells clanged. Shouting, screaming hordes clogged the streets, shinnied up lamp posts or telephone poles, or leaned with abandon from the windows of hotels and office buildings. A cutting wind off the Lake made wind tunnels of the canyon streets of the Loop but failed to subdue the crowds. Shopfronts remained locked. It was a workless day for nearly everyone, as the great mid-west metropolis rocked with wild rejoicing. Victory had been won in France! The war was over, said the news flashes. Confirmation was yet to come from the War Department, but everybody was too wildly excited to bother about an official statement.

Mamie was buffeted by Chicago's tumult. It was nip-and-tuck whether she and "Icky" would be stranded completely during the five-hour wait between trains. No redcaps to carry bags, no taxis, no food! Sympathetic fellow passengers carried her luggage from her inbound train to the taxi stand, only to find it empty of cabs. After a long delay a bus pulled up, but in the wild scramble with other travelers to get aboard, Mamie was pushed aside. Fortunately, the driver was aware that the victim was a woman burdened with a crying infant. He collected her bags, and rearranged his passengers so that she could squeeze in. Under normal traffic conditions the crosstown trip from Union Station to the LaSalle Street terminal requires at most twenty minutes. That day the unheated bus was lucky to nudge its way through the jammed streets in two hours.

At LaSalle Street the checkroom, dining room and lunch counters were closed, and the bus driver settled Mamie and "Icky" and their luggage in a waiting room. "Icky" was fretful with hunger and Mamie grew desperate. She fished some biscuits from a bag and gave him water from the drinking fountain; then, finding herself surrounded by people too preoccupied to be helpful, she had just about decided to leave her baggage unguarded and appeal for aid in the station master's office when a porter appeared out of nowhere. Bless that bus driver! He had told the redcap of her predicament! Could milk be found for "Icky"? It would take a lot of finding—so many eating places were shut tight—but if she was prepared to wait, he would do his best. The minutes ticked into an hour, but back came the porter with a bottle of milk and two ham sandwiches. He also had a hand truck on which he stacked the suitcases, promising to put them aboard the Denver train, scheduled to leave in about two hours. Mamie filled a nursing bottle and settled back to feed "Icky". While he drank and grew sleepy, she chewed at the sandwiches.

Now, for the first time, she was able to reflect on the deep import of the armistice. No longer frightened by the day's frustrations, she could think of the sudden ending of hostilities with thanksgiving tempered only by the sorrow that waited at the end of the journey. Cradling her sleeping son, she rose, searched out the telegraph office and wired her husband. Then with a newspaper she settled down in the waiting room until train time.

Relief turned to bleak despair next sun-up when the train pulled into a station and word was brought aboard that the truce reports were false. No armistice had been consummated, fighting was still going on, said the staring, hateful headlines of a local paper. It was mid-day of November 11 when Mamie embraced her family in Denver, then drove home to Lafayette Street to leave "Icky" with Dawson, the cook, and change clothes for her sister's funeral. After the final rites at Fairmont Cemetery, "Buster's" casket was lowered into a grave adjoining that of Eleanor, the oldest Doud daughter, who had died in 1912.

Back in the stillness of their home Mr. and Mrs. Doud turned naturally to the happy innocence of "Icky" for comfort, and Mamie, strung tight by sorrow and disappointment and physically spent, closed herself in her room to sleep. Early in the night she awoke in terror; sirens were moaning. At first she thought the sound was nightmare; then came whistle blasts and the tolling of church bells. In the hall she heard her father's step, then her mother's hushed voice; "Mike" was calling out. Opening the door, Mamie followed her parents downstairs. Papa tried to telephone one of the newspapers, but hung up when they said "busy". Lights were on all up and down the block; neighbors peered from windows. And still noise and more noise; just like the false armistice, Mama said. Could this be the real thing?

Papa Doud disappeared to dress, then was off in the Packard. He was back within the hour with the answer: the War Department had made official announcement that the German High Command had asked to meet with Allied generals aboard a train in Compiègne Forest to sign an armistice.

Wary from one disappointment, Mamie waited through the night, as did everyone up and down Lafayette Street, in all Denver; in all the nation. While it was still dark, boys began bellowing the first extras. Yes, Mamie could see, as she read over her father's shoulder, that this *was* the Armistice.

Mrs. Doud kept Mamie in bed all day. Every few hours her father popped in with fresh newspapers. Then came a wire from Ike warning that until the Army could unsnarl the swift shutdown of combat all orders stood, but he didn't think he would be going overseas. It was a week before Mamie left her room; meanwhile her husband was at Camp Dix, wondering if perhaps he wouldn't be sent to France after all. When orders came assigning him to Camp Benning, Georgia, as a supply officer, he telephoned. He didn't think that Benning would be permanent— so would Mamie concentrate on getting well?

In March he was transferred back to tank training and reported for duty at Camp Meade, halfway between Washington and Baltimore. Meade, a raw, thrown-together wartime cantonment, was a confusion of tanks and tankmen recently returned from the theatre of war. It was to be reorganized as an armored training center. Ike was given command of the heavy tank brigade. A colonel who had led American tanks to victory in France commanded the light tanks. His name was George S. Patton, Jr.

Battle-tested Patton, already an impressive and colorful leader, liked Ike on sight. Ike, five years behind Patton at West Point, regarded the older man with respect. He also envied him: Patton had fought in France—in tanks. During the three years they were associated at Camp Meade their teamwork in the training command helped to overcome widespread opposition to armor and laid the foundation for the upbuilding of a tank program in the years before World War Two, when Patton again commanded fire-spitting vehicles and smashed the German defense.

Out in Denver, "high dander" described Mamie's state of mind when Ike kept on writing that it would be months before wooden barracks could be converted into family housing; meanwhile he was living in bachelor officers' quarters under wartime conditions. Mamie couldn't see why she couldn't set up housekeeping in Washington or Baltimore; commuting would be only twenty miles either way, and surely he could be home at least for week ends. But Ike was adamant. Later, always later, fumed Mamie. Young and impatient, she could not understand why, now that the war was over, she must go on waiting. Inaction made things worse; she hated to get up and face the dull days. Dawson and the family took turns at spoiling "Icky" and there was nothing she could do about it, short of a quarrel. Afternoons she played cards or rode around town with her mother. Evening parties were out; Mamie felt too conspicuous without her husband. On Sunday, after dinner at noon, there was invariably a two-hour drive out Colfax and Broadway, past the Phipps Sanitarium, down a road that led to the cemetery and the family plot to place fresh flowers on the graves.

For Mamie, spring came slowly in the Rockies. For Ike at Camp Meade, it came even more slowly. No headway was made toward conversion of the barracks into duplex houses. Then June arrived and an unbelievable shift: Ike was borrowed to be an observer with the Army's first transcontinental truck train that would start from Washington, D. C. early in July and head out to the West Coast. It was to be a test of the practicability of mass motor transportation. General Pershing first used motor vehicles to support troops when he probed into Mexico in 1915 seeking Villa. Trucks had proved valuable in France, and now the General of the Armies wanted his faith to be justified; so he instigated the grueling test of a mid-summer motorcade across the United States. Could—and would—the truck replace the Army mule?

With today's trucks and trailer-trucks thundering on every

highway it seems fantastic that in 1919 there could be any question about motorized transportation. But roads were few; concrete highways were unheard of, and asphalt paving was still in the experimental stage in cities. The Army trucks were in for a terrific beating; men who rode them would be peace-time heroes.

The line of trucks planned to pull into North Platte, Nebraska for an overnight halt. Ike thought Mamie might like to be in North Platte as a welcoming committee of one. This would be some time in August, if the trucks held up; so there was plenty of time for her to decide. He cautioned against bringing "Icky." The 200-mile train trip from Denver would be tiresome, and hotel accommodation in North Platte none too comfortable in the summer's swelter. Also, it was only an overnight stop; then the motor train would head on west.

Mamie finished her husband's letter and flew upstairs to find her father. Blotting a column of figures and laying aside his pen, Mr. Doud listened carefully while his daughter breathlessly read him Ike's letter. Train indeed! Here was a just excuse for that motor-trip-with-a-purpose he'd been trying to drum up since spring. Just the two of them, Mama and "Mike" could stay home and mind "Icky." It would be rough through the foothills, roads not much more than trails! The Nebraska prairie-land would be a bake-oven with not much in the way of roads. If Mamie was game, the trip was as good as made. She *was* game, and she kissed him extravagantly.

The Army's endurance test with mechanized motor transports became front-page news as soon as the trucks roared out of Washington. Papa Doud and Mamie charted each day's run with pins on a map and did not need Ike's wire to tell them when to start for North Platte. At sun-up next day, dressed in dusters, goggles, and pull-down hats, father and daughter made a final recheck of supplies, which included blankets, vital if they stalled overnight getting across the mountains. It was a risky journey, through the uninhabited foothills of the Rockies and sparsely settled Nebraska prairies. A breakdown almost anywhere along the route might isolate them for several days, in which case the trip would be in vain, for Ike would be with the motorcade when it headed west. Food a-plenty was packed in the rear of the Packard. Cans of water, extra tins of gasoline, a portable stove, coffee pot and frying pan rested on the floor. Papa's tool kit, spare tires, tow rope and shovel were stowed in outside compartments. Mama Doud, none too happy about the trip, had insisted on a first-aid kit. "Mike" contributed some extra film for Mamie's camera. Dawson handed up a box of Papa's cigars and a thermos of soda pop that "Miss Mamie" had overlooked.

With spirits as high as the snow-clad peaks that lay ahead, father and daughter sped out of town. All morning they snailed up the rocky grades. Often the Packard steamed like a teakettle, forcing them to halt to cool off the radiator. Only once was Mr. Doud involved with a minor problem with the starter. After noon, they dropped down to the sand and stubble of Nebraska, to mile after mile of emptiness. Only wagon tracks, that had probably never been used by automobiles, guided them to North Platte.

They reached the riverside town by early evening, having averaged about fifteen miles an hour, nearly always in second gear. Mr. Doud, divested of his duster, and spruce as usual except for a dusty face, casually remarked to the hotel clerk that he had driven in from Denver with his daughter to meet the convoy of Army trucks. The clerk spread the news of Papa's feat. North Platte was still a horse-and-wagon town. Curious stares from bobbing heads at the dining-room door added to the gaiety of the meal Mamie shared with her father. If the travelers had just dropped in from Mars they could not have caused more stir. Even the Packard parked at the hotel hitching rail was scrutinized. Western courtesy deterred the ring of spectators from touching strange property, but more than one inquisitive nose accidentally grazed the windshield and side-curtains.

Papa was flattered. He said half the fun of cross-country driving was turning up in small towns and surprising people. Mamie told him to stay up and have fun; she was punch-tired from the day's bouncing. Next morning she decided that Papa must have stayed up quite a while—he was calling a lot of people around the hotel by their first names.

Dressed in frothy cotton with black velvet at her wrists, her shining hair dipped and coiled to neat perfection, Mamie was without a doubt the prettiest girl in all Nebraska as she popped into and out of the hotel awaiting the sunset arrival of her husband. At last, the ponderous, dust-masked convoy rolled down the street. Mamie flashed her handkerchief, searching the faces of the fast-moving riders. Men yelled and waved wildly as they blurred past. Finally she heard a voice bellowing her name, and Ike, a grin on his dust-powdered face, leaned as far as he dared from a front seat, "hollering like a kid on a roller-coaster."

Mr. Doud said that Mamie shouldn't get dusty and wrinkled driving out to the camp site, but she insisted. Once there, no need to search among the trucks for Ike; he spied the Packard first and broke into a run. Sunburned and dirty, that was Ike, but he had never looked happier or healthier. What a contrast from that awful day of good-bye in the Harrisburg station!

Alone with her husband, Mamie began to state her intentions, expecting disagreement. Quarters or no quarters, she was going to Meade, if she had to live in a tent. Instead, Ike was all for having her go to Meade, provided she left "Icky" in Denver until they moved into permanent quarters on the post. If she didn't expect too much and was willing to live off post in some small nearby Maryland community for a few months, he might be lucky in finding a couple of rooms in a private home. For the first time since her marriage, Mamie felt reassured. The "war to end all wars" was over; now she and Ike could really begin solid planning. Rented rooms! That was an inconvenience she would accept gladly, knowing the sketchy arrangement to be a prelude to honest-to-goodness married life on the post.

Unhappily, the Meade tour of duty was to be her time of greatest disillusionment and tragedy. But as they planned their future her happiness was boundless.

A short time later, Mamie had to summon up all her reserves of courage to leave "Icky." He was a busy two-year-old, pedaling his tricycle up and down the block; a backyard sandpile operator, and fast as a monkey around the front porch pillars. "All boy, and a yard wide; just like his father," in his mother's opinion.

Mamie left for Camp Meade in September bag and baggage. A few weeks later her father would be driving, as usual, to San Antonio. A family conclave resulted in the decision to have Mrs. Doud, "Mike" and "Icky" go by train. Landers, his Army service over and done with, and Duncan went with Mr. Doud in the Packard. It was planned to keep "Icky" in San Antonio at least until Christmas. Mamie hoped to have quarters at Camp Meade by then; in any event, she saw no reason why she and Ike could not spend the holidays at the McCullough Street house in San Antonio, then take him back with them to Camp Meade. It was all as simple as that.

She had yet to set foot in Maryland and learn defeat the hard way. Mrs. Eisenhower confesses that she "threw in the sponge just once." That was when she found it impossible to go on living at Odenton, Maryland, a little rail-stop seven miles up the road from Camp Meade. It was not the seedy furniture, the grimy rug or the torn curtains at the single window of the room she and her husband occupied in a slatternly Odenton house that were unbearable. Even the frigid dampness could be borne. She had arrived prepared for the worst. On the way over from Baltimore, Ike had prepared her for the lodgings. They weren't much better than a rural tenement, but they would have to do; no other living space was up for rent in the whole Camp Meade area.

Trouble started the first morning with what seemed to be temporary failure of the electric current. The landlady told her that due to a local power shortage there was a daily six-to-six shut-off of electricity. Mamie didn't mind doing her personal laundry, or even hanging it in the room to dry, but she rebelled at having to do the ironing at night.

That year there was no Indian Summer. Shut up in the clammy room, with not enough daylight filtering through the window, even when the curtains were pinned back, to permit reading, Mamie was the prisoner of her thoughts. The landlady was frugal with coal, and Mamie was forced to huddle in bed or bundle in blankets if she wanted to sit in a chair and stare out the streaked window at the intermittent traffic. Her breakfast came out of a paper bag. There wasn't a particle of sense in dressing and driving over with Ike to the Officers' Club, for that meant standing around and waiting for a return ride in a jitney. To slop through the rain for noon-time food at a lunch counter in a local drugstore didn't seem worth the effort. As a rule she ate a dried-up sandwich, picked up the previous night on the drive back from dinner at Camp Meade.

After several weeks of this existence, Mamie knew that she was doomed unless she found better accommodations. She questioned Odenton's few storekeepers without success, then went over to Laurel, but had no better luck. Ike was right; the war had brought too many new people into the area. No one showed any desire to move out. No one except Mamie Eisenhower. In dark defeat she packed up and caught a train for San Antonio.

Chapter 6

CAMP MEADE, MD.

1919–1922

Mamie rented a furnished apartment on Grayson Avenue in San Antonio, halfway between the Doud house in McCullough Street and Fort Sam. She chose to set up her own small apartment, as she felt she had already imposed too much on her parents' hospitality during the long Denver visit. Papa Doud liked her go-it-alone spirit; a stiff backbone in married people was one of his cherished ideals. Mrs. Doud also approved, rating her daughter's independence a sure sign of maturity. If anything, family ties were closer than ever. There was the usual visiting back and forth; "Icky's" playtime was spent in the spacious yard and big white house, but Mamie made her apartment the center of her life. Her part-time maid served as baby sitter whenever she played cards or went out to dinner with married friends on Infantry Row. Ike had retained his wartime rank, which meant that as the wife of a lieutenant colonel Mamie had a much broader social horizon compared with the days she lived on the post as a first lieutenant's wife.

The interlude on Grayson Avenue lasted a bare three months. Ike came down on Christmas leave with the glad tidings that he had been allotted quarters in one of the converted barracks at Camp Meade. They would move in any time after the first of the year.

Pressed to describe the housing, he said the rooms were large, with plenty of windows. Unlimited electricity was also available. The kitchen and bath had new plumbing, but they would have to depend on a coal-fed stove for heating upstairs and downstairs. The stove was a round, cast-iron contrivance, the usual Army issue, and should keep them comfortable without being too much of a burden. He and other married officers had arranged to pay a man to make the rounds of married quarters, do the heavy stoking and bring in extra scuttles of coal. Ike said he had ordered the barrels and crates of household belongings sent from storage at Camp Colt as a start toward getting settled as quickly as possible. Several borrowed Army cots would do until Mamie bought beds. The standard Army allotment of a chest of drawers, dining table and chairs had been moved in. Not much of a beginning, but at least they had light, heat and plenty of room.

"Roofed-over camping out" was Mamie's mental picture of the housing, but she was willing to start again from scratch to make a home. There were no savings to draw on, so she knew it would take financial wizardry to fix up such a place without going into debt. Had it not been for her travel expenses and the cost of the apartment in San Antonio, they would have had extra funds for new furniture. Going into debt, even for necessary purchases, was unthinkable.

From the day of their marriage the Eisenhowers have paid in full for everything. Adherence to this stern principle has often meant weeks, or even months, of frugality and self-denial until enough cash was at hand for the acquisition of new things. Mamie has always been the family banker and economist. Except for pocket money, her husband has never handled money. When new quarters had to be made homelike, her own clothing allowance was absorbed into the household budget, and they were transferred on an average of every two years during General Eisenhower's military service. Mamie, who has lost count of the many domiciles (she thinks twenty-seven is nearly correct), terms herself "a move-body as well as a home-body."

When it came to furnishing the Camp Meade duplex, she knew she would be lucky to find second-best at the prices she could afford to pay. There would have to be a lot of improvising, such as packing-case tables and barrel chairs, disguised with paint and chintzes. If she found the right bargains, she estimated quickly that it would take at least six months to accumulate all they needed. At this point, Mamie boiled over, remembering her $90 give-away of the furnishings in the apartment on Infantry Row. What smooth sailing it would be if she had not been a "cotton-topped imbecile!"

Later, when creating a dressing table for her Camp Meade bedroom out of orange crates and a remnant length of flowered material, she indulged in further self-reproach. If she had not been such a fool, she thought, thumb-tacking each pleat of the material with angry pressure, the Circassian walnut table with the triple mirrors, not this confounded makeshift, would be lending beauty and comfort to the room. That was the piece of furniture she regretted losing most of all.

Day-long rounds of auctions and second-hand stores in Baltimore were tiring as well as time-consuming. Bargains were not easy to find. Ike would drive Mamie the seven miles to either West Laurel or East Odenton for a train connection, then pick her up in the evening. These Maryland towns were linked to Baltimore, less than twenty miles away, by local trains operated by separate railroads. During the trip that took well over an hour each way, Mamie usually rested her feet by sitting sideways while reading a newspaper. In 1920, only old ladies wore "sensible" shoes; young women who followed fashion contorted their feet into high-heeled footwear with "needle-pointed" toes. Mamie believed in being fashionable, so she paid dearly on those long shopping tours. When her purchases were delivered, there were always extra cartage fees added to the price of items that could not be wrapped as carrying bundles. Ike showed great interest, but he could never be coaxed into going to shop in Baltimore. Mamie thinks he became allergic to shopping in general ever since she disposed of his two tailormade suits at Fort Sam. At any rate, since then he has confined his personal buying to jewelry and florist shops, leaving even the selection of his civilian attire to his wife.

Between Baltimore excursions, Mamie kept house, aided by a succession of maids. The unexciting rural location of Camp Meade dampened their spirits and few maids stayed longer than one pay-day. Mrs. Eisenhower says she kept two maids—"one coming and one going"—and did most of the housework herself. The coal stove in the living room was a real heart-breaker. It was always at extremes—either overheated or stone cold. At no time did it heat the upstairs. The twice-daily rounds of the stoker by no means satisfied its appetite. Though the kitchen plumbing— a sink and a washtub in the back entry—was new, an old coal range, backed by a hot water boiler, was an insufferable nuisance. It made the kitchen cozy in winter, but once summer set in, the room became an inferno! Ice never lasted through a day in the wooden refrigerator. So the Eisenhowers invested in another electric hot plate—a fine-and-dandy arrangement until the needs of bath time or a wash-tub session required lots of hot water and the coal stove necessarily blazed away.

Ike, who had learned to cook on a coal range in his mother's kitchen, knew how to coax just the right heat from the stove. He shook the ashes, never too much, never too little; opened the damper a crack or a handspan, depending on what was to be cooked; banked the fire at night, or lifted off a top lid for fast boiling or frying. He taught Mamie all these tricks, and in time she ran him a close second; but she detested the mess and bother, and was always glad when he volunteered to cook a meal—even though she knew he would scorn potholders and ruin the dish towels by grabbing hot handles with them.

On June 30th Ike dropped back to his permanent rank of captain; and two days later was promoted to temporary major. His brilliant record as an executive officer caused the Army to make this unusual peacetime promotion. The $21.67 reduction in pay

—he would be drawing $320 a month as major—called for greater economy. Mamie, who now needed only incidentals for the duplex, revised her budget downward and went on wearing mostly made-over clothes. Her only luxury was a rented piano.

The close friendship between Ike and George Patton was never matched by their wives. Much as Mamie and Beatrice Patton liked each other, their widely separated personal interests left them little time for intimacy. Mrs. Patton liked to sail and fish; she was an excellent horsewoman and aspired to match her husband's talent as a poet. A globe-trotter from childhood, she had married George, her childhood sweetheart, when he graduated from West Point five years ahead of Ike, and had thereafter adapted her ways to the Army way of life with the same intense devotion to the service that filled her husband's brave heart.

Mamie's only interest in sports was as a spectator at football games; her reading was confined to current events and an occasional novel. Although her family had better than average means, she had not traveled widely like Beatrice Patton, nor had she been associated with internationally prominent people. Mamie's orbit was domesticity. Her sparkle, wit and charm, her laughter, keen card sense and entertaining music, all made her the popular wife of a popular officer.

Bea Patton kept a good house and liked informal parties but she left her housekeeping in hired hands. She was away a great deal—visiting her family near Boston, sailing the Chesapeake in season, deep-sea fishing off Florida, riding with a hunt club on Maryland's Eastern Shore, or dropping over to Washington for a few days. Innately shy, she was able to check-rein her ebullient husband without seeming to exercise any control. Swaggering, arm-waving Patton, with a poet's heart and a soldier's blade-sharp mind, was always a considerate husband.

The Pattons were then in their early thirties and had many high-ranking friends in the Army. A man of independent wealth (his wife also had a tidy fortune of her own), Patton, though always scrupulously respectful with military superiors, was never awed by general officers. This won him steadfast friends and bitter enemies in high places. While at Camp Meade, he was bent on proving to "doubting Thomases"—one of his gentler epithets—in the War Department that the tank corps was the key to forward ground assault. Military budgets had been cut way down and Patton feared the tank corps would be shelved unless Army policy-makers put aside old prejudices and underwrote an intensive training, research and development program for tanks. A firm believer in deeds, as well as words, Patton used many a social occasion to induce staff officers to come over from the War Department and see for themselves how tanks performed.

One such group of War Department officers on a tour of Camp Meade exasperated Major Patton (he also had been demoted from his wartime rank) to the bursting point by refusing to accept his invitation to ride in one of the well-varnished tanks lined up for inspection. The star-spangled visitors walked in silence up and down the rows of armored vehicles. Only the occasional clap of a swagger-stick could be heard. This diffident curiosity and such stand-back tactics reminded Patton of circus ticket-holders viewing a line of hobbled elephants.

His guests were ready to conclude the inspection just as the enthusiastic and excitable Patton was ready to settle himself in the driver's seat of one of the behemoths. As for accompanying him over the countryside, his guests refused with cold superiority. Someone said cuttingly that tanks were known to blow up, topple over and even turn turtle on a steep hill. With a snort of disgust, Patton turned, beckoned to his wife, and with a sweeping theatrical gesture invited her to enter a small whippet tank. Though dressed fit for a garden party, she disappeared nimbly into the turret. Patton let out a yell of triumph; howled to his visitors over the racket of thundering motors to wait—and watch—and was off. He handled the tank as he would a polo pony (he was the Army's high goal player), spinning in lightning turns, jarring to abrupt stops, thudding down the field at break-neck speed. The onlookers saw a rare demonstration of the maneuverability of armored cavalry. His performance produced dry smiles. The top brass, having taken one look at bruised, begrimed and topsy-turvy Mrs. Patton, were still determined not to sample any of Patton's tankmanship.

When Mamie heard the exploit described cattily around camp, she defended Bea's sportsmanship. Unladylike? Fiddlesticks! Bea had shown her mettle. The tank-shy Army bigwigs had stood by, not because they were afraid of a bump or two, but to preserve the press of their uniforms.

"Icky," with a child's sensitivity, was aware that it would soon be Christmas. For a three-year-old he showed much wisdom. He shadowed his father at every opportunity. When the post football team had practice, "Icky" was out with his father watching the play. If there was tinkering to be done on the Ford, "Icky" hung around and handed his father tools. At bedtime mother read stories from books about never-never fairyland, and that was fine; but father told wonderful tales about Indians and soldiers, his quiet voice rumbling along from thrill to thrill. Father and son crowded much happiness into their time together.

On Christmas morning the tree glowed brighter than the living-room stove. "Icky" explored his packages, tugging wonderful gifts from their tissue wrappings. He had a full day of excitement and went up to bed on leaden feet, tired as all small children are after a day of Santa Claus's bounty.

In the morning he was listless with a slight temperature; nothing alarming, but to be on the safe side his parents decided he should stay abed. By night he was much brighter, but he still ran a fever and he slept fitfully. During the following day his father slipped away from duty several times to check on "Icky's" progress, and when the fever worsened that night, more as a precaution than because they feared a serious illness, the parents bundled him up and took him to the post hospital. The strange room, the strange people in white, and the odd odors frightened the little boy, so his father sat beside him through the night.

Mamie went home to the cold and empty house and to bed, plagued by nameless fears and teeth-chattering chill. In the morning her voice was gone and she sneezed continually.

Ike returned to snatch a hurried breakfast and make himself presentable for the day. He brought word that "Icky," after a night of tossing and small-voiced demands that his father stay close, was still fever-wracked but had drifted off to sleep. Ike was deeply worried, but he realized that Mamie's labored breathing might be the forerunner of another respiratory attack, and hid his fears for his son. All too vividly he could remember her, lying still in the Fort Sam hospital. Now, of all times, she must guard her health and remain in bed until she was rid of the congestion. With a promise to report back as soon as he had learned the results of a fresh examination of "Icky," he sped to the hospital.

Long before noon, a medical officer gave Ike the dread diagnosis. "Icky" had scarlet fever. Days would have to pass before the crisis. Meanwhile, the doctor thought Mrs. Eisenhower should be kept at home until her infection disappeared. His emotions finally in check, Ike turned away and left the hospital to find a telephone. He had to speak to Mama Doud without fear of interruption. He reached her quickly in Boone, Iowa, where she and Papa and "Mike" were spending the holidays. Mrs. Doud heard him through. Without betraying the fear that filled her stout heart, she replied, "I will come immediately."

By the last day of the year, Mrs. Doud arrived. She found her daughter almost well physically, but sunk in silent emotional torment—an acute locked-in hysteria. Ike, who had been at the hospital almost constantly, looked to his mother-in-law to comfort Mamie while he remained constantly beside the sick child.

Mamie had not been entirely alone; anxious friends had tried to hearten her, but these gestures of sympathy only increased her inner fear. She refused to talk except in halting monosyllables. Mrs. Doud took firm hold and soon had her daughter talking freely. Once Mamie had unburdened her fears, she became able to handle herself rationally, and for the next two days mother and daughter sought to speed the hours with all manner of household tasks, a welcome distraction. Still, Mamie only pecked at her food, and she swung to another extreme of tension: she talked constantly. She resented not being able to share Ike's ceaseless vigil at the hospital, even though she realized that she could not defy the bitter winter gales that lashed the wooden sidings of the house with sleet and rain. Each time the telephone bell shrilled, Mamie froze with sheer terror as she listened to her husband's quiet, weary voice. Night and day, over and over, he repeated that there was still no improvement in "Icky's" state. George Patton and other officers called, and did what they could to divert the uneasy loneliness of Mamie and her mother. Mrs. Doud's greatest strain was when she talked long distance with her husband. She forced herself to speak with firm conviction, when she told him that "Icky's" strong constitution would bring him safely through the crisis. She dared not let Mamie detect any discouragement in her voice.

During the bleak mid-evening of January second—a night like the others of storm and ice—Ike phoned to say that the doctors believed "Icky's" crisis was at hand. Mamie heard him through. She murmured a few choked words, replaced the receiver and fanned her fingers across her haggard face. Mrs. Doud waited in silence, expecting a torrent of weeping. Instead, her daughter withdrew her hands and sank against the chair back. Her eyes were closed but she was conscious. Though her skin was waxen, she breathed deeply.

A knock at the front door took the troubled Mrs. Doud into the hall. She closed the living room door, before she admitted the visitor. One of Ike's favorite lieutenants stumbled into the passage-way out of a world of driving sleet. Wordlessly, he backed the door shut and followed Mrs. Doud into the kitchen.

Striving to keep her voice matter-of-fact, she told him what had just happened. Ike's call must have been bad news, she said; Mamie was too upset to talk. He said he already knew that "Icky's" life hung in delicate balance. That was why he had come. Because of the storm, it was important for a man to be in the house. The electric power might be cut off or the roof spring a leak. With a look of deep gratitude, Mrs. Doud thanked him. He shook up the stove, and she put on a pot of coffee. She also brewed tea for Mamie, and for minutes they rattled around in a brave show of commonplace activity, confining their remarks to the weather. Mamie, who had overheard, now joined them and asked casually if she could help. Flushed, her eyes over-bright, Mamie held herself erect. She took a cup and led the way into the living room where they pulled chairs into a semicircle around the stove. Talk about the storm lasted as long as they could sip the hot beverage. Then the cups were put aside and there was no further pretense at conversation.

The fall of cinders in the stove and the squeak of straining fibers whenever one of the trio stirred in a rattan chair were nerve-racking. Mrs. Doud could stand the sounds no longer and spoke up. No one felt like talking, she said; perhaps music would give a measure of inner peace. At least it was better than the silence. Mamie stared and was about to refuse to touch the piano when her mother asked their guest, who was more than an average musician, if he would care to play. He hesitated and looked questioningly at Mamie. In a voice as firm as her mother's she said it would help if he gave them some music.

Mamie watched him as he played. At first she appeared alert and interested, then she settled back in her chair, averting her face and slowly pleating and repleating her handkerchief. For two hours, except when the greying embers in the stove needed attention, the young musician played on. Sometimes he played so softly that the spatter of the sleet on the windows could be heard. Suddenly, without warning, his hands crashed in a discord. He sagged forward, his head bumping hard against the upright wooden panel of the music-rack. Mamie and Mrs. Doud bolted from their seats, but before they could be of assistance he pulled himself together, got up and strode into the kitchen without speaking.

Even as mother and daughter were wondering what they should do, the Lieutenant returned from the kitchen and walked directly to the piano. He resumed his playing at an accelerated tempo, as if seeking to make up for his lapse. He had been playing for perhaps twenty minutes when feet sounded on the porch and the front door opened. The pianist rose instantly and turned. Mamie started to her feet, and her mother moved behind her, a protective hand outstretched.

Ike crossed the threshold and advanced toward his wife. Mamie looked at his agonized face; her own grew unbelieving, horrorstruck. When he attempted to speak, he could not. She shook her head slowly and moved into the protection of his arms. The two officers who had accompanied the distracted father looked helplessly about—first at Mrs. Doud, then at the young man beside the piano. There was nothing anyone could do. Led by Mrs. Doud, they filed quietly into the dining room, closed the door, and left Ike and Mamie alone in their grief.

Mrs. Doud, who related the events of that night of anguish, says that when after many years she saw the young officer who had collapsed at the piano, she recalled the incident and asked if he could explain the break in his playing. He told her that something had snapped in his mind. He knew with stabbing conviction that "Icky" had died. Later he learned that the child's life had ended at that exact moment.

When "Icky's" body was taken from Camp Meade to Baltimore, a guard of honor rode in the slow procession. At the railroad station, solemn soldiers stood beside the flag-draped wooden case that held the white coffin until it was time to lift it, so pitifully small, into the baggage car of a westbound train. Farther down the platform, Major and Mrs. Eisenhower and Mrs. Doud boarded the train and closed themselves in a drawing room.

During all the tragic preliminaries to the journey, Mamie had remained repressed and tearless. As the train sped toward Chicago she showed no signs of normal grief. Even during the final phase of the journey, when her sister "Mike" boarded the train at Boone, and rode across Iowa for several hours, Mamie's only act was to try and stop "Mike's" tears. They parted at Carroll and "Mike" returned to her aunt's home in Boone. Mr. Doud was already in Denver.

Last services for "Icky" were held in the Doud living room and the flower-smothered casket rested before the fireplace where his parents had stood to repeat their marriage vows. Mamie continued in a bottomless despair. Though the eyes of everyone around her streamed, she found it impossible to cry. Nor did she break even when she faced the finality of the open grave. For two years she mourned in dry-eyed desperation, hiding her grief beneath an outward show of normal living. Only when another family crisis arose, did she weep at last for her lost child.

Mamie would not hear of her husband returning to Camp Meade alone to face the sights and sounds that cloaked the tragic death of their little boy. Ike's grief, as all-consuming as her own, was pitched to frightening intensity. In contrast to her suppressed sorrow, he gave vent openly to his devastation, causing her to fear for his health. They have never put aside their cross of sorrow.

The Infantry Tank School had been established at Camp Meade and Ike found a degree of surcease from his dark grief in the rigorous training. He did his share to prove to Army policy-makers the vital need for armored support of ground troops.

George Patton really raised his sights when he was notified that Brigadier-General Fox Conner would inspect the corps. Here was the chance to impress one of the great strategists of the war, now serving as Chief of Staff to General Pershing in Washington. As wartime Chief of Operations in France with Pershing, General Conner and his wife had been intimate friends of George and Bea Patton since pre-war horse cavalry days at Fort Riley, Kansas. Lieutenant Patton reported there for duty with the largest saber seen in Army circles since the War of 1812. The Pattons and the Conners had boarded the same train in Kansas. Midway to Fort Riley, Colonel Conner, who had not taken his eyes off the serious young man holding the massive weapon, walked down the car and introduced himself.

Mamie has often speculated on what course her husband's

military career would have taken if General Conner had not visited Camp Meade. Ike was already on his way up, no question about that. But it was a chance conversation between the General and George Patton, during a lull in the tour of inspection, that set events in motion which would cause Dwight D. Eisenhower eventually to be recognized as a military genius and leader of men.

During a break for coffee, General Conner mentioned that he was due to take over command of Camp Gaillard in Panama in a few weeks. He confided to Patton that he was faced with the problem of selecting a young man for his staff. As he had been out of touch with young officers during and since the war, he wondered if Patton could recommend a promising junior whom he could take to the Canal Zone as his executive officer. Patton enumerated the qualifications of Ike Eisenhower, and General Conner asked to meet the young major. Patton produced Ike, but there was no intimation during the brief exchange of words with General Conner that Major Eisenhower was being sized up for a new job. As a climax to the day's tour, Patton, up to his old tricks of tank salesmanship, suggested that General Conner take a trial run. The General assented, and his wife, who knew of Bea Patton's experience, spoke up and asked to go along. Since the whippet tanks held only two persons, she was turned over to Major Eisenhower, who was told to give her a short and easy ride. Mrs. Conner remembers Ike's solicitude; he handled her as carefully as a crate of eggs; but even so her teeth were "nearly jarred loose."

After the visitors departed, Patton told Ike about Panama, and advised him to accept if the job was offered. It was Patton's opinion that if Ike served under General Conner, one of the Army's "great brains", he could learn a lot.

Mamie has never forgotten her husband's homecoming that night. He walked in with a bemused and wondering look. Patton's generosity in proposing his name, more than the prospect of a fine opportunity, was what overwhelmed him. He told her that even if nothing came from the recommendation—General

Conner had the whole Army to choose from—the fact that Patton had spoken out for him was what counted. All evening, Ike could talk of nothing else.

General Conner did choose Ike. In accordance with strict military procedure, the General sent a formal letter within a week inviting Major Eisenhower to become his executive officer in Panama. Ike's formal acceptance was in the next mail. It was early October. He was to report at Camp Gaillard late in January.

Now that a time limit had been set on living in the troublesome duplex, Mamie joked about the inconveniences and looked ahead to the inviting prospect of Panama. She had taken a tourist whirl through the Canal Zone with her parents in 1914 when their Caribbean cruise ship stopped for a day at Panama. Six years had not blurred her memory of the monolithic canal locks; of Gatun Lake, cluttered with tropical vegetation except in the lanes kept clear for traversing ships; of Culebra, the mile-wide, man-made ditch; of the steaming jungles, constantly threatening to encroach on the narrow tracks of the under-sized trans-zone railroad. She remembered the Chinese and Indian shopkeepers with their tempting wares in the alley-like streets of Panama City. Foreign and wonderful, that was Panama! She could forget coal scuttles, frigid bedrooms and snow and live close to the sun—with servants to do her every bidding.

In December, Mamie began sorting their clothing and household possessions. Everything—from the kitchen match-safe to the Khiva rug—went into the Panama shipment, but winter clothing, with the exception of warm outfits that she and Ike would wear the first few days aboard ship, was moth-balled for storage. A new owner was found for the Ford. The piano went back to the rental agency. Ike, well supplied with summer uniforms, had no tropical clothing worries, but Mamie's wardrobe was anything but adequate for Panama's heat. She had been told that for proper grooming, two complete changes of clothing would have to be washed and ironed every day. Clothing was the last thing she had any interest in, but she dared not venture into the tropics with only a few dresses. She decided to go to New York two days before the scheduled sailing of the Army transport *Cambrai*, to see if she could find some inexpensive summer things, even though it was the dead of winter. As a last resort she was prepared to use Papa Doud's Christmas check for cotton yardage, trusting that Panama had dressmakers.

On sailing day the Eisenhowers' cabin bloomed with a great bouquet of red roses, Mamie's favorite flowers, a remembrance from her parents. Telegrams, candy and fruit in baskets, testified to the love and thoughtfulness of family and friends. When the ship was cleared of visitors and a prolonged blast signaled that mooring lines were being cast off, Mamie and her husband stood by the rail. The vessel inched away from the dock.

Below them on the afterdeck, troops were packed sardine-fashion. The men stamped and yelled good-bye to well-wishers on the receding pier. Fine snow began drifting from the cheerless sky and eddied down to the steel-grey water on a sharp wind. During the few minutes the vessel swung in midstream before heading toward the open sea, the soldiers ceased yelling and began singing. "There's a Long Long Trail" . . . farewell to home and loved ones. The haunting refrain made Mamie breathe uneasily, and she fled the deck.

Chapter 7

"A double-decked shanty, only twice as disreputable," said Mamie Eisenhower in disgust, as she and her husband peered through a tangle of vines and a wall-like growth of bushes and trees for their first look at the house the Army had assigned them in Panama. It was perched on a shelf of jungle-clogged ground overlooking Gaillard Cut, the "Big Ditch" of the canal. The ghostly structure belonged in a nightmare. Even Ike admitted that the rotting thing looked unreal.

Hot and gasping, horrified by her struggle up a steep path infested with slithery, crawly things, Mamie scarcely knew how to give vent to her sense of outrage. Angrily she stamped a muddy shoe in the damp undergrowth. Ike, hot and chagrined, merely shrugged and pushed through the heavy foliage toward the desolate house. His movement dislodged a fat lizard that scurried for cover. A mosquito whined at Mamie's ear. Afraid to follow her husband, yet more afraid to be alone in the eerie green stillness that buzzed and writhed with unseen life, she tried to steady her nerves by taking deep breaths, but the humid air, rank with the must of over-ripe vegetation, was revolting. Fighting faint-ness, she edged forward. Slipping and sliding but keeping her footing, she reached the clearing of the one-time garden and clung to her husband, who now was calmly appraising the wretched decay of the house. Aware of her trembling, he offered to take her back to the car at the foot of the path to wait while he checked the inside. She turned aside the suggestion; she would be more comfortable within earshot of him, she said.

During the ten years the house had been untenanted, the steaming tropic heat and creeping jungle had worked swift destruction. The steps had rotted away; grey-green mold covered the clapboard walls; such shutters as survived were acant; only wisps of screening remained in the frames of the lop-sided down-stairs porch, and the thick arms of storm-felled trees still lay in deeply dented sections of the roof. Several stilts of the high, open foundation had buckled crazily and now were knotted by vines to planks that had slipped through from the upper floor.

Mamie was sure the place was beyond repair. Better to with-hold judgment, said her husband, until he made a circuit of the interior. Would she stay right where she was while he had a look around? Would she stay! Wild horses couldn't have dragged her inside. While he felt out the side supports of the steps for a foot-ing she called a warning: Would he tread carefully? She wouldn't put it past the tipsy house to lurch under his weight and slide downhill into the cut. Ike made no reply. He crossed the porch gingerly and inserted a key in the mildewed door. Rewarded by a squalling of rusty hinges, he shoved the panel gently open and disappeared within.

While she waited, Mamie played mental tick-tack-toe—and lost. Suppose the house could be repaired—how was she going to know a minute's peace of mind living in such isolation? It had been scary reaching the house in the daytime—what would the steep path be like after dark? Those moldy walls teemed with creatures that bit and stung—how could they be kept out of food, furniture and clothing? Already she visualized furry, many-legged insects nesting in shoes, snakes slumbering in the bed-clothes and regiments of ants assaulting the kitchen.

She also had time to review the spine-chilling experience of the drive over from Balboa. Was she going to have to be first cousin to a tight-rope-walker every time she went to and from Balboa and Panama City? Men with sharp knives could slash back the vegetation; poison could be sprayed at insects; but the cat-walk crowning the 47-foot gates of the Pedro Miguel Lock was as permanent as tide and taxes. How could she learn to keep her heart out of her throat driving or walking across the closed gates? Perhaps now, when she returned with her husband to the Tivoli Hotel, where they were quartered temporarily, she might feel less of inner panic when the driver stopped midway on the steep cliffs, stepped out and shouldered the rear wheels of the car around the sharp V of the center closure. How could familiarity ever breed contempt of that cat-walk?

Now Ike was back and reported to his wife. A few new timbers here and there, plenty of paint after an all-over scrubbing, new shutters, screening, and steps, and the dilapidated house would come alive again. Mamie made a wide, disgusted gesture toward the encroaching jungle. Oh, *that* could be cut back and replanted, maybe with some orchids—local labor was plentiful. Ike radiated optimism, trying to kindle a response in his wife.

Before she could speak her mind—and she had plenty on it that glaring January morning—a tiny woman in a crisp dress as white as her aureole of hair darted round the house. Her blue eyes twinkled as she spoke in a casual deep voice of dramatic timbre. Would the Eisenhowers cheer up and forget the "awful, awful house" and come along and see what she had done with an even worse lame duck? Major Eisenhower ramrodded his back, stole a quick look at his wife, then presented her to Mrs. Fox Conner. The General's wife!

As Mrs. Conner clasped Mamie's hand the earth crunched and rumbled, the house rattled and swayed, the trees creaked. Tighten-ing her grip, Mrs. Conner looked at the perturbed Eisenhowers and smiled widely. "It's just another one of those confounded slides, they happen all the time," she said, with no show of concern.

Less than a hundred yards offside, through an opening in the high hibiscus hedge, Mrs. Conner led the way into a well-kept garden and up painted and varnished steps into the screen-enclosed living porch of the General's quarters. Pale yellow paint covered all outside walls. Bright green shutters, doors and window-sills gave the house fresh newness.

Mrs. Conner showed that she understood perfectly the depression of her guests. She darted from sight long enough to allow Ike and Mamie to take stock of the colorful comfort of the porch; then she was back with a house-girl bearing coffee. Wasting no time, their hostess launched into a discussion of the seeming magic she had wrought in restoring the house in less than six weeks. This beachhead established, she indicated that Ike was to relax in a long chair, and drew Mamie indoors. Together they went from room to room. Underfoot were gleaming floors; all around them, walls and ceilings were enameled in cool off-white. The house, not primly formal, abounded in possessions. Color was at every window. Splashy draperies were looped back; silver and crystal bowls spilled bright tropical flowers, there were low chairs and low sofas; the dining table was a fine plateau of waxed wood. Upstairs were bedrooms in cool pastels that dramatized the simplicity of mahogany. It could have been a vacation house anywhere in America—except for brocade wall hangings, fine pictures, and silver massed on the dining-room buffet.

All housewife, Mrs. Conner centered her running conversation ("I talked against time that morning," she recalls) on the restoration of the house. She showed where sections of flooring had been replaced, and what new lighting and plumbing fixtures had been set up; she dwelt on the difference all this made. Paint, planks and plumbing, and days of scrubbing and repairing—those were the miracles that had made "the total wreck into a home."

Here was a senior Army wife guiding a young Army wife, leading without seeming to lead; giving hope and comfort. Mrs.

Conner, mother of two grown daughters, fully understood what "Icky's" tragic death had meant. But as her rich voice moved smoothly on, it touched only household matters. She was determined to spark Mamie's hopes—and she did.

When they returned to the living room and Mamie paused by the piano, marveling that a piano had been trundled across the lock of Pedro Miguel and wormed up a jungle path, Mrs. Conner could touch the responsive chord of music. The General's wife said quickly that she hoped the piano would stand up under the tropic heat and moisture, ordinarily ruinous to stringed instruments. Time would tell whether the electric bulb suspended behind the upright strings would generate enough heat to prevent warping. Perhaps some day soon, Mamie would come and try the piano. Mrs. Conner's violin was being given the same heat treatment in an upstairs wardrobe that had been wired for a bulb outlet.

Mamie nodded. The General's wife was a musician too and they would be neighbors. That was a good bond—but also rather an awesome one. Mamie was young enough to be a daughter of this spirited woman; she was junior in every way. Inflexible Army rank did that (Ike was now a permanent major). This reaching down of a general's wife to the wife of a "little sir" was breathtaking and must be handled so very carefully. Mamie knew her place—you just didn't become chummy with a general's wife. All the same, she warmed to Mrs. Conner's humanness; it was almost like being in tow of Mama Doud.

A happier Mamie followed her husband's broad shoulders down the trail to their waiting car. She still couldn't help jerking with fear reflexes—unseen creatures slipping through the moist green tangle or crunching underfoot, but she laughed now instead of crying out in revulsion. Even the return ride over the locks was easier. Mamie told her husband that while she wasn't prepared to move in with mold and rust and gaping holes, she would be willing to take a chance once the house steps were replaced and workmen had started scraping and painting.

But she didn't wait. "I shoved a floor broom like everybody

else—and I scrubbed—maybe not on my knees, but I sure used a mop," declares Mrs. Eisenhower when she recalled the reconditioning of the Panama quarters. Labor was plentiful, but not overly vigorous—always the case in the slow-moving tropics; so Mamie found it necessary not only to boss the clean-up, but to slosh and scrub with bristles and water, while men hacked out the garden's undergrowth and other men scraped away mold and hammered new boards and fixtures into the house.

At last the porches were screened, and a cook and houseboy helped to unpack and arrange the familiar stateside belongings in the freshly painted rooms. The help was willing but untrained in American ways, and the language barrier was a problem. Eventually Mamie strung together an odd "kitchen vocabulary" of Spanish and Portuguese nouns and verbs that didn't always convey her meaning. But since other wives on the post were having equal trouble, she took to laughing instead of scolding when minor mishaps occurred. However, since the cook stubbornly refused to keep the meat off the kitchen floor and went on adding great hunks of lard when he fried bacon, life in the hillside house was stormy. Mamie was never able to enforce her rule that chickens be killed out of earshot. Sure as fate, a final flutter and squawk would break the afternoon stillness when chicken was on the night's menu. That put an end to Mamie's appetite.

Mrs. Conner had just as much difficulty. Her chicken story was for many a month the prize among the "cook crimes" swapped among the wives. Her instructions to prepare "curry with diced chicken" was taken literally by her cook, who served up the dish with the chicken diced—bones and all. The same cook boiled six potatoes for a buffet salad for thirty people, this being the usual number of potatoes she cooked for the General's family.

None of the housewives trusted her cook to do marketing, either at the post commissary or aboard the fresh fruit and vegetable barge that tied up shortly after daybreak in the big ditch below camp. Mamie, like the rest of the wives, would collect baskets and string-bags and set out on foot shortly after six o'clock for the tramp down the steep slanting road to the brink of the cut. The walk was always one long ache for her feet; but no walk, no fresh food for the day—it was as rudimentary as that. The barge, operated by the Army Quartermaster Corps on a strict schedule, had to transact its business and be on its way before the day's regular ship traffic began moving through the canal. Prices were fixed and the provisions had already passed inspection for quality; so the women had nothing to do but make hurried selections, stow their purchases in bags and baskets, and climb into a mule-drawn wagon that would take them up the hill on a half-hour ride of talk and laughter. In many ways it was the most fun of the day.

Languidly cool these bright mornings—cool and carefree, for the common bond that drew the homemakers together made the rides as rousing as a women's club on wheels. If dry staples and cold-storage meats were needed, the wives hopped off at camp, turned their burdens over to waiting houseboys, and made a bee-line for the commissary and post exchange, hoping that they could snatch up a few dollars' worth of English china or Irish linens if a sporadic shipment filled a counter. There was never any advance notice of the arrival time of these low-priced lux-uries. Individual purchases were small, never more than a few plates, napkins, or doilies in favorite designs to piece out what had already been started. Dinner services accumulated in this manner took months, sometimes years, to complete. It was invariably the last two of a dozen butter plates, or demitasse cups that plagued buyers of sets. On days when china and linen were on sale, wives let food-buying slide. "Most of us had to choose between Spode and steak—and Spode won," says Mrs. Eisenhower, who is proud that she still has most of the original set of china she accumulated at the Gaillard post exchange.

Panama City was a delight for bargain-hunters. No duty was levied on imported merchandise, but shopping required pro-longed dickering. The Bombay shops and Chinese stores, not much more than stalls tucked away on ancient narrow streets, had stocks of both sleazy and tempting top-quality oriental goods. Carved teak and sandalwood screens, tables, trays and boxes; brass and *cloisonné* lamps, candlesticks, bowls and ash trays; jade, ivory and crystal jewelry and figurines; gay silks and cotton prints; heavily embroidered shawls, and teak and rattan furniture—all from lands east of Suez and west of the Rising Sun. Army people prepared to pay higher than commissary prices could find glass, china and silver from England and France, and linens from Ireland and Spain, in shops belonging to Panamanian merchants, who also carried stocks of French perfumes, *bijouterie*, laces and underwear. Panama hats (made in Colombia), baskets, clay pots, passable wood carvings, silver-wire baubles, overflowed the little shops around the foul-smelling markets.

During the boom days when tens of thousands of American and European workmen and engineers were funneled in and out of the Isthmus, Panama City was as rip-roaring as it had been when California Gold-Rush hopefuls fought, gambled, and drank their way over the narrow strip of land to make sailing ship connections up the Pacific Coast, and ships down from San Francisco brought the quick-rich winner and drained-out loser from the gold-lode country to travel by muleback through the steaming fifty miles of jungle and along flooded rivers to Cristobal on the Caribbean side. A few shriveled ancients, drowsing in the shadows of the Cathedral in the Plaza Independencia, could still hark back seventy-three years to the bartering, bludgeoning and blood-letting of the gold-mad Argonauts. But mirror-clear in the minds of all adults, the shopkeepers especially, were the dollar-free ways of the big-fisted men who drove steam shovels, concrete mixers and dredges, or tossed red-hot rivets under the noon sun as they welded "the giant's footprints in the jungle" into Gatun, Miraflores and Pedro Miguel locks.

Mamie, like most newcomers to the zone, soon found that shopkeepers upheld the age-old tradition: all foreigners were fair game for bilking, if only by a few centavos. No matter how long the dickering, the short end of every bargain was hers. The smooth-voiced Bombay men and bland, clucking Chinese never settled for rock-bottom prices. They preferred to sell their wares at kited prices to free-spending crews from Navy vessels and one-day visitors off cruise ships and inter-coastal liners. It was only during slack times—on "freighter days," when unpromising cargo vessels were in transit in the canal—that the oriental merchants of Panama City would not insist on "first price" from Zone residents.

The fetid closeness of the tucked-away shops and the drawn-out haggling never quite overcame Mrs. Eisenhower's hankering for the modest treasures she searched out. For several months, until her husband bought a car—this time a used Buick—she rode a jitney into the city, after walking down the hill from camp and crossing the lock gates to a huddle of shacks. Progress over the cat-walk no longer made her giddy, but plodding up the hill to her house in time to beat darkness was hateful. Every so often a slide, mushrooming up out of the waters of the big ditch, would weaken the banks, and as likely as not the road gave way. The knowledge that this could happen without warning assailed the hearts of all pedestrians, but since there was no other way to go to and from camp, everyone took the chance. Oddly enough, in spite of the frequency of the slides, no one ever was caught when sections of the road tumbled toward the water.

Mamie's husband, as executive officer to General Conner, found himself drawn professionally and personally to his senior. Mrs. Conner has vivid memories of their relationship. "I never saw two men more congenial than Ike Eisenhower and my husband," she said. "They spent hours discussing wars, past and future. Fox always felt that the Versailles peace treaty had been a perfect breeder for a new war that would take place in about twenty years. Gradually Ike became convinced that Fox was right. Ike has often said that my husband had more influence on him than any officer he served under."

The minds of General Conner and Major Eisenhower met—there was no mistaking that. Ike was a good listener, prompt and efficient in carrying out orders—excellent qualities in a young officer working directly under a brilliant senior soldier. Mornings they rode together in the back jungle country while the sun was still too weak to lather their horses and themselves; week ends they often went fishing. Camp Gaillard was manned by Puerto Rican recruits, officered by Americans. In those lean, between-war years, when Congress hacked and hacked at military appropriations, many officers felt that their careers were being hamstrung, and fell into easy ways; but Ike, fired by General Conner's convictions, made every day a solid foundation for the future and spent many nights studying in his veranda office, to the benefit of the subsequent history of the free world. One can see destiny in this relationship.

General and Mrs. Conner saw to it that the post had a lively social life. There were weekly dances at the Officers' Club. Though not much more than a porch with enough side-walling to ward off the rains—as much as thirty-nine inches could pour down in one round of the clock in the wet season—the Club was also the get-together spot for bridge tournaments and basket suppers. A small swimming pool had been dug close by, and on clear, hot nights movies were focused on an outdoor screen.

Mrs. Eisenhower thinks she might have borne the heat and near-jungle living if only her house could have been divested of wild life. Mosquitoes, lizards, ants, and snakes—pests of the first order—were mild in comparison to the nightly presence of bats. No amount of screening, or careful closing of doors and windows barred the flying mammals. Every so often one would flatten its way between boards to zoom through the rooms and go smack on walls or ceilings. Before Mamie provided her husband with a bat net, he did battle with his sword against the intruders. Miserable under a sheet, pillow or towel—anything she could grab to protect her head—Mamie's terror verged on laughter as she watched her home's defender leap from chair to table to bed, lashing and slashing at the elusive quarry.

"Ike was so grim and earnest, I didn't dare laugh," she says. "His long leaps and fancy sword-play on the furniture were a riot. I kept thinking of Douglas Fairbanks, the great leaper and jumper and swordsman of the movies. Only Fairbanks didn't fight bats."

By early spring, down to steaming Camp Gaillard from high Denver came Mr. and Mrs. Doud and their daughter "Mike," now a soft-spoken, beau-busy miss of sixteen. Pretty, too—"Mike" was growing more like her sister every day. The trip was ostensibly for pleasure, but there was an undercurrent of serious purpose. Mamie's letters to her parents during her first months in Panama, while not exactly woeful, had not been full of cheer. She disliked the heat, the lack of stateside conveniences, the perpetual battle against bats, bugs and reptiles. Now that a second baby was in prospect, Mr. and Mrs. Doud thought it was wrong to leave Ike to deal alone with Mamie's geographic unhappiness.

Mrs. Doud liked the breeze-swept quarters; she approved the new purchases for the house and chuckled over the cook's vagaries. Mr. Doud was in his element: cigars were cheap, his son-in-law's company lively as ever, and there was plenty of opportunity evenings to sit in on friendly poker games. "Mike" was whirled into a teen-age heaven by the attentions of the bachelor officers. Not content with the goings-on at the club on the post, her swains took her dancing in the barn-like Tivoli Hotel, still the top social spot of the Zone, and then to night-spots in Panama City. "Mike" felt that she was rapidly becoming a woman of the world; she had clipped her hair to the fashionable shortness of an Irene Castle "bob"; she danced the Charleston and wore hoop earrings and lipstick.

Mamie's hair was also short—and now she wore bangs. Mrs. Eisenhower is positive that she cut her hair for comfort, and not to conform to prevailing fashion. She cannot recall the circumstances of her first clip. The bangs that have since become her distinguishing feature were also so casually come by that she hasn't the faintest recollection of adopting them.

"I don't remember having my hair cut," she says. "It must have been right after we settled in Panama. I guess the bangs took the place of the dips of long hair I wore to cover my high fore-

136

head. I just have photographs to go by. Pictures taken before we went to Panama show me with long hair; after that I was bobbed and banged."

Night life in Panama City ceased abruptly for "Mike" after she succumbed to the urge to cover the seven miles to Pedro Miguel Lock in a pony-cart *calesa* instead of a racing jitney. Papa Doud—of all people—became a stern disciplinarian after waiting up half the night, and decreed that her future social life on the Zone should be confined to Camp Gaillard. "Mike" knew she had really overstepped, and what happened to her escort is no longer in her memory-book. She thinks that her brother-in-law must have scared him stiff with a reprimand, because from then on she was shy one attentive second lieutenant. Her mother's and sister's disapproval helped to build the incident into a life-long memory.

She arrived home to find her family groggy from lack of sleep in the darkness of three o'clock in the morning. They had stopped playing cards, but were still on the veranda on look-out duty. When she tried to laugh off their withering remarks, her father took charge; for "Mike" it was the time when he displayed his greatest anger. *Calesa* is still a word to make her shudder.

Family amity was restored in a few days when the fleet came in, and with it Lieutenant Commander Charles "Swede" Hazlett, one of Ike's boyhood friends. "Swede" looked up Ike, as well he should. They had been high-school classmates and members of the same Abilene poker parties in the years they worked around town, before each went his respective way as appointees to Annapolis and West Point.

"Swede" was the person who had influenced Ike to seek a career in uniform. In 1911, himself all set for Annapolis, he encouraged Ike to seek the sponsorship of Kansas Senator Joseph L. Bristow. When the appointment was won, "Swede" turned to and helped Ike cram at night for the entrance examinations. Just to play safe, Ike took both the Annapolis and West Point tests. He came out high Annapolis man with an 87.7 score, only to discover that his age—he was twenty-one—barred him from becoming a midshipman. In the West Point trials he ranked second. When the top West Point contender failed the physical examination, Ike moved up and qualified, twenty-one being the age limit for entrance to the Military Academy. Though one went by land and one by sea, the young men kept in touch by mail. Now, during joint military exercises for defense of the Canal Zone, the old friends turned their hours off-duty into a two-man "old home week" at the Eisenhowers' quarters. Mamie and all the Douds liked the young Kansan. When the fleet hoisted anchor, "Swede" Hazlett continued to be a week-end visitor for the month his submarine was undergoing an overhaul at Coco Solo Naval Base near Balboa. When his underwater craft was back in commission he suggested that Ike go on the trial run. Mr. Doud listened alertly to the invitation, but continued smoking in silence. The gleam in his father-in-law's eyes did not escape Ike, and he asked casually if Papa Doud could also make the run. Mamie caught her husband's wink as he broached the subject to "Swede," who said he might be able to stretch naval regulations and take a civilian passenger. Mr. Doud almost bit through his cigar. His wife sniffed and looked slightly bewildered. "Mike" hooted like a boat whistle and waltzed off the veranda.

It never occurred to Mamie, or to her mother, that the trip would include a dive, otherwise some stiff objections would have been raised. Next day mother and daughter buzzed cheerfully around the house while their men-folk were guests of the Navy. By dinner-time they knew the awful truth. Ike and Papa Doud outmatched each other describing what happened after the hatch was battened down and the S-32 submerged. Something about "canted decks. . . . We slid, but recovered our footing when the 'pig boat' levelled off. . . ." Gay and frankly envious, Mrs. Doud, a woman who has always liked high adventure, had a suggestion: Now that her husband and son-in-law had savored an underwater experience, perhaps they would consider the air; flying machines seemed to be coming right along as a mode of transportation. Mamie was furious; risking your neck in a submarine was bad enough, but knowing that she was out-numbered as a fearful person, she sat tight, telling herself, "I am to be a mother again, I must remain calm."

The hot humid days of Panama's "winter" passed, and the time drew near for her family to leave. Mamie and Ike reached the sensible conclusion that she should go with them. Funny thing—leaving the once-hated house wasn't going to be easy. Mamie had grown to love her "stilted ark." She no longer noticed the quiver and quake of the slides; the cook had become merely a woman of strange convictions, and post life was close and friendly. But looking things in the eye—something Mrs. Eisenhower has always been able to do—brought out in sharp focus the fact that Ancon Hospital, some miles toward the Caribbean on the far side of the cut, might be unreachable in an emergency. Why take chances? It was a small hospital, concerned mainly with treating tropical diseases and accidents, and without special provision for maternity care. Mamie didn't doubt that she would be well looked after at the hospital, but she was haunted by the fear that she would never make it down the hill from her home and across the locks, then down a poor jungle road to the hospital—in time. Many a day, going to Panama City, she had been forced to wait a good hour while Pedro Miguel Lock inched in and out for ships; fate might abandon her in just such a fashion in her hour of greatest need.

Her husband was even more upset about the hazard of the open gates. Much as he hated a separation, he knew that the only safe course lay in sending his wife home with her parents in May. He would use his accumulated leave and join her in Denver late in July, just before the baby was expected. Mamie accepted the arrangement, but went away not too gay in heart. She could not help feeling that something would intervene to prevent Ike from making the trip, in spite of General Conner's parting promise that he would "get our young man out of here in plenty of time."

Back in Colorado scarcely a month, Mamie had word from her husband that he was leaving on the next Army transport.

Here was news too good to be true—something was up. Skeptical always of a sudden shift in Army routine, she awaited Ike's arrival with foreboding. During the drive from the railroad station to her parents' home, her misgivings were confirmed. He had come north to enter Fitzsimons Army General Hospital in Denver to have his chronically bothersome appendix removed.

The operation, however, was without complications; Ike was home in ten days and was completely recovered as the hours narrowed down to his wife's confinement. In the early morning hours of August 3, he roused Mr. and Mrs. Doud. Mamie's time had come; she was dressing. He suggested that all three of them get their clothes on as quickly and quietly as possible—she didn't want "Mike" disturbed. In a matter of minutes Mr. Doud had the Packard backed out of the garage. The night was paling. With his wife beside him and Ike and Mamie on the back seat, he drove carefully to the Park Avenue Hospital. By breakfast time John Sheldon Doud Eisenhower was crying lustily in the manner of all healthy new-born infants.

Never was a little boy more wanted. His father, mother, and grandparents reached a pinnacle of happiness that August morning. In her large, airy room in the private hospital Mamie was surrounded with every comfort, including special day-and-night nursing care. Mrs. Doud had insisted on making these arrangements; she was taking no chance of a repetition of her daughter's previous ordeal in an Army hospital. Moreover, Mrs. Doud had located a nurse, Kathryn Herrick, who would watch over Johnnie when he was taken back to Camp Gaillard.

Ike had to return to his Panama duty the following week, but he left easy in mind. His wife was smiling from her heart out; Johnnie was husky and hungry. Ike liked capable Miss Herrick and knew she would supervise Mamie's care of Johnnie with a sensible, professional eye. Above all, he didn't want Johnnie spoiled—it would be easy to spoil such a charming cherub, destined to be doted upon, even by himself. That was something to guard against.

Scratch, scratch—day after day, Mamie's pen raced over pages and pages of letters about Johnnie. His father gained the impression that the zenith of infant precocity had been reached. Radiant and once more beaming fun and laughter, Mamie withheld from her letters—and from her family—her anxious moments about the boy. She knew that she shouldn't hover over him or watch his breathing, feel his squirming, healthy body apprehensively for signs of fever—but she couldn't help herself. He was so doubly precious.

"It took me years, many years, to get over my 'smother love'—it wasn't until Johnnie had children of his own that I finally stopped all worry," said Mrs. Eisenhower, with the startling frankness she shows in self-evaluation. "We've had Korea in the meantime, with Johnnie in combat," she added. And Korea, she admitted in response to a question, had been even more distressing. "It was different. All mothers can understand that who have awaited the return of their sons from war. I no longer worried about his health—he had that in abundance. It was his very life that was at stake, if a 'numbered' bullet or piece of shrapnel found its mark."

All she could do, she said, was "pray without ceasing—just as I prayed for his father. Only with Johnnie, Ike prayed with me—and that helped."

Over the years, President Eisenhower has come forward as a dedicated soldier and statesman who declares his faith in God. His wife, though she has not been articulate in a public expression, has equal religious conviction, and turns daily to the Bible and books of spiritual comfort and guidance. Only the frail health that has plagued her in recent years occasionally prevents her from going to church with her husband. No invalid, she suffers from a recurrent nervous digestive disorder, the obvious result of the pressures that life has brought to bear on her.

But ill health is rare with Mamie. Usually she dresses with distinction, applies a modicum of cosmetics, for her clear, fresh complexion needs no more, and goes out among people—friends or strangers, four, forty, or four thousand—with blithe spirit. "Hi," she says and "Hi!" she means, for she uses the greeting just as other Americans do. Mamie knows how to "rise and shine." That is a term the Navy, the Army—to say nothing of the Marines and the Air Force—have considered "standard wake-up" since our country was very young. The President learned to "rise and shine" at West Point. Perhaps Mamie has absorbed some of this bravura from him. She says, "I don't like to get up early. I never do unless it is necessary, but once I'm up, I laugh and 'shine'."

John Eisenhower was three months old when his mother took him to Panama. For the next two years he lived a normal and healthy babyhood in the big, screened house overlooking Gaillard Cut. Treasured as he was, he was never pampered or spoiled. There was one minor upset soon after his arrival, an ailment actually almost superficial, with never a hint of complications, but Army doctors felt it best to give him medical care for several days at Ancon Hospital. It was a somber experience for Johnnie's mother and father, still fearful after the loss of their first son in a hospital. They stayed within call of Johnnie at the tropical medical pavilion until he was discharged.

When Johnnie was back, kicking and squirming again in his nursery, his mother resumed her morning habit of "beating the trail" through the hedge to visit next door with Virginia Conner. The General's wife, mother of two daughters of marriageable age and a son at West Point, was a good counter-balance for her young neighbor. A forthright, free-speaking woman, her motherly nature understood completely the lingering sense of tragedy, and she met Mamie's fears with common sense. Warm and vibrant, an organizer and a doer, Virginia Conner continually urged Mamie to activity outside the confines of homemaking. It was fortunate that this wholesome impulse came to the wife of a junior officer from the wife of her husband's commandant. It could not go unheeded, and it radiated courage and purpose.

Of those times, Mrs. Conner has said, "Mamie and I had much in common besides our love of music and children. She hated Panama, but after Johnnie began growing strong and healthy, she developed a sure and steady hand. Many a time I saw her gay laugh smooth out Ike's occasional irritability."

On her first morning visit to Virginia Conner after Johnnie was back from the hospital, Mamie told the General's wife that while she was grateful for her son's care in the Ancon institution, she thought it "a crying shame" that no children's or maternity ward was provided for the families of enlisted men from Camp Gaillard, most of whom were Puerto Ricans. Mrs. Conner leaped to the idea. She had long wanted a post maternity hospital for the prolific Puerto Ricans, whose babies were delivered in a "hit or miss" fashion in the enlisted area at Empire, just behind Camp Gaillard. Sick infants and children had to be carried across Pedro Miguel Lock, then driven three miles down the other side of the cut to Ancon.

It was deplorable but unavoidable, she told Mamie, unless a collection could be taken up to outfit a small post hospital. The Army had no funds for such an undertaking, but probably would hack through enough red-tape to assign some run down building at Empire that could be converted into a small hospital. If Mamie would agree to head the fund-raising committee for the project, Mrs. Conner would act as sponsor and get the go-ahead light from the General.

Mamie accepted the challenge, though she knew it would be a long and difficult job to obtain donations totaling over a thousand dollars from the limited number of officer families living on the post, most of whom needed every cent of pay for personal expenses.

Fun, games and parties—that would be the only way to lure philanthropic dollars. Mamie organized her finance committee, whipping up enthusiasm among other wives; Mrs. Conner located an empty building at Empire. Even the men, though skeptical at first, warmed to the project and undertook to organize a volunteer clean-up squad to repair and paint the building. One officer conceived the idea of enlisting the aid of two Hollywood stars, Lila Lee and Thomas Meighan, who were making a picture in the Zone, and Mrs. Conner made sure of them by hurrying to the Tivoli Hotel and inviting the screen stars to the dinner and the post dance that would start the fund drive. Accepting her bid, they offered to arrive with a print of their latest picture for a preview showing. News of this social coup raced to other posts across the Zone via the bamboo telegraph, that speedy word-of-mouth system of communication indigenous to the tropics. Ticket sales soared and a gala evening was assured.

Caught up in the spirit of the fun-making, Thomas Meighan gave several robust renditions of Irish ballads, with the audience roaring each chorus. Lila Lee danced fox trot after fox trot with dreamy-eyed officers. Prohibition being in force, the strictly "ginger-ale evening" in no way dampened the hilarity. When the band packed up and went home, lingering guests gathered around Mamie at the piano to harmonize old favorites.

Mrs. Conner was among the "honor guard" formed to escort Lila Lee and Tom Meighan down hill to the locks. The glint of the moon on the water-filled cut enchanted Mr. Meighan. He paused, and was eulogizing the sight in ringing tones when the roar of a slide drowned his oratory. Wild-eyed, certain that he was meeting his doom, the actor swayed as the road rocked crazily. Miss Lee shrieked and clutched the nearest masculine arm. Though only a small slice of the road went out, no amount of explanation could convince the visitors that they had not been on the brink of catastrophe.

It took more parties to amass enough money to underwrite the hospital. "Bingo" had not been devised, but "Lotto," a similar game of chance, was played for prizes. There were bridge tournaments, box-lunch parties, even cake-baking contests and white-elephant sales. But it was not on the entertainment side alone that Mamie showed she could be a whirlwind organizer. Terming herself "a clean-up expert," she directed the volunteers who scrubbed and painted the long narrow building and helped to furnish the wards and nursery. Mrs. Conner gives Mamie credit for having been the hardest-working wife engaged in the project, but Mrs. Eisenhower asserts she was only one member of a team of determined women who refused to sit by and see the wives and children of enlisted men deprived of prompt medical care.

Interest and assistance continued long after the ten-bed infirmary opened under the supervision of Mathilde Simoni, a Red Cross nurse. Army doctors made regular and emergency visits from Ancon Hospital, but Miss Simoni carried the bulk of the load. Like her brother, Father Aristides Simoni, the post chaplain, she was Italian born and dedicated to the service of others. A trained and experienced nurse, as well as a linguist, she cared expertly for the fearful and frightened Puerto Rican mothers and their solemn, sable-eyed children. Mamie and all wives on "the team" furnished layettes for the new-born babies and clothing for older children. They also kept the hospital supplied with fresh flowers, toys, and special convalescent foods.

As there was no Protestant chaplain at Camp Gaillard, it fell to Father Simoni to conduct joint religious services in the small, tin-roofed post chapel. He overcame the language barrier rather neatly by reciting his sermon phrase by phrase, first in Spanish, then in English. A cultivated Italian, he had been educated in Rome and had celebrated his first mass in St. Peter's before being sent to the United States as a young priest. Tolerant and wise, he was as much beloved by those outside his faith as by the thousands of Catholics he served at the Army post and in the jungle hinterlands. He was also a strict disciplinarian, so far as religious observances were concerned, though at times he found himself unable to cope with the near-comic aspect of the musical portion of Sunday services. The fervent Puerto Ricans invariably sang off-key, over-shouting the Americans to such an extent that the hymns became a loud babel of Spanish and English. Father Simoni, like a stern schoolmaster, would end the shrill discord by rapping for silence, then would exhort the well-meaning Puerto Rican soldiers and their families to sing *"voco ce bassa"* so that the Americans could also be heard. Mrs. Conner would stand, violin at her side, through the priest's admonition, struggling to suppress her amusement at the schoolroom atmosphere. She would keep her eyes on the rough planks of the floor

145

to avoid seeing the meek and serious faces of the wrong-doers, and Ike and Mamie, like other Americans in the congregation, needed to exercise utmost control of their facial muscles.

The good padre knew he was wasting his breath. Sunday after Sunday he explained the need for more harmony and less *fortissimo*; then he would nod to Mrs. Conner and the soldier at the wheezy organ to resume playing, only to have the Puerto Ricans, after dutifully muting themselves for a few bars, raise their voices with ear-splitting effect.

General Conner and Ike were often absent from chapel, for the General liked Ike as his fishing companion on week-end excursions to offshore areas, such as the Pearl Islands. During these absences their wives overcame their solitude by joining forces and entertaining post friends. Mrs. Conner, who loved music and laughter, usually planned a Saturday night buffet supper at her house, with singing afterward. She would play her violin for hours to Mamie's piano accompaniment. Songs ranged from operatic arias to ragtime, with some of the more talented guests venturing to give impersonations of famous singers.

Charades were also popular, but the biggest all-star production was a mock wedding, on a week end shortly before Mrs. Conner's oldest daughter, Betsy, was to be married. For weeks the post had been agog with plans and counter-plans for Betsy's wedding, and Mrs. Conner's guests were eager to participate in a mock ceremony. It was to be an all-male masquerade. The men chose the "bride" from among the shorter officers present and escorted him upstairs, along with the "groom," the "preacher" and the "bridesmaids." Mrs. Conner and Mamie helped ransack chests for suitable wedding garments, then waited downstairs to play the wedding march. The "blushing bride" descended slowly on the arm of her "father." "Her" gown was an elaborate draping of bed sheets; a lace curtain was attached to a frilly nightcap aslant her brow. Her bouquet was a mingling of feather duster and flowers from the buffet table centerpiece, and "she" was rouged and lip-sticked like a circus poster. In careful step to the nuptial music, the "bride" was halfway across the living room when a loud whistle sounded outside the house. There was no mistaking the high clear notes: General Conner was announcing his homecoming. In panic the bridal party streaked toward the stairs, only to meet the General head-on in the hall. A man of humor, he took one look at the oddly outfitted group and roared. He wanted to rout out Ike from next door and continue the "ceremony," but the embarrassed masqueraders fled to the upper floor to help the "bride" out of her wedding dress.

The following summer, when General Conner's Panama duty was due to end in a few months, his wife decided to go on ahead and resettle the family in Washington, where he would again be attached to the War Department. As word of Mrs. Conner's intentions penetrated Camp Gaillard, numerous proposals cropped up for giving the first lady of the post a surprise farewell dinner-dance. Some officers and their wives wanted the party held in a club in Panama City, where there were no liquor restrictions. Ike stood firm for an on-post affair, even though he realized that he would be letting himself and Mamie in for a lot of exacting work when other officers and their wives backed away from the responsibility of trying to put together a top-notch party in the small Officers' Club. Ike took this first hurdle neatly by arranging to use one of the large dining halls serving enlisted men and turn it into a garden-like banquet hall. So far, so good. Beyond seeing that the post band turned out for rehearsals of Mrs. Conner's favorite melodies and arranging for guest speakers, Ike left all the thousand-and-one details of the food supply and service up to his wife.

It was the first time Mamie's talent as an organizer of smooth-running social functions had to wrestle with a large and important party. And wrestle she most certainly did. Often the success of the undertaking hinged on a narrow margin of ingenuity and improvisation. Starting out with a sheaf of check-lists, she put first things first, beginning with the menu, then working over into table decorations and table service. On the last she had her most difficult problem, for she wanted the tables to gleam with silver set on fine linen; finally she canvassed the homes of other officers' wives and was able to borrow the needed articles. She also prevailed upon her friends to lend their houseboys along with the table settings. In the afternoon before the party the boys, accompanied by the officers' wives, each keeping an eye on her precious possessions, converged on the mess hall, now a bower of ferns and forest greens. At this point, Mamie was called upon to show generalship. Check-list in hand, she assigned the boys to serving stations, then supervised the unpacking and placement of the silver. Slowly, carefully, with great patience, in halting Spanish, she conveyed her instructions by means of pantomine and chopped-off verbs. Without seeming to boss—Mamie couldn't be "bossy" if she tried—she instilled confidence into the nervous boys, and they served the meal without a hitch. But her real triumph came next day, when no silver or linen was reported missing. She never discovered how the boys kept track of their employers' property during the excitement of serving.

On tenterhooks until the banquet ended and the party moved over to the Officers' Club for dancing, Mrs. Eisenhower now looks back on the undertaking as her first success in party management. "I had to find lettuce, when there wasn't a head on the Isthmus," she says. "It took fifty dozen red roses to decorate the tables! That meant buying up just about every rose in Panama City—and praying that the vendors would keep their word and make delivery. The china was another headache. I couldn't ask the girls to risk breakage of their Wedgwood and Minton, so we rented dishes from the Tivoli Hotel. It was a lot of hard work, but a wonderful experience that has made all other parties easy by comparison."

As one of the mementos of that occasion, Mrs. Conner keeps a tall silver vase on a table in her living room. It was the Eisenhowers' bon-voyage gift, presented the night of the farewell party. Nearly two decades and another world war were to pass into history before they would again sit down to dinner with Mrs. Conner. In 1947, when the young officer in whom her husband had placed such faith during the sweltering years at Camp Gaillard had risen to become a five-star general of the

Army and leader of the victorious Allied troops in Europe in World War Two, Mrs. Conner found herself a guest at the quarters of General and Mrs. Eisenhower at Fort Myer near Washington. Living alone in a small apartment—her husband had died the previous year—Mrs. Conner had wanted to entertain her old friends from Panama at a hotel, but Mamie begged to be allowed to be hostess, explaining that Ike was now a "marked man" and could no longer eat in public without being subjected to constant interruption by autograph seekers. When her host, with the same diffident pride of his youth, took her into the trophy room to see his many decorations for distinguished military service, Mrs. Conner found it difficult to reconcile the awards from grateful nations with the demeanor of the quiet, plain-speaking man at her side. Ike Eisenhower and General Eisenhower had remained the same.

"Ike displayed that rarest of all qualities, the humbleness of true greatness," she said. "In manner and voice, in the quick gestures, the robust laugh, he was to all outward appearances the same intense young man who had been my husband's assistant." And Mrs. Eisenhower was "the same full-of-fun Mamie who used to sit on my front porch in Panama and discuss the problems of the day."

When the nearly three years of close association between General Conner and young Major Eisenhower ended, the older officer left for Washington promising to use his influence to assure Ike the opportunity to qualify for the Command and General Staff School at Fort Leavenworth, Kansas. During their innumerable into-the-dawn discussions of military strategy and international danger signals, General Conner had become convinced that he was dealing with a young officer possessed of the rare qualities of leadership and perception requisite for victory in the next world war, a war that he said was bound to come within twenty years. The fact that Ike had not attended his infantry service school—a prerequisite for enrollment at Fort Leavenworth—did not seem to General Conner an insurmountable obstacle. He admitted that he would have to bring a certain amount of pressure to bear, but since he expected to be made Deputy Chief of Staff, the General felt he would be in the right position to wield influence; he considered it urgent that Ike prepare himself as soon as possible and start moving up in rank and responsibility.

Mrs. Eisenhower remembers distinctly the dawn of the long night when this talk was held. She heard her husband come in and go directly to the nursery where Miss Herrick was giving Johnnie his get-up bottle. Minutes later he came breezily in from his son's room, as fresh and untired as if he had just bathed and dressed. With fatherly pride he remarked that Johnnie was getting to look more like football material every day. When Mamie replied she presumed he meant the West Point eleven, Ike made a quick mental calculation and said cryptically "Class of '44— that will just about be it." Then he switched quickly to tell her of General Conner's premonition of another world war and of his promise of sponsorship.

Just before he went overseas in 1942 to command the Allied forces in Europe, General Eisenhower, sitting at dinner at Fort Myer with his wife and son, who now was wearing the uniform of a West Point cadet, harked back to his eighteen-year-old prediction. It was then that Mamie learned he had been thinking of Johnnie in reference to the prospect of another war, not of Johnnie's chances of making any one year's West Point football team.

Chapter 8

U.S.A. AND FRANCE
1924-1935

MAjor and Mrs. Dwight D. Eisenhower, happy to be back in the United States after nearly three years of isolated tropical duty in Panama, had to cope almost at once with a difficult situation. Ike got orders to return to Camp Meade, Maryland, where he was assigned as recreation officer and coach of the Third Area Football Team. They were unhappy at the prospect of living once again on the post filled with memories of the death of their first-born son. They were disappointed over the nature of Ike's job. But since it is not the prerogative of an Army man—or his wife—to question the wisdom of orders issued by a superior officer (at least not audibly) the Eisenhowers had no choice in the matter; orders were orders, and that was that.

Knowing it would be a great tug at their hearts to see Johnnie toddling around the company streets of the post that had been so closely associated with the happy playtime of his dead brother, the Eisenhowers weighed sending their two-year-old and his nurse Kathryn Herrick to Denver to stay with Mr. and Mrs.

Doud. From a practical point of view, there was every indication that Ike's coaching assignment would not last beyond the football season, and they vetoed the separation.

Living conditions at Camp Meade showed little improvement. If anything, the passage of three years had added to the bleakness. Mamie, back at housekeeping in tinder-box quarters in a section of one of the old remodeled wooden barracks, noted a grim innovation. A coil of knotted rope was attached to a stout hook, screwed at the side of a window in each upstairs bedroom—a means of quick escape if fire broke out. Coal was still lugged in for the downstairs stoves. Rain and sleet still clattered against the windows when winter storms lashed in from Chesapeake Bay. Rainy wash days still meant clothesline rigged in the kitchen and dining room. On the bright side, day help was now easier to hire. A less fastidious homemaker than Mamie would have unpacked only necessities and dispensed with trying to create the air of a permanent home during the few months she expected to occupy the quarters. Makeshift living arrangements and clutter irritated her too much. She emptied every crate, box and barrel; she rehemmed curtains to fit the odd windows; she put her much-prized Minton china and other treasures from Panama on display. Temptation to rent a piano was strong until it turned out that cartage fees to bring an instrument from Baltimore and return it were equal to three months' rent.

The football season had barely ended when Ike was directed to report as recruiting officer at Fort Logan, Colorado. Happy to be going practically to the doorstep of her family home (Logan is less than ten miles outside Denver) Mamie had a sobering thought. She knew that the appointment to Command and General Staff School at Fort Leavenworth, Kansas, was still uncertain, and she was disturbed for fear her husband might be forgotten and passed over. She told herself it was silly to doubt the intentions of General Fox Conner, Ike's commander in Panama. It had been he who proposed cutting corners and getting Ike appointed to staff school. If anybody could push the appointment through it would be General Conner, who was back in the War Department as assistant chief of staff for supply.

Her suspense was short-lived. General Conner sent word to his protégé to go West, enjoy the climate, enlist recruits and above all—study. Mamie twinkled. Ike didn't have to tell her in so many words that General Conner's advice to study meant he would not let the Leavenworth plan evaporate.

In terms of intensified family affection, the eight months the Eisenhowers spent in Colorado were richly rewarding. Not only was Mamie in closer relationship with her parents, but Ike seemed truly their son. The "closed family corporation," as Mrs. Doud defines the devoted interdependence of her family, put down very deep roots in 1925. Her grandson Johnnie, in the heyday of little-boyhood, focused in himself the love and harmony of the merged families. Spoiled? A little, perhaps, but he was well and happy, and that was what really counted. Johnnie insisted stubbornly on calling his grandfather "Poopa." He also adopted the practice of yelling "Ike" when he wanted his father, a habit that continued until he was in grammar school. Mamie has always called her mother "Momma" but Johnnie chose "Nana." Since he also had an "Auntie Mike" it seems strange that he never tagged his mother with a nickname but called her "Mamie" in those early years. She has since always been "Mother" to her son, though his wife and children call her "Mimi."

"Mike" Doud at eighteen was enjoying the same popularity that had spun her sister Mamie in a teen-age whirl in San Antonio until Lieutenant Eisenhower came along. Among Mike's many swains was Richard Gill, one of the older boys who had lived up the block when the Douds wintered in San Antonio. Young Gill was visiting Denver on what was ostensibly a vacation trip, so his attentions weren't taken too seriously. Then, early in August he and "Mike" eloped. The marriage rocked both families, but no harsh words followed and the young couple soon had their own home in San Antonio. While the elopement was still causing repercussions, Ike and Mamie were busy with another bout of packing. This time they were making ready for the long-anticipated move to Command and General Staff School at Fort Leavenworth.

Mamie took one look at Otis Hall, a red-brick and white-trim former barracks reconstructed in three-story units to accommodate four families, and vowed that the Army had assigned them to really fine quarters at last. Ike commandeered the top floor's two extra bedrooms as his private study, where he could get away from normal household distractions and work undisturbed—nights, Sundays and holidays. Night after night, he shut himself away from everyone except Major Leonard T. Gerow, a close associate since the days at Fort Sam, when they were bachelor lieutenants with West Point fresh behind them. Now the two close friends, brought together again at the staff school, "spelled" each other preparing for the tough oral and written examinations, and found the teamwork mutually profitable.

Like other ambitious wives of officers attending the school, Mamie kept her household in motion around Ike's need for tranquillity. Even little Johnnie sensed the situation and would go quietly to sleep after his father's final goodnight.

Mamie was constantly on the alert for any lag in her husband's appetite that might be a forerunner of nervous exhaustion, but he seemed to thrive on his driving routine—a snatched early breakfast and a hurried dinner after day-long classes. Rarely did he wait for Major Gerow to arrive, so anxious was he to begin his evening grind. Mamie would ease back with a book, knit or twiddle the cat-whisker of a crystal radio set, and so pass one more heavy, silent set of hours. About midnight, Ike would put in an appearance en route for a foray on the refrigerator.

Looking back on those nine months, Mrs. Eisenhower still marvels at her husband's tireless capacity, at his ability, after such study, to compose examination papers with a clarity and accuracy that brought consistently high marks. His genius for absorbing every detail of class work counted double because of his facility in writing. There had never been any doubt in his wife's mind that he was destined for military distinction; now she knew it would be something extraordinary.

"I knew as true as I sat in Otis Hall that Ike was going to be a great general," she said. "I couldn't talk to anybody about it until after graduation—even then I confided only to Papa and Mama—but I *knew* he would make it."

Fort Leavenworth was sharply divided into two worlds: one of class-going men, the other, their waiting wives. By common unspoken consent, the women built their social life in the daytime. As at all Army posts, the wives made up small cliques, determined as a rule by neighborliness. They helped mind each other's children; loaned and borrowed anything from a cup of sugar to a samovar; played twenty-five-cents-a-corner afternoon bridge, and rivaled each other preparing and serving surprise luncheon dishes at small parties. In the morning at the commissary, the talk was mostly about dollar-stretching recipes, but, being daughters of Eve, they traded gossip also, as housewives do in a market place the world over.

The men were free of classes only on Saturday afternoons and Sundays, but since many of them used their free time for extra study, week-end parties happened only now and then. The desk-bound routine was a source of physical staleness, and so a part of their brief leisure was needed for outdoor exercise. When the weather was fine, out came the golf clubs and off went the husbands. Some wives played the course with their husbands, but most of the women, including Mamie, disliked walking, particularly over open country. When he went to Leavenworth, Ike didn't know a brassie from a putter—and cared less. A triple-threat football player from his high school days until a knee injury in 1912 benched him permanently from the West Point eleven, Ike was mildly amused to see other one-time Army athletes spend so much free time on the Leavenworth golf course. Mrs. Eisenhower does not remember who induced him first to try whacking balls down the fairway, but once he got the feel of a driver he thrilled to the challenge of a game that demands complete mental concentration of the player as well as muscular coordination. She saw at once that she was destined to become a "golf widow", but far from being resentful, she urged Ike to consider the game as a future hobby, when he had finished staff school. Golf is now his principal recreation. "The only thing I know about golf is that you can't have a low score card if you worry about something else," she says. "That's why golf is good for Ike. He can really get his mind off his problems for a few hours a week."

Golf wasn't in anybody's mind that July, as graduation day drew near for the 1926 class at Fort Leavenworth's Command and General Staff School. Student officers, free of classes, went around either in a state of repressed nervous tension or openly a-jitter, wondering what class standing their marks would merit. Ike was neither jittery nor tense. On the contrary, he had mellowed, and as far as his wife could see was only "normally anxious." His marks had been consistently high, but he had no way of knowing how his over-all average would stand in class competition. Up to and including the day of graduation, secrecy cloaked the final ratings.

During the school's last-minute fever pitch, Papa Doud arrived from Denver—having eaten up the highway as usual in his Packard. He was in expansive good humor, all ready for the morrow's graduation festivities. There was nothing like a long drive through open country to bring John Doud to top form. The blue-suited dignity of his mid-fifties was neither pompous nor self-righteous, for he had never let the flame of adventure grow dim in his spirit. His automobile touring satisfied an urge to explore new horizons that had gripped him since boyhood. At fourteen, he had decamped from his father's well-provided home in Chicago and worked three months as fourth cook on a Mississippi river boat. Once before and once after this independent sally, he had scooted off for brief periods. His father, Royal H. Doud, one of the first men to set up a meat packing plant in Chicago, finally cracked down. Young John went to work then, graduated from the University of Chicago, got a job in the stockyards at Omaha, Nebraska, and later formed a partnership with his uncle James Doud in a private enterprise, buying and selling livestock in Boone, Iowa. At twenty-two, he married Elvira Matilda Carlson, a local girl. By the time Mamie, the second of his four daughters, was born in 1896, John Doud was prospering in business. Eight years later, with a sufficient fortune to permit his retirement from day-to-day office demands, he took his family to Colorado.

In 1907, he bought his first automobile, a Stanley Steamer. Soon tiring of Denver's streets, he began juggernauting in a powerful Winton Six touring car over the wagon-rutted roads that joined Colorado's towns. Acquiring a Packard in 1910, he set out with his family on his first long-distance run—a trail-blazing thousand miles—driving on roads through open range, farm and ranch lands to San Antonio. Now a quarter-century veteran of highways and byways, he sat merry-eyed in the Eisenhower quarters at Fort Leavenworth, drawing deep drafts on his long cigar, and listening to Ike and Mamie detail the hard-working days and months of the school. At dinner, Papa Doud remarked that if Ike didn't come out top man, then he had been overrating his son-in-law's capacities for a good many years. Flattered, but noncommittal, Ike muttered something about "not thinking he was that good."

But Ike was "that good." In the morning, the word traveled all over the post: "Eisenhower's first!" Mamie, finishing up the breakfast dishes, with her eye on the dragging hands of the kitchen clock, ran with wet hands to answer the telephone's piercing bell. Half past eight, it was. A friendly man's voice said, "Major's made first place, ma'am", and the line went dead. Interrupting her father as he was playing with John, she told him the good news. She had barely finished, when a neighbor banged on the door. Congratulations! News got around fast in the Army. The big parade was on: front door, back door, telephone. Papa Doud finally grabbed the phone between conversations and called his wife in San Antonio. Ike came in, happy, of course, but with a new seriousness.

By tradition his honor status marked him an Army "comer." Barring physical impairment or some tactless blunder, he would rank some day as a general officer. Physically strong, sensitive to the moods and manners of others, intellectually a giant, but unspoiled by false pride, his simple directness engendered friendship and confidence. That morning he thanked Mamie from his heart for all she had done, saying that he couldn't have driven himself during the difficult months of study without her patient understanding and self-effacement.

The long day and the longer night of hand-shaking, back-slapping and well-wishing for the top classman were over at last. Mamie, hoarse with laughter and excitement, called goodnight over the stair rail to her husband and father at dawn. They were headed in the direction of the kitchen.

"I knew, every hour of every month at Leavenworth, that Ike would come out Number One," says Mrs. Eisenhower. "But when he made it, I was so tumbled inside with gladness, it was days before I could eat properly."

Excitement notwithstanding, she faced another round of "pack up and go." This time they were headed for Fort Benning, Georgia. Ike was to take on the routine duties of battalion commander of the 24th Infantry Regiment, and would coach the post football team. But before leaving Kansas, they drove 150 miles to Abilene for a reunion with Ike's mother and father and five brothers.

The Fort Benning duty lasted from July, 1926, until January, 1927. Major Eisenhower was ordered then to Washington to the Battle Monuments Commission. There would be no living on an Army post during this tour. Mamie was expected to go house-hunting in the capital, and to try to find living accommodation priced within Ike's quarters allotment. She shied away from the maintenance expense of a house and concentrated on locating an apartment. An influx of civilian and military personnel during World War One had spurted apartment building in Washington. Now, in the post-war era of shrunken population, there were vacancies all over town—especially in the new multiple-unit structures that old-time Washingtonians considered detestable commercial encroachments in the city of homes and embassies. Like all newcomers to Washington, Mamie was puzzled by the star pattern of streets and avenues converging into the numerous "circles." Never a walker, and unable to afford unlimited taxi trips, she gave up trying to find her way through the maze. Consulting the phone book, she called several real estate agencies and inquired after two-bedroom apartments, in a good neighborhood, at the right rental.

There were many offerings. On the advice of Army friends who knew the town, she settled on the Wyoming Apartments, located on a residential avenue of the same name just behind broad Connecticut Avenue—the "Embassy Row" of that era. An imposing six-story building encrusted with heavy stone cornices, and with a pillared entrance, the Wyoming was in the luxury class in everything but rent. There was a little park nearby where Johnnie could play, and neighborhood stores were handy down Columbia Road. Trolley service was available for the short ride downtown.

Mrs. Eisenhower's first favorable impression of the Wyoming has never changed. Not long ago she recommended it to a friend seeking roominess and the quiet of a good neighborhood, asserting there were no better apartments in Washington. She should know. She lived at the Wyoming for a total of nine years.

Moving-in delighted Johnnie. He watched the unloading of his family's effects from the elevator (an elevator was something new in Johnnie's life); then he packed off with his nurse for a short walk in the sharpness of the January day. He returned to linger in the lobby, fascinated by the lights and buzz of the switchboard. In the course of this exploration, Johnnie made conversation with Kenneth White, the building's janitor.

An enduring friendship began that day between the chattering four-year-old and the soft-spoken Negro. Christmas and birthdays, they still exchange cards. "Whitie", on his days off— he is still a fixture at the Wyoming—keeps up-to-date on the President, Mrs. Eisenhower and John when he goes out to work part-time at the Klingle Road residence of Mrs. Moore, John's "Aunt Mike." Mrs. Eisenhower and her mother often motor out from the White House for what Mrs. Moore calls "sitting around as we always have done." One afternoon shortly after the Inauguration, Mrs. Eisenhower's sharp ears and sharper memory caught Whitie's voice in the rear of the house. Instantly she asked her sister, "Isn't that Kenneth White?" Not waiting for a reply, so sure was she that she knew who was speaking, she was on her feet and greeting him through the breakfast-room door. The grizzle-haired man blinked back tears until she eased his feelings with news about Johnnie, who had just returned to Korea.

"I knew Mamie had a good memory, but not *that* good," remarked Mrs. Moore. "A good dozen years had passed since she last saw White. I had not mentioned he was helping me, yet in a split second she recognized his voice. Mama and I were dumfounded."

Kathryn Herrick stayed on as Johnnie's nurse until August, 1928; then she gave him a good-bye squeeze when he left with his parents and grandparents for France. The months she cared for him in Washington had been packed with stirring new experiences for the child. On his first Easter as a city-dweller, he joined the crush of squealing children, who plunged and straggled over the White House lawn after President Calvin Coolidge gave the starting signal for the traditional Easter-egg hunt. Mrs. Eisenhower is certain that was the first time her husband and son entered the White House grounds. In the spring there was the zoo, close by the Wyoming, to charm Johnnie. On summer afternoons, as a very special treat, he was taken scudding across the Tidal Basin, holding tightly to the swan seat of the flat-bottomed motor boat. Some Sundays he motored with his parents to visit at Fort Myer, reached by a bridge over the Potomac River. Trains with out-stretched smoke plumes could sometimes be glimpsed on the railroad bridge downstream, but what sent Johnnie's heart thudding was being able to watch a locomotive nose toward a station bumper. In Union Station, held high in his father's arms, peering through the bars of the iron fence at incoming trains, Johnnie's joy was complete. On one such occasion, he even saw his Grandfather and Grandmother Doud waving from a stream of passengers. "Poopa" and "Nana" had come for another visit, bringing new toys, new bedtime stories and their gay laughter and pranks to fill his happy days.

Mr. and Mrs. Doud rejoined the Eisenhowers in 1928, on a sticky July day, for the first phase of the overseas journey they would soon be making with their grandson and his parents. Ike had been tapped for a wonderful foreign assignment. He was ordered to go to Paris with the Battle Monuments Commission to do field work on data which would be incorporated into a history and guidebook of the World War One battlefields in France. Passage was already engaged on the *America*, top luxury liner flying the American flag in the transatlantic service, and there remained only the usual packing and storage problems before the two families would be ready for an early August sailing. Besides fulfilling a lifelong desire to visit Europe, Mr. and Mrs. Doud were going along to keep an eye on Johnnie, while his mother found a Paris apartment and his father assumed his new duties. Foot-free and travel-minded as always, the Douds were as agreeably flurried as Ike and Mamie over the prospect of living abroad.

The ocean crossing was in the best of weather until heavy fog held up the *America's* departure from Southampton, England, for the short Channel crossing to Le Havre. They did not dock in the French port until after dark. After a long wait for the discharge of baggage, there was the baffling customs examination. None of the inspectors spoke English and the snail's-pace clearance consumed hours. It was after midnight before the *America's* passengers were permitted to take seats on the boat train. "Headachy" from the dragged-out inspection and worried over Johnnie's weariness, Mrs. Eisenhower was dismayed to find that all seats in the train compartment were occupied. There was no space for bedding down the child, who was curled uncomfortably on his father's lap. After much platform commotion, the wheels started turning and the train sped through the night toward Paris. A whole new set of troubles broke out when Mamie and her family left the compartment at the Gare St. Lazare. Ike had expected that someone from the Commission would meet them, but evidently the lateness of the hour—it was then half past three— precluded any assistance. It was a serious situation. Neither Ike, Mamie nor the Douds spoke a word of French. A hotel reservation had been made for them—but where? Major Eisenhower and his father-in-law swore with exasperation. Even "The Man from Cook's" had gone to bed; at least no travel agency man was in evidence. While Ike and Mr. Doud were coming to a decision, a quartette of slouching porters snatched up the bags, rattled some unintelligible French and disappeared. Was this the act of bandits, or an old French custom? Mamie wanted to know. Her husband made an end-run around other groups of weary humanity on the platform and caught up with the porters as they were neatly stacking the baggage in a waiting room. Just as he started to backtrack to pick up his family, one of the men ran at his side, trying vainly to tell him something. Ike thought it was a plea for money until a cart loaded with trunks went by, and his companion shouted and pointed. Trunks! More trouble. After getting his family settled near the hand luggage, Ike went off to claim and check the trunks. One look at the pile-up in an enclosure—which everybody else seemed to be ignoring—and Ike shook his head. It would take hours to tussle through that mess.

Now came the time for a bold decision: should they spend the rest of the night in the station, or attempt to find a hotel? Operation taxi won. Ike hoisted sleeping Johnnie against his shoulder, growled "taxi" several times at the porters—and bobbed his head toward the station entrance. His temper was growing fouler by the minute. The men parroted back "taxzee," followed by an incomprehensible torrent, but at least they understood. Outside, a cabby as red-faced as the paint on his battered taxi pulled up. Over the remarks of the porters, already dumping the baggage in the front and rear sections of the cab, Ike tried a simple English

162

sentence on the driver using the word "hotel." Grinning, the man asked, "Name?" Ike shook his head. After a short reflection, the cabby sprang into action with a loud "Ah!" He ushered Mrs. Doud, Mamie and Mr. Doud into the vehicle, helped Ike hand Johnnie in and fixed a baleful eye on the line-up of porters. Bossy as a mother hen, the driver examined the denomination of the bills Ike extracted from his wallet, plucked out two, and signed to Ike that he must wedge himself in on top of the suitcases in the back compartment. He then slammed the door, thrust the money at one of the porters and climbed behind the wheel. Deaf to the maledictions splitting the air, he drove off into the night. The bounce of the cab over cobblestones reminded Mamie of her famous tank ride. The cab seemed to be galloping at runaway speed, except for the time it took corners at sharp right angles. "The Headless Horseman of Sleepy Hollow" had nothing on this driver, she told herself: only this man had a head, and gave every indication of knowing where he was going.

Once out of the narrow streets, he increased his speed on the boulevards, plunging at other nocturnal strays with a *beep* of his rubber horn. The ride ended before a stone building with a large arched gate, bolted fast against the night. Hopping out, the driver ambled over and rang the bell. Many times he rang the bell. It resounded clearly through the thick wooden gate, so funereal was the silence in the narrow thoroughfare. A small door in the gate opened; the taxi driver and the concierge exchanged a few words, and then all was well. Mamie hesitated to step over the two-foot sill of the door into the inner driveway, but her husband urged her to follow her mother. Feeling each step across the shadowed courtyard, Mamie climbed low stairs and entered a small, well-furnished lobby. A recumbent form unfolded from a chair. A tall young man, blinking sleep out of his eyes, said "Good evening." Ike laid Johnnie on a sofa and discussed lodgings with the clerk. Two rooms were available and already the driver and the concierge were trundling the baggage into an elevator not much bigger than a bird-cage.

The registration cards and identification formalities were at last over. Ike turned to the beaming cabby and asked the fare. The driver shrugged and looked pointedly at the clerk. The two men spoke briefly, then the clerk explained that the driver was willing to accept whatever was reasonable for his services. Hearing Ike's explanation of the grave predicament that had been averted by the driver's assistance, the clerk suggested a modest but generous fee. Ike added some extra francs and shook hands with the cabby, who saluted smartly and took himself off. Escorting his guests to their rooms, the clerk praised the reliability of the driver, saying that not all night-prowling taxi men possessed such integrity.

Refreshed with sleep, but still seething from the previous night's trouble, Ike vowed to his wife next morning that as long as he was in Paris he would enforce a rule at the Commission: anyone—clerk or general—was to be met by a staff member regardless of the time of arrival. He made the rule stick and more than once went himself to meet new staff people.

By Christmas, Mamie found Paris less trying. Nothing went right the first few months, though she had ferreted out an inexpensive, handsomely furnished apartment at 68 Quai d'Auteuil on the left bank of the Seine almost in the pleasant suburb of Passy. Then as now, an acute lack of housing prevailed in the French capital. At first Mamie's frantic search turned up either fourth-floor walkups in dingy crowded neighborhoods at outrageous prices or de luxe apartments fit for royalty—at royal rentals. French-speaking wives of officers attached to Ike's group helped her run down leads. Wives at the American Embassy also lent a hand, but she found her prize by reading the want-ads. The place she rented was on the ground floor, with a sunny exposure; it contained three bedrooms, a salon, a dining room and a library. The plumbing was antiquated; there was no ice box in the gloomy kitchen, and the heat was never sufficient. But by Paris standards it was a superior, modern apartment, and had the advantage of being a short walk from the offices of the Battle Monuments Commission. Major Eisenhower always went home for lunch.

Like any housewife living abroad for the first time, Mrs. Eisenhower, unable to convey her wants in a foreign language and encircled by strange customs, doubted at first that she would ever get her Paris home on an even keel. Trying to tell her cooks—she had a procession of them the first few months—what she wanted from market each morning was a major problem in mathematics. Used to the American method of purchasing dry grocery staples weekly instead of day-to-day, she had to accustom herself to small paper cornucopias and little packets instead of tins and generous cardboard containers. Owing to the lack of refrigeration, it was impossible to carry fresh foods over. Eggs for the day, dabs of butter, milk in old wine bottles, all took getting used to. Worse still, the cook of the moment, unable to speak English, would assert her rugged individualism by refusing to tackle American recipes. French food was fine for the grown-ups, but Mamie considered the sauces and seasoning far too rich for Johnnie. She ended by preparing his meals.

No one ever tried harder to learn French. While they still lived in the hotel, she began daily lessons in the hope of being able to communicate her wants in the kitchen, and to deal with tradesmen. In spite of a sharp memory and a keen ear—her excellent piano-playing is entirely by ear—she bogged down on French grammar and was forced to cull rudimentary verbs and nouns from a pocket dictionary. Meanwhile, Johnnie, a pupil at the MacJannet private day school, was rattling along at a great rate. Ike, brushing up on his own school French, wasn't doing too badly either. Unlike his wife, who was involved in household problems, he had opportunity to meet and mingle with many Frenchmen, especially when he left Paris on field tours of historic battle sites. It was not until good spring weather made country travel pleasant that Mamie was able to accompany him into Brittany and Flanders.

Mrs. Eisenhower recalls the time she sat in an automobile watching her husband work his way through fields and forest lands, beating down the undergrowth, his eyes sharp for hidden battle markers. Eleven years had passed since the Armistice; and nature had thrown a heavy green carpet, spattered with scarlet poppies, over the scenes of bitter conflict. Major Eisenhower's work was to seek out and chart accurately all battle areas, preliminary to a history which would keep fresh the memory of those who fell in World War One. Convinced that another even more disastrous war was inevitable, he found it difficult not to be greatly depressed when confronted with evidence of war's waste of human life, so dramatically revealed by the rows on rows of white crosses in the big military cemeteries. Mamie and Ike have spoken often of those massed graves as the world's most tragic symbol of war.

To get away from the depressing March wetness, and in the hope that a spell of sunshine would bake the winter legacy of chill from their bones, Mr. and Mrs. Doud proposed a family trip during the Easter holidays to San Remo on the Italian Riviera. They made the overnight journey in *Wagon Lits* compartments of an express train that reached the border in the chilly dawn. Ike, wearing an overcoat over his nightclothes, joined other passengers similarly attired in the customs shed and nursed his family's baggage past the inspectors. Inspection was perfunctory, but it took a while to get the luggage hoisted back through the right compartment windows and start the train on the final hundred miles into San Remo.

The seaside holiday turned into a fiasco in less than twenty-four hours. Johnnie came down with whooping cough. His mother and grandmother took turns easing his discomfort while their menfolk lounged on the beach or drove over the picturesque countryside. Neither Ike nor his father-in-law liked such a one-sided vacation, but their wives thought it sheer folly for the entire family to be cooped up in the hotel. When Johnnie was well enough not to require further nursing, it was time to return to Paris.

Springtime in Paris was heart-lifting. Pink cabbage roses banked in the flower stalls behind the Church of the Madeleine; brisk trade in the sidewalk cafes; the Tuileries and Luxembourg gardens at their loveliest; goat carts and puppet shows to beguile toddlers on the Champs Élysées; week-end pleasure craft on the Seine; the Eiffel Tower glinting in the sun—all were delights for the annual crop of tourists and were a renewal of joy for Parisians too. Mrs. Eisenhower had never been gayer or lighter of heart. She bought several hats; stood patiently for costume fittings in the apartment of an unknown but clever dressmaker, and window-shopped the jewelry, leather and dress accessory shops in the Rue de la Paix, the Place Vendôme and the Rue St. Honoré.

Mamie's social life during the winter had revolved within a small, tight circle of couples connected with the Battle Monuments Commission and younger people from the American Embassy. The small parties; the card games; the visiting back-and-forth pretty much duplicated Army post life at home. Living costs were high, pay checks low; gala nights at the opera or dinners at the Ritz never happened. None of the military men among their friends had sufficient rank to be on the list for important state dinners, balls and receptions; the State Department people attended these functions in line of duty, but otherwise enjoyed quiet family life much as they would in the States. The crowd gravitated to the Eisenhower apartment, there to join Mamie around the piano in nostalgic songfests. A homesick lot, their hearts and souls went into the choruses of American ballads and jazz. At such times, Ike attended to the cooking, sending batches of everyday American food steaming to the buffet table where everyone helped themselves. As jealous as any chef of his recipes, he would beam mysteriously when asked the secret of his truly remarkable stews, hamburgers, fried chicken—and on special occasions, *filets mignons,* done to a turn but in sharp contrast to French cuisine, and with no suspicion of a rich sauce.

Mrs. Eisenhower and her family would probably have missed out altogether on the colorful and fashionable spectacle of a Longchamps race meet, if Lewis and Marie Kayton hadn't turned up from San Antonio bent and determined to spend an afternoon at the track. Tickets to the Club House enclosure were wangled from a friend at the American Embassy. Mannequins paraded about exhibiting clothes from the great Paris dressmakers; Indian potentates were accompanied by their wives in gleaming saris; there were American, French and British women, bearing famous names and in breath-taking finery; South American beauties, the last word in *chic,* ablaze with fabulous jewels—a dazzling display! The soberly clothed men were nothing more than background for the fashion parade.

Mrs. Eisenhower can still remember some of the costumes she saw—and who wore them—so remarkable an index is her memory.

By way of contrast, Mrs. Doud got off on the subject of the "old days" in San Antonio during dinner that evening, and started a round of riotous reminiscences. Lew Kayton won hands down with a 1915 incident that has become more hilarious over the years, but which when it occurred was a maddening misfortune for Mamie. Lew had been one of the young Texans who kept Mamie Doud's social calendar so full she didn't have a spare evening for Dwight Eisenhower, a brand-new West Pointer on duty at Fort Sam Houston. Owner of a yellow Oakland speedster, Lew was the most dashing of Mamie's many beaux. He suggested celebrating her nineteenth birthday, which fell on a Sunday, with a fast spin eighty-seven miles north of Austin. Her parents gave permission. Mr. Doud had looked over the Oakland on numerous occasions when it was parked in front of his house, and he estimated the round trip would take between seven and eight hours. So, with time out for lunch in the northern city at the home of Mr. and Mrs. John La Prelle, Lew and Mamie would have a nice all-day outing.

Dressed in her best, wearing her mother's duster coat and a long veil as protection against clouds of sand and adobe dust, Mamie sat back in the low leather seat of the Oakland. For forty-odd minutes the car ran like a sewing machine, racing ahead at a giddy thirty-five miles an hour. Then disaster struck. It might have been a horseshoe nail, a sliver of glass, or a sharp rock; anyway, they had a tire puncture. Lew was prepared for just such an emergency. He got out, pumped the hand jack, and quickly replaced the flat with one of his two spare tires. Half an hour later, there was a repeat performance. That was only the beginning.

They reached Austin by the light of the November moon after thirteen punctures and three blowouts. Mamie was crying and angry, knowing that Mrs. La Prelle would have every reason to feel put out with unexpected house guests. It was all Lew's fault. Why hadn't he learned how to patch an inner tube really instead of cementing on pieces that wouldn't hold. She called her mother and explained. Lew talked to Mr. Doud, who laughed so hard he had to hang up. The young motorist bought a new set of inner tubes and a spare tire Monday morning, figuring that if he drove back slowly, the tires on the wheels would hold. They did, but during the four-hour ride, Mamie stared ahead, tight as a clam. At her house, she scurried out, slammed the car door and ran up the steps without a word. It was weeks before she was on speaking terms with Lew. Meanwhile, she had started giving dates to Lieutenant Eisenhower.

To this day Mrs. Eisenhower can't understand why she didn't insist on turning back after the third puncture, unless it was fear of being thought a quitter by her father.

"Papa brought us girls up to always finish what we started," she says. "Even though I got so mad I couldn't talk—mainly because Lew teased me—I would have died before asking him to turn back. I wanted to show him I could match his stubbornness."

Major Eisenhower was ordered to staff duty in Washington in October, and so the Paris visit came to a close. Ike and his family arrived in New York on the *Leviathan,* then the largest passenger liner afloat. They went directly to the capital, and resettled themselves at the Wyoming Apartments in a commodious, two-bathroom apartment. Mamie, gay as a lark with that confident secure feeling of being truly at home, counted her blessings. Johnnie had entered the second grade of Kalorama Day School; Ike was dug in at his desk at the War Department, transferring his studies of French battlefields into a guidebook and history; Milton Eisenhower, married to pretty Helen Eakin whom he met while attending Kansas State College, was working at the Department of Agriculture and lived in the same section of the city. Mamie warmed with sisterly affection toward the wife of her husband's favorite brother. She enjoyed her bright mind and mid-west breeziness. Included in the family hobnobbing were Harry and Ruth Butcher, who had become friends of the Milton Eisenhowers during Ike and Mamie's absence overseas. "Butch," rated a man on the way up in the new field of radio broadcasting, was running Station WJSV, just opened by the Columbia Broadcasting Company. Tall, blonde, open-hearted Ruth and Mamie liked each other instantly. Ever since, they have remained intimates. The Carl Beaches—he was a well-known local physician— helped make up many a table at evenings of bridge.

Instead of being transferred back to troops when his guidebook was finished, Major Eisenhower was kept on staff duty at the War Department for the next five years. Senior officers, gratified with his clear, concise reporting on his overseas research, recommended him to Assistant Secretary of War Patrick J. Hurley who set him to work evaluating the production and conversion potentials of light and heavy industry, should it become necessary to make a quick switch to defense manufacture of military equipment on a large scale. The outgrowth of this M-Day assessment was the Army's Industrial War College, which Major Eisenhower helped to found.

Mrs. Eisenhower says her husband had a hard time convincing many industrialists of the need for such a program. Isolationism was entrenched over the country, causing many big-business executives to take a dim view of any plan relating to military preparedness. The great economic depression of 1929 had forced many industries out of business; those that survived were all working with skeleton forces. Military leaders, convinced that another war was being fomented by Adolf Hitler's build-up of the German Army and Air Force, feared a repetition of World War One when the United States was caught unprepared for conflict. In the event of a war emergency, they wanted to have a workable plan for re-tooling American industry quickly to arms production. By exercising his strong powers of persuasion and conciliation, Major Eisenhower contributed much toward making the program a success. He also gained an insight into all phases of industrial production, later to be of incalculable value to the Allied cause when he tackled the titanic problem of logistical supply for offensives in North Africa and Europe.

Explaining in detail the fact-finding done by her husband, Mrs. Eisenhower says proudly, "Ike made the most of his opportunity. He learned supply from the factory up, and knew by heart production man-hours on everything from a bomber to a mess kit."

In 1932, General Douglas MacArthur, then Army Chief of Staff, was so impressed with Major Eisenhower's clearcut reports and tactful relations with businessmen that he requested the able young officer for his staff. Major Eisenhower had one bond in common with his superior. Both had graduated first in their class at the Command and General Staff School at Fort Leavenworth. The going was very rocky for General MacArthur in the last year of President Hoover's administration. His Commander-in-Chief had ordered him to use stern measures to break up the encampment of jobless World War One veterans around the Washington Monument. MacArthur used troops to disperse the Bonus Marchers, touching off a prairie fire of criticism that took years to die down. Major Eisenhower, working quietly in the adjoining office to his chief, put his pen to work to rebuild public esteem for General MacArthur. This uphill grind continued until the General left in 1935 for Manila, to create an army for the Commonwealth Government of the Philippines. He was accompanied by several hand-picked staff officers, including Dwight D. Eisenhower.

Mrs. Eisenhower sums up her seven years in Washington after returning from France—she stayed on in the Wyoming Apartments a year after her husband was transferred to Manila—as being a period of "pleasant and uneventful housekeeping, when every day was a carbon of the day before." This didn't mean that they were stay-at-homes every evening. As popular with top-ranking Army couples as with their own coterie of intimates, the Eisenhowers were constantly going off to formal and informal military parties where Ike would be the only officer present below field grade—an unusual state of affairs. Far from being self-conscious when entirely surrounded by high-ranking superiors, Ike and Mamie remained themselves and had great fun.

Mrs. Eisenhower, who openly hero-worships her husband, explains that the invitations started when his brilliant staff studies, plans and reports made his superiors realize the caliber of this young officer who was making good in a job ordinarily delegated to an older and higher-ranking man. From the Secretary of War on down, the War Department policy-makers liked and respected Major Eisenhower. Witty as well as keen-minded, he was stimulating company for these older men when he relaxed from the responsibilities of his job. So it followed quite naturally that his superiors and their wives disregarded social red-tape and welcomed Major and Mrs. Eisenhower to their parties. Superiors would have recommended him for promotion, but the slim ranks of the budget-bound peacetime Army—only 138,000 men were in uniform—had stalled all up-grading.

Entertaining was not all one-sided. Mamie was frequently hostess; sometimes she had the wives of her husband's bosses in for an afternoon of cards, sometimes she gave small home dinners for several couples. Her food was never elaborate, but it was served on her best china and on a table centered by a carefully planned flower arrangement. The meals achieved elegance without being pretentious. Sometimes her flowers cost as much as the meal—and those were lean years when every cent of her husband's pay counted. Believing that the right flowers are as important as the right food, she has never considered them an extravagance.

Mrs. Eisenhower ruled out a home dinner when it came time to return the hospitality of the Hurleys—he was now Secretary of War—and decided that the atmosphere and faultless service of a fine hotel would honor her guests better than turning the apartment upside down and getting in extra help. It would cost much more than dinner at home, but she was going to do it right, or not at all. Her husband said he guessed she knew what she was doing to their bank account, but her practical mind soon solved the financial aspect of the undertaking. They would dine at the Willard Hotel where special reduced rates were given to the Saturday Night Dinner Dance Club. This was an organization patronized by members of Congress, young military couples, civilians in government and a sprinkling of local business and professional people. The Eisenhowers had become members before they went abroad, and usually attended with a large "Dutch treat" group. Mrs. Eisenhower, with all the aplomb in the world, reserved a table for four, then sat back calmly and waited for the big evening. She now laughs at her temerity, saying that while there was no rule against a major and his wife being formal hosts to such exalted superiors, it probably had never been done before.

"Ike and I liked Secretary and Mrs. Hurley. They had been wonderfully kind to us, so we couldn't see why we shouldn't return their hospitality," Mrs. Eisenhower says.

The dinner went off as planned and they danced until late. All the following week, as they dined on stew and meat loaf to equalize the bank account, Major and Mrs. Eisenhower told each other that next time—if there was a next time—they would go easier on the flowers.

"The party flowers cost almost as much as it took to feed us a week. Added to the dinner check, they really upset our budget," Mamie says.

Stored away these many years in a warehouse vault with other valuables is a silver tea-set of Early American design that was given piece by piece to Mrs. Eisenhower by her husband. The pieces mark each of her birthdays and wedding anniversaries while they lived in Washington. Because Ike paid for the silver with dimes, quarters and dollars hoarded from his weekly lunch and cigarette money, none of her possessions is more cherished.

"The day Ike gave me the kettle I knew he really loved me," says Mrs. Eisenhower with a twinkle. "He had to just about stop smoking to afford that."

Years later, he did stop smoking, but not for reasons of finance. He found that without tobacco he was less edgy under the press

173

of his command responsibilities. The opposite is true of Mrs. Eisenhower. She has continued to smoke moderately. Tobacco soothes her nerves, she says. Her brand is a well-known extra-mild, filter-tipped cigarette. She has never smoked in public places, or even at a large social affair. Several years ago she was deeply hurt by false rumors about her use of alcoholic beverages. The author can state positively that Mrs. Eisenhower consumes nothing but soft drinks; in fact she is personally straightlaced about strong drink but not critical of her husband's occasional highball. She would never think of giving a cocktail party, and no liquor is served at White House receptions. At state dinners, when foreign diplomats are present, wine is poured. The international guests, who are accustomed to wine with meals, would consider failure to provide such refreshment a breach of official hospitality.

It was not easy for Major Eisenhower to leave his family behind and sail for Manila in October 1935. Chary of taking his wife into the tropics until she was rid of a mysterious stomach complaint that had been resisting medical treatment for many months, he convinced her—and himself—that she must wait in Washington until the condition cleared up. There was also the matter of their son's education. Johnnie was in his final term at the John Quincy Adams Junior High School, almost around the corner from their apartment home; if he was allowed to graduate with his class in the spring, he would be ready to enter a prep school at Baguio, in the Philippines.

Mamie dreaded the separation from her husband, but she agreed to remain in the capital for the sake of Johnnie's education. Meanwhile, she would rest and relax and do her best to be rid of an ailing stomach. Johnnie was forlorn over the separation, but his father boosted his spirit, asserting that any break in his studies before prep school might impair his basic scholastic training—something thirteen-year-old Johnnie could not afford to risk if he intended to become a West Point cadet. Johnnie's eyes lit up like Christmas candles at the mention of West Point and he manfully promised his father he would try to finish school with straight A's. Mrs. Eisenhower listened to her son's enthusiastic acceptance of his father's dictum with mixed feelings. She thought this talk of her son wanting to be a cadet was a boyish urge that would disappear after he passed through adolescence. On the contrary, her husband was sure his son could and would become a soldier.

Long visits from her parents helped speed the months of waiting. Mamie's health improved spasmodically; she felt fine one month, wretched the next. Under her mother's watchful eye— Mrs. Doud has never stood for disregard of doctor's orders— Mamie adhered to a strict diet and tried not to worry. The diet came easily, but blocking her fears was something else again. Ike's boundless energy overflowed in his letters, but his wife, who remembered Panama's heat, insects and makeshift quarters all too vividly, was not concerned about the glamorous and comfortable life he led in Manila. It was when he went into the wild *bontok* (jungle) and mountain districts of Luzon that she worried. She knew many Army people who had served in the islands, and was well briefed on conditions.

Many an evening, to enliven family spirits, Mrs. Doud and Johnnie would get out their harmonicas and play bright tunes. Instructed on a series of progressively larger instruments by his grandmother, Johnnie had got to where he could play fast harmony. Competition was keen between them, but Mrs. Doud always kept a slight edge. She is really mistress of the mouth organ. Johnnie also played the piano by ear, like his mother. They often joined in duets, leaning toward Ike's favorites, such as "Abdul a Bul-bul Ameer," and Army songs. Johnnie could sing word-perfect, in an unpredictable mixture of bass and tenor. Much as he liked school sports, the boy avoided rough games out of consideration for his mother's fears. Mrs. Eisenhower, who is always ready to admit mistakes, says now that her close guardianship of her son amounted almost to a phobia. From the hour of his birth, she had lived in mortal terror that Johnnie would contract some serious illness or injure himself. Except for colds and mild attacks

of a few children's diseases, however, he'd come through childhood unscathed; and his mother's obsession about his health was
modified the following year when it grew clear that he meant to
undertake the stern training and subsequent hazards of a military
career.

Chapter 9

THE PHILIPPINES

1936–1939

There was only fitful happiness for Mamie Eisenhower in the two and a half years she lived in Manila while her husband was assistant to General Douglas MacArthur, the military adviser, Commonwealth of the Philippine Islands. This was a newly formed military mission that came into being in 1935 when the United States granted commonwealth status to the islands as a preliminary to complete independence.

Lieutenant-colonel Eisenhower had been hard at work for a year in his staff job before he was joined in the fall of 1936 by his wife and son. John's education and her own bad health had, as we have seen, kept Mamie in Washington during Ike's settling down period in Manila. Though he wrote glowingly of comfortable living conditions that almost duplicated stateside standards, and said he had found a top-rate private school for John in the mountain capital of Baguio, Mamie put off the long trip until John graduated from high school and she had been assured by specialists at Walter Reed Hospital, the Army's great medical center in Washington, that her stubborn stomach condition had been brought under control. Putting aside her intense dislike of all things tropical, she decided to give Manila a trial—maybe it would live up to its sobriquet, "Pearl of the Orient." "Very fine," she told herself, "only who wants to live in the Orient?" In a skeptical spirit she packed and placed in warehouse storage all the apartment furnishings. Ike had said that the attractive rattan furniture everybody used was cheap—in case she should decide against long-term living in the two-room apartment he was occupying in the Manila Hotel. The hotel sounded like a good idea. Mamie didn't feel up to another siege of offshore housekeeping—Panama's makeshifts were still vivid. Besides, Johnnie would be at boarding school, 175 miles away in the pine-crested Benguet mountains. So why bother to keep house?

Actually, Mamie was still far from well when she arrived in Manila in October. She and Johnnie had journeyed by easy stages, stopping off for a visit with her family in Denver, before continuing on to San Francisco to board an Army transport for the twenty-seven-day voyage across the Pacific, with port visits to Honolulu, Yokohama and Shanghai. As the grey transport, after lying hove-to all night between the island of Corregidor and Bataan peninsula, upped anchor and slipped quietly across the pond-like waters of Manila Bay in the blinding new sun, Mamie could barely discern the flat grey-and-green city beyond the glassy water. She braced herself, though her mind felt as wilted as her dress. Was this to be Panama all over again, with the added filth of the Orient? Yokohama and Shanghai had been modern cities too, but her nostrils still were affronted by their stench.

Of that long-ago morning, Mrs. Eisenhower says: "I built myself up for a let-down. I wasn't counting on finding anything delightful or delicious in such a hot place. I guess it was because the bad dream of three years in Panama was my only comparison."

Mamie stood quietly at the rail while the ship was made fast to the pier. Johnnie, keyed to the same high excitement as the rest of the passengers who were seeing Manila for the first time, was big-eyed with wonder. Ike, in whites, waved and shouted up from the dock and Mamie waved back, at the same time keeping a restraining arm on Johnnie who had climbed a steel rung of the ship's rail and was leaning far over to attract his father's attention.

At the dock end of the gangplank, Mamie paused, put her left foot forward—her left for good luck—and stepped on to the asphalt. Then came her first shock. Ike hurried forward and swept off his hat as he embraced her—and Ike was bald! Seeing her start of surprise, he explained ruefully that, the weather being what it was, he was cropping his hair to keep cool. With a horrified glance at his pate, Mamie retorted, "Crop—what?"

To avoid the furnace-like heat that suffocated the city except in the three months of balmy "winter" weather, Mamie rarely moved by day out of her hotel apartment, unless it was to be pleasantly chilled in the air-conditioned public rooms on the main floor. At sundown, when the off-shore breeze drove the day's humidity inland, she often motored with Ike around the green stretch of the Luneta to the Army and Navy Club, or down wide Dewey Boulevard and into traffic-clogged Calle F. B. Harrison to the Polo Club in the suburb of Pasay. Their car was a tidy Ford, fitted with eye-blinding white seat covers. It was a nimble and dependable vehicle in the hodge-podge of local traffic. Ike had learned to drive Manila fashion, a method quickly adopted by most Americans as a means of self-defense. Mamie's heart skipped a beat the first time he rushed full speed ahead at a tootling brass band of strolling fiesta celebrants. When he found he had no road clearance to pass the merrymakers, who were wholly unconcerned, he stomped on the foot-brake and simultaneously jerked back the hand-brake. A traffic-tested Manila driver, that was Ike. He told his wife pridefully that he had yet to bowl over pigs, chickens or puppies, and always avoided small children that came arrow-like from the by-ways. He slowed down for more formidable contenders for the right-of-way, such as lumbering carabaos (water buffalo) and the juggernaut public buses that clipped off fifty miles an hour. Grown dogs who took their nocturnal rest on the relatively cool highways required many a swift twist of the steering wheel, but Ike kept his record unblemished. He was adept at scooting around the *calesas* and *caromettas*, the pony taxis that trotted people and produce over city streets and rural roads, and he never unwheeled one of these quick-turning two-wheeled carts even in the crooked Escolta, Pinpin or Avenida Rosario in downtown Manila.

When she felt well enough, Mamie enjoyed a moderate amount of the social life that made prewar Manila, next to Shanghai, the gayest and most hospitable city in the Far East. The discomfort of a flare-up of the old stomach complaint prevented her from accepting more than a few of the invitations showered on her during her first winter of residence. From late October through February, party-giving became a way of life in Manila, indulged in by rich and poor alike. The rich and influential gave parties honoring the great and near-great, or parties just for fun's sake or for repaying social obligations. The poor thronged to the great mid-winter carnival on a sweep of land close to the white-pillared Legislative Building, or held noisy neighborhood fiestas of religious significance. On October 31, All Saints' Eve, candles blinked from thousands of graves in Del Norte Cemetery. During the brief winter cycle, the bay's night breezes were often bone-chilling, and even at noon the rainless blue skies reflected only moderate heat. The fresh cool air also discouraged mosquitoes, mankind's relentless enemy at other seasons.

The most coveted bids were to Malacañan, President Manuel Quezon's official palace. Originally the residence of Spanish governors, the two-storied cream-colored mansion was situated in a terraced garden on a curve of the north bank of the Pasig river in the heart of old Manila. Though modernized by additions built during the thirty-odd years it served as the official residence of American governor-generals (after the Spanish-American War when the Philippines became a United States possession), Malacañan has never lost its ancient heritage. It was spared from destruction during three years of Japanese occupation in World

War Two, and was unharmed when American forces liberated the islands in 1945.

Balls and receptions at Malacañan were events of breath-taking splendor and courtliness. In the great paneled rooms that opened on to wide verandas, and down broad staircases and in and out of the garden, guests moved with elegance. Under the sparkling crystal chandeliers and in the diffused light of garden lanterns, it was the lavishly gowned Filipina women, wearing flashing jewels and golden glitter against the satin sheen of their vibrantly colored *turnos,* who created the illusion of Spanish court life. Each was a Velasquez canvas in motion. By choosing to appear in a native *turno*—a traditional costume consisting of a tight wasp-waisted bodice, diaphanous balloon sleeves cuffed at the elbow, and a sheath skirt ending in a narrow train—the Filipinas far outshone women of the western world wearing Paris-inspired creations. The most provocative aspect of the *turno* was a stiff-ened fichu worn over the deep square neck of the blouse to con-ceal—or reveal—lovely shoulders, for it could be removed and looped over the wrist of the hand that kept a fan ever in motion.

Many Filipino men preferred traditional *barong-Tagalog* to the short white mess-jacket, stiff shirt, white tie and black trousers worn by American and European guests. Here again was a harking back to Spanish times. The *barong-Tagalog* is a long-tailed shirt that hangs outside black dress trousers. Exquisitely embroidered on gossamer *pina*—a native fabric woven from tough pineapple fiber—the *barong,* because of its beauty and value, is an heirloom handed down from father to son. It is worn with the neckband buttoned to give the narrow turn-down collar a snug fit. Jeweled cufflinks are permissible, but no tie is worn. Both the *turno* and the *barong* are still favored by the élite of the islands, though some of the men, unlike the women, resort to western dress for formal functions.

A woman of fashion considers herself lucky if her dressmaker can produce a *turno* for as little as the equivalent of $500. Wealthy women never wear a *turno* more than a second time, since the distinctive sequin designs on the skirt and bodice make each garment a conversation-piece. Present-day prices for *barong-Tagalogs*, which, alas, do not compare in workmanship with the heirloom garments, range upwards from $100, depending on the fineness of the embroidery and the clearness of the spider-web thread of the fabric.

To this day, Mrs. Eisenhower is ecstatic when she discusses the breath-taking beauty of *turnos* and the marvel of the fine stitching of the *barongs*. Malacañan balls and receptions she remembers as events of surpassing beauty that rekindled the past. During the early months of her time in Manila, Weldon Jones was Acting High Commissioner for the United States, and Malacañan's guest-list was duplicated when he gave diplomatic parties in his official residence on Dewey Boulevard. But the stark simplicity of the modern mansion made such gatherings less colorful than when President Quezon received in his ornate palace.

Next in importance was the Manila Hotel. Here were held official parties given by, or in honor of, Vice President Sergio Osmena, and legislative leaders of the Philippine Assembly. Top-bracket Filipinos, Americans and Europeans swarmed to these affairs and also turned out in full force when the exclusive Spanish Club honored officialdom. Otherwise, except for a scattering of cocktail parties and receptions tendered by foreign legations and consulates, there was a dearth of cosmopolitan parties the rest of the winter season. Entertaining went on at a giddy rate in the villas of wealthy Americans fronting on Dewey Boulevard, or set back in floral paradises in secluded streets in the districts of Malate and Pasay. Invitations to these galas were hard to come by for anyone outside the Sacrosanct Number 1 or Number 2 sets of the American community. Of the approximately 5000 Americans then living in Manila, not more than 500 persons—mostly married couples—had the requisite business, professional and financial background to be acceptable as leaders of the dollar aristocracy. There was also a fringe Number 3 set, composed of some 1500 bachelors and married couples living on limited incomes derived from secondary jobs, who might be expected some day, by reason of promotion to executive responsibility, to find themselves in an upper social stratum. They belonged to at least one club and so enjoyed a vague, nodding acquaintance with their social superiors. The rest of the civilian community was socially untouchable.

Regardless of the sharp distinctions among themselves, nearly all Americans shunned the company of Filipinos except to win professional and business good will. American clubs did not welcome Filipinos, either as members or guests, and American hosts and hostesses would choose the Manila Hotel pavilion or a less expensive restaurant when it became necessary to give a "mixed" party. Among the Americans only the very rich or very poor or intellectually independent risked neighborhood condemnation by entertaining Filipinos in their homes. On the other hand, hospitality in Filipino homes was accepted by even the most wary American. This rock-bound condescension toward and ostracism of Filipinos did not cease until American military forces liberated the islands from Japanese occupation in 1945.

Filipinos resented this discrimination, yet pride or politeness—perhaps a mixture of both—caused them to accept discrimination with impassive grace. In her own years in Manila, the author often wondered if they did not take wry satisfaction in observing the tri-caste system that cleaved the American community and fostered dollar-sign protocol. And yet it would be unfair to condemn all Number 1 husbands and wives as haughty and standoffish. From personal experience the author knows a few who disregarded the social barriers to befriend her and other young women struggling on the earnings of their husbands who were in subordinate positions. But among peso-counting juniors, protocol usually was set aside only for good-looking bachelors and attractive husbands whose wives were stateside.

Mrs. Eisenhower, as wife of a military aide to the Philippine Commonwealth Government, was in the fortunate position of being able to ignore the dubious code that civilian Americans thought right and proper with regard to Filipinos. If her health had been normal and she had been living in a house instead of a small apartment at the Manila Hotel, she would have had many gay and impartial gatherings for her Filipino and American friends. Living in semi-retirement, she sometimes taxed her strength to give bridge and mah-jongg teas, or set up a few tables for cards after dinner for eight or twelve. Fast and successful at bridge like her husband—who was known in club circles as Manila's most formidable bridge player—Mamie had also fallen under the spell of the ivory mah-jongg tiles, but found herself up against stiff competition when playing with Filipina women who preferred the old Chinese game to cards. Ike held to bridge and poker, sometimes sitting in on the stag poker sessions President Quezon gave at Malacañan. Quezon's poker skill was second to none. Though warned by doctors to conserve his strength—he was then in the early stages of a tubercular condition that cost him his life in 1944—the Philippine President was happiest when playing poker far into the night.

The Eisenhower apartment, in the west bayside wing of the six-story grey and white hotel, soon lost its barren transient look after Mamie began to explore the Chinese shops in the Walled City and invested in a low rosewood chow-chow bench, nests of tables, vermilion cinnabar boxes, porcelain lamp bases, carved camphorwood chests, and vases and bowls for flowers. She arranged these new possessions with Manila-made split bamboo settees and lounge chairs, bought to replace the angular wooden hotel furniture. The bamboo pieces were low and comfortable, and the seat and back cushions upholstered in boldly designed cretonnes served to create a cool, garden atmosphere. Underfoot were ice-slick hardwood floors which shone like a mahogany table-top. They were skated each morning by room-boys balanced on split coconut shells, who then burnished them with burlap pads. Flowers were brought in daily and massed in bowls. Small roses, Mamie's favorite bloom, could not be obtained in the market stalls during the nine months of heat and rain, but there was always a year-round profusion of zinnias, marigolds, royal-purple or wine-red bougainvillea, scarlet hibiscus, small butterfly orchids, and trailing sprays of tiny-belled pink and white cadeña. When the spectacular flame-trees erupted just before the start of the rainy season in May, clusters of the fire-red blossoms were gathered from a row of the blazing trees growing on the road leading to the hotel.

The apartment was kept shadowed all day by the closed latticed windows composed of dozens of squares of translucent mother-of-pearl shells. These unique typhoon-proof windows also mellowed the staring sun; on clement nights they slid easily into wall recesses. Inexpensive as well as practical, they were used in the *nipa* huts of the poor and the mansions of the rich. Mamie, who detests closed-in rooms, found the diffused light depressing. Her bedroom would have been attractive except for the large ceiling fan and the mosquito bars over the beds. At sundown a room-boy arrived to pump clouds of spray from a flit-gun over and under the beds in preparation for unfurling the nets and tucking the hems securely under the mattresses. Sleeping inside a net was a nightly ordeal for Mamie, who had suffered from claustrophobia since childhood, but she knew there was no other way to escape Manila's winged marauders, those hardy fighters that could zoom through clouds of smoke in the living room, where coils of burning punk were set out from dusk to bedtime, to conduct relentless warfare against humans.

In time, Mamie came to tolerate the cream-colored little chin-chook lizards that "chook-chooked" up and down walls and, defying gravity, raced upside down across the ceilings in successful pursuit of mosquitoes. It was only when a chin-chook came loose from the ceiling and flopped into her lap or "spanged" on the dressing table or into the bathtub, that Mamie shrilled with horror. She has never forgotten inadvertently slamming the door of a wooden wardrobe on one of the small creatures.

Unlike Jean MacArthur, the General's wife, who made a hobby of searching out fine examples of richly carved and inlaid Spanish furniture, Mamie had neither the strength nor the money to motor over the countryside ferreting out antiques. The contents of the MacArthur seven-room, air-conditioned penthouse atop the hotel included furnishings quite as fabulous as Malacañan's treasures. The cream-paneled living room was a jewel-like salon containing many fine examples of Louis XIV furniture and bric-a-brac. The added splendor of General MacArthur's glittering decorations displayed in glass cases and cabinets emphasized the regality of the setting. A Manila matron who knew Mrs. MacArthur well says she always felt transported to the Petit Trianon when she stepped into the MacArthur salon.

A combined library and study, opening off the main hall, held tiers of books, map cases, a wide carved desk, and several fine old Spanish chairs. Great quantities of heirloom silver were set out on the massive buffet and serving tables in the dining room; there were antique, high-backed, intricately carved banquet chairs and a long dining table gleaming with the mellow beauty of time. Glass doors that sealed the room for air-conditioning gave access to a large terrace affording a sweeping view of all south Manila and the bay. Mrs. MacArthur's bedroom and the one occupied by her husband both had fine Spanish furniture. With the windows kept closed in air-conditioned rooms, there were no unsightly mosquito nets and ceiling fans to intrude on the splendid décor. Additional sleeping quarters, including a nursery for infant Arthur MacArthur, were furnished more simply.

The MacArthurs were perhaps the greatest stay-at-homes in Manila. They lived much to themselves, appearing only at a limited number of state functions and confining their own hospitality to occasional dinners for dignitaries. Infrequently Mrs. MacArthur invited women to tea. Her simplicity and charm, her quick intelligence and unhurried Southern manner kindled a warm response in others, but her husband preferred to remain aloof and she conformed to his desires.

Ike, like other members of the staff, worked closely with General MacArthur at headquarters, but in off-duty hours had practically no contact with his superior. Among Ike's associates, however, were several officers who would rise to become generals and serve under his supreme World War Two command in Europe.

The staff work on which they were then engaged was important, for they were training and preparing a Filipino Army to defend the 7000-island archipelago in case power-hungry Japan, already swarming over Korea and Manchuria, should decide to try to gobble the Philippines. All of them shared General MacArthur's conviction that each day's dawning brought Japanese aggression nearer. Most Filipinos and civilian Americans resented having the Commonwealth Government embark on an $8,000,000-a-year defense program, but President Quezon informed his critics that he would not have accepted independence for his country had not General MacArthur promised to build an adequate defense against "the danger from the north."

While winter held, Mamie knew it would be next thing to a polar expedition to drive to mile-high Baguio to visit Johnnie, who was enrolled with other American boys at the Bishop Brent School. During this first long separation from her son, Mamie lived heart-in-mouth between Johnnie's letters. Ike said that when Manila began to fry in the heat of March and April would be time enough for Mamie to seek chilly Baguio. It was a hard 175-mile drive through the rice-bowl provinces of northern Luzon, followed by a rapid, blood-curdling climb up the steep, one-way zigzag trail. The route could be covered in from five to eight hours, depending on the length of time spent at the trail check-off stations waiting for downgrade traffic to be cleared. Air time to Baguio was less than two hours, but Mamie preferred four wheels racing over the rocks and rubble of the dust-filled roads to the butterfly motion of a two-seater plane. She feared flying, especially to Baguio, where Ike's good friend Major James Ort had been killed when his light plane crashed approaching Camp John Hay.

There had been a dreadful wrench for Mamie when she learned that her husband was determined to become an aviator. He had broken the news at breakfast on the morning of her arrival in Manila; he told her that he started his work day at six o'clock with an hour's flying instruction at Zablan Field. One look at the light in his eyes, at the roll and tilt of his hands as he explained take-off and landing procedures, and Mamie knew Ike was really "wing happy" and eager to solo. She knew too that there was nothing she could do about it. It wasn't a good sign either to have Johnnie gaping worshipfully at his father and asking excited questions. Such shared enthusiasm could lead to anything—and it did.

After breakfast Ike announced that he had made arrangements to fly to Baguio with Johnnie in a light observation plane piloted by Captain William E. Lee, his instructor. Mamie's knees all but turned to water. But Ike's mind was made up; there was no use arguing. He contended that thirteen-year-old Johnnie was living in an "air age" and should start to take flying as casually as riding a bicycle. The air route to his new school, over some of the wildest and most beautiful provinces of Luzon, would provide Johnnie with an unforgettable first flight, said his father. Then and there, Mamie did some flying of her own—into the bedroom. She did not want her churning feelings to get out of hand.

On the day of Johnnie's departure, Mamie acted out a carefree farewell and was rewarded with appreciative hugs from her son and his father. Mrs. Eisenhower says she prayed hard that morning for the two people she loved better than life itself, bouncing and fluttering in a flimsy plane toward the wild mountain country. It was well that she prayed, for before the day's end Lieutenant-colonel Eisenhower and Captain Lee were in need of the Lord's mercy.

The flight up was fast and uneventful and vastly enjoyed by young John. Ike took his son over to school, checked him in at the principal's office, then rejoined Captain Lee at the Baguio Country Club for lunch. Toward three o'clock, they muffled themselves in overcoats and left the roaring fire in the lounge to return to the Camp John Hay flying field. A sharp cross wind had risen, which made a take-off on the narrow strip too chancy, Bill Lee said; they would have to wait until sundown, when air currents usually veered in another direction.

The wind lessened with gathering darkness, but it did not

change direction. The pilot said, however, that if it was all right with Ike, he thought he could get the plane airborne without difficulty, and Ike, who had complete confidence in his friend's flying ability, said "Go ahead." They took off with a laboring motor, but gained enough altitude to wobble into the valley ahead. There the single-engine craft, even with wide-open throttle, was unable to develop enough power to clear the ridge pines. Captain Lee banked sharply into another valley, but again the weak motor could not overcome the down draft. As a last resort, he made another vertical turn into a narrow, rocky ravine where there was barely wing clearance. Now the only way out was up. Miraculously, the plane responded to the pilot's straining hold on the stick, and with its wheels almost in the pine needles, cleared a jagged peak. Captain Lee, now an Air Force general, has termed the close call "operation wing, muscle and prayer."

In April, it was Ike's turn to worry about his wife's first trip to Baguio. Against his wishes, she was leaving with friends in a large, fast car, chauffeured by a Filipino who was reputed to know every town, barrio, cluster of nipa shacks, and time-saving detour, from years of shuttling back and forth to the mountains. His record so far was accident-free, but Ike had ridden behind the young man on occasional one-mile trips to the Caloocan Golf Club, just north of Manila, and thought him wild beyond reason. But there was no use trying to convince Mamie of this. She was too impatient to be willing to wait several weeks until she could go up with Ike in the family Ford. Months of separation from Johnnie, added to the bake-oven heat of April in Manila, made her long desperately for Baguio.

A bit on the grim side, Ike said good-bye, insisting that she phone him on arrival. When the call came through, hours overdue, her voice was barely audible. Jerkily she said that the car had skidded and knocked over a little girl in a barrio when the driver braked suddenly to avoid hitting a plodding carabao. The child was shaken but uninjured, but for seconds everyone thought the four-year-old was dead, and there had been hours of questioning by local police and posting of bail for the driver. Knowing his wife's intense devotion to children, Ike realized that she had been badly shocked, but it was his hope that supper with Johnnie and a good night's sleep would cancel out the experience.

Two days later he froze to the telephone when "Bootsie" White, wife of his good friend Major Sam White, stationed at Camp John Hay, told him his wife was very ill in the post hospital. It was never determined whether the accident or the altitude, or a combination of both, had induced the stomach hemorrhage and coma that almost snuffed out Mamie's life. Fortunately, the Whites were in an adjoining room when the attack occurred; if "Bootsie" had not been there to watch over her while Major White routed out a medical officer, the consequences might well have been fatal.

Ike flew up at once and remained until Mamie's recovery was certain; then he made week-end visits during her month of hospitalization. John sat gravely with his mother every afternoon. As soon as she was well enough for sustained conversation he talked to her by the hour about school sports and his classroom problems. Mamie perceived that her son was maturing rapidly. He was stretching toward six feet, was hardening muscularly, and becoming purposeful in voice and manner. He regarded his academic instruction and athletic periods as serious preliminary training for West Point, and his mother was resigned to the realization that his new-found independence was directed toward working and planning for a military career. She resolved to try never again to stand between him and the world, for her days of careful mothering were over—Johnnie was going to be as independent and determined as his father. Already she could foresee the high hour when she and Ike would watch their son march in with his West Point graduating class. Only seven short years and Johnnie would be a second lieutenant!

As Mamie's spirits revived and she became strong enough to reach into the world around her, "Bootsie" and Sam White took her daily surprise packages of oddments collected at the Post Exchange. Propped in bed, a pink ribbon binding her short curls, every hair of her bangs evened above her lovely face, Mamie would chuckle and wrinkle her nose as she unwrapped anything from a packet of peppermints to a batch of hair curlers. The morning she riffled gaily through a deck of miniature playing cards, the Whites knew that Mamie's days in the hospital were numbered. Next day they took her a bridge score and a jumbo pencil.

Ike wouldn't hear of his wife risking the sodden heat of Manila; so she stayed on in Baguio until summer was nearly done, feeling very guilty in the cool comfort of the mountains, while her husband worked on through the lowland's ugliest, angriest season. All of the Philippines—coastal areas, plains, and mountains alike—is lashed by torrential rains and high winds that sometimes reach typhoon intensity. The big storms sickle trees and utility poles like grass, flatten *nipa* houses, unroof mortared structures, and wash away bridges, roads and docks. May, sundered by ball lightning, has little rain besides the flash storms. Typhoon warnings are broadcast regularly in June, and from then on, during the next four months, fierce winds flail the deafening rain. Manila rarely meets a typhoon head-on, but there is always seasonal damage.

Humanity is abused in other ways as well. When the hot sun streams past clouds, the ground steams; the rotting algae floating on the Pasig River slimes to a fearful stench that blankets city and countryside; the mud wallows of the *carabaos* and the tidal flats along the bay are black-crusted with mosquito larvae; mildew coats houses, clothes, paper, leather, furniture and food. The acrid mustiness of the grey-green mold lodges in throats and nostrils. Everyone and everything—except the fish in the bay—are clammy and foul-smelling. In the mountains it is wet and windy, but the cool air does not breed stench and rot. September may close the year's accounts with final eighty-mile winds and lashing rain. Late October, however, is more likely to wind up the tempests and play host to the onset of winter's clarity and freshness.

In her last year of residence in the Philippines, Mrs. Eisenhower felt trapped in Manila's summer cycle of discomfort. She admits she was never able to adjust as happily as many American women to the heat, smells and rain-letting skies, and thinks that the inaction of hotel living was the primary reason. "If I had not been hotel-bound, it would have been easier," she says. "Women with household responsibilities seemed as contented as their hard-working husbands—even on days when a duck would have drowned. But there I was, cooped up in two rooms with too much time on my hands."

On her initial visit to Baguio, Mamie clung to the Army set at Camp John Hay. Late in the season, as she grew stronger and felt equal to going off the post to the country club and to homes of civilian friends, she delighted in visiting Mrs. George Fairchild, whose hobby was horticulture. Senator and Mrs. Fairchild, one of the "first couples" of the American community, had befriended Ike during the year he awaited Mamie's arrival; now they enjoyed his wife's refreshing naturalness. Simple and direct, with a background of nearly a quarter of a century in the islands, the white-haired, Hawaiian-born Senator and his vivacious wife were also truly "simpatico" to the culture and aspirations of the Filipino people. The Fairchilds summered in Baguio in a home almost as imposing as Mansion House, the official residence of Acting High Commissioner Weldon Jones. When she was not busy in the blazing beauty of her garden, Mrs. Fairchild liked to bring American and Filipino friends together for small dinners and luncheons without the press of formality. The talk always aired island politics, past, present and future, but Mamie remembers best an evening on which Weldon Jones and Senator Fairchild recalled the "old days" when Igorote tribesmen knifed and speared pioneer American missionaries and mining prospectors with reckless savagery—all this in tribal settlements or on mountain trails in wild valleys and mountain crests not too remote from Baguio. When the spine-chilling conversation switched to the Southern Islands, Mr. Jones had vivid memories of the sorties on Palawan, Sulu and Mindanao of extremist Moros who went "hermantado" and hacked up Christian Filipinos and Americans. Once in a while, he added, a fanatic still armored his arms, legs and body with bamboo and whirled screaming into a village, wielding a razor-sharp *barong* to slash innocent bystanders to eternity, and then raced back to the hills. On that evening, the accounts of the malefactions of the Igorotes touched Mamie's sensibilities much more directly than Moro bloodthirstiness, for the Igorotes lived at trail-traveling distance from Camp John Hay.

Friday was market day in Baguio. Igorote tribesmen, "dressed for town" in cast-off Army shirts that hid their g-string nakedness, sat indifferent and aloof behind displays of their produce and handicrafts. Their women, cackling among themselves, in indigo-blue shifts, also treated customers with beady-eyed disinterest. Wood carvings, silver trinkets, hand-loomed yardage—parrot-bright, or of indigo-blue and maroon stripes interwoven with yellow—attested to the primitive artistry of the Igorotes. Here were people of a race that had stood still through the ages and tolerated no interference with their aboriginal way of life; the money they took in exchange for their wares was their one concession to civilization. Vending over, they hoisted pack-baskets and dog-trotted single-file toward the mountain paths, not to be seen until the following week. Transactions with the Igorotes gave Mamie a feeling of being uncomfortably close to aboriginal savagery, but she bought numerous souvenirs to take back to Manila.

Just before Christmas, when John was down from Baguio and settling in for a long holiday at the hotel with his mother and father, Mrs. Eisenhower found that she must abandon all plans for her son's vacation. Her husband came back from a bridge session at the Army and Navy Club with an adventurous gleam in his eye. Lieutenant-colonel and Mrs. William M. Hoge had detained him in the lounge to unfold their coming trip to the Southern Islands. They would be gone a month while the Colonel made an inspection of Army facilities in Moro towns and villages. They would be accompanied by George, their eighteen-year-old son, and the Hoges suggested that Johnnie go with George; two boys would have more fun than one. Ike said that he had accepted the invitation, provided Johnnie wanted to go. *Did* Johnnie want to go! He barely let his father finish before he was war-dancing around the furniture, gleefully singing several stanzas from the old Army ditty, "The Monkeys Have No Tails in Zamboanga." Visions of Moros going "hermantado" leaped before his mother's eyes, but Mamie hadn't the heart to be a wet-blanket. Besides Ike had already approved the trip, and what Ike said went. She knew that she would worry every second Johnnie was away—it would be his first trip on his own—but the Hoges were a solid, conservative couple who would never welcome needless hazards.

Mrs. Hoge well remembers the fun she had excursioning with the boys. Her husband, now a Lieutenant-general commanding all United States Army ground forces in Europe, sharply regrets to this day that his official duties at military installations denied him a close-up view of the wide-eyed wonder of Johnnie and his son in the primitive market places of the Moro towns and villages.

The 700-mile south-bound voyage in a small inter-island steamer was rough, noisy, and reeking. Deck passengers—human and animal—wailed and bellowed night and day while the boat wallowed through the seas of Sibuyan, Visayan and Mindanao. In and out of many ports, including Calapan, Cebu, and Dumagate, the creaking little vessel made its way, tying up to wharfs, discharging passengers, freight, and mail, then stowing aboard new cargo and passengers. To avoid the squawling, high-smelling jumble of docking, the Hoges and John rushed ashore as soon as the gangway was made fast, and put off returning until the sailing whistle blew. Mrs. Hoge, a sportswoman of stamina, needed all the energy she could command to walk through countless markets, old Spanish buildings, and streetside tiendas that sold conglomerate wares ranging from native straw mats to Japanese alarm clocks; John and George priced and handled everything in sight, but refused to part with their spending money; Colonel Hoge exchanged courtesies with government officials.

At Zamboanga they transshipped from the steamer to a small coastwise vessel that took them in and out of other Mindanao ports, then cut across the Sulu Sea to Jolo, traditional seat of the Sultan of Sulu. The sights seemed more than ever like pages out of the Arabian Nights—reception committees of Moros in violent-hued silk sarongs and peaked head-cloths; unseen gongs vibrating welcome from inshore jungles; flapping copper-colored lateen sails up-masted from bright red and blue "proas" carrying pearl divers to work; village after village built on stilts over the water.

Back again in Zamboanga, John laid down pesos for a Moro knife, spears, and brass gongs, mementoes for his father and himself. He debated his mother's gift until his last hour ashore, then hurried back to the bird and animal mart and bought her a white cockatoo. Mrs. Hoge had tried vainly to steer him toward a silk scarf or wide silver bracelet, but John remained undecided until the snowy bird captured his fancy. He weighed its purchase overnight. At breakfast he was sure the pet would surprise and delight his mother, and no amount of persuasion could alter his resolve. It was the cockatoo or nothing.

Confined in a bamboo cage that became progressively dirtier and smellier during the six-day return voyage, the cockatoo grew frayed and greyed with travel. At Colonel Hoge's suggestion, John and a deckhand undertook to slosh down the cage at dawn-light as the steamer swung into Manila Bay, but the bird fanned its wings and drove them off. John looked helplessly at the wretched creature in the spattered cage. If he had been able to substitute so much as a small basket or a string of shells, he would have given the cockatoo to the deckhand.

As the steamer warped to a dock in the Pasig River, John quickly identified his father standing on the running board of the Ford, yelling and waving over the jostling crowd. Ike's joyous welcome turned to indignation when Johnnie lugged the squawk-ing cockatoo ashore; under the remonstrance John stood speechless, waiting for his father to cool off. Sure enough, Ike clipped his anger and began to grin; he chatted amiably with the Hoges and beamed at John. Seated in her car while she waited for the chauffeur to collect the family goods, Mrs. Hoge enjoyed a mild hysteria watching her husband, Ike, and the boys debate the problem of putting the cage on the white cover of the rear seat of the Eisenhower Ford. Ike settled matters by buying a newspaper, and he and John spread the sheets over the seat. George Hoge helped to wrestle the cage through the narrow door. It was "operation flying-feathers and bird seed," Mrs. Hoge recalls, with Ike again voicing damnations. When the cage was wedged firmly on the seat, Ike slammed the door and shrugged it all off.

Tactfully, the Hoges refrained from probing into the cockatoo's fate. A week or so later they observed that the bird was not in the Eisenhower suite and deduced it had been banished. It was a correct assumption.

Seventeen years later, Mrs. Eisenhower is still wistful over the fate of her son's bedraggled gift. She says she tried to argue that a new cage and several baths would make the bird presentable, but her husband refused to put up with its rackety squawking. After a night spent in the servant's quarters at the end of the hall, the cockatoo was sent out to Fort McKinley to become a permanent boarder in the quarters of Army friends. John was disappointed, and deeply embarrassed by the unfitness of his gift. His mother is positive that her son, whom she termed "an apartment house child deprived of all pets," was gratifying a deep-seated longing when he bought the cockatoo. "Johnnie really bought the bird for himself—that's why it just about broke his heart when his father sent it away," she says. It was not until after World War Two, when John was junior officer on duty with his father in England, that he finally had a pet of his own. It was a Scottie pup named Julia, one of a litter from his father's dog Telek. Julia, still going strong, is the constant companion of John's three children, David, Anne, and Susan.

In the spring of 1938, after months of mounting physical misery, Mrs. Eisenhower was advised by doctors to submit to a gall bladder operation as a possible cure for her distressing stomach condition. Ike would not hear of her returning alone to the Black Clinic in Pueblo, Colorado, and promptly "put in" for three months Stateside leave. As soon as it was granted they booked passage on the fast transpacific liner *President Coolidge,* and with John they sailed early in May for San Francisco. Scarcely a month later, the surgical ordeal successfully completed, Mamie was mending at her parents' home in Denver. While she was gaining strength, her husband made a hurried trip to Abilene to see his mother and brothers. She was still, as she terms it, "in the tottering stage," when she started for Manila early in August with her husband and son. They were passengers out of Vancouver, in the *Empress of Japan,* the Canadian Pacific's "Speed Queen of the Pacific." In eighteen days they were back in the heat and sogginess, under the lowering typhoon skies of Manila's time of heavy rains. Mrs. Eisenhower knew exactly what lay ahead, but she was determined not to let the tropics and the squirrel-cage hotel life get the better of her naturally gay heart. Over and over she told herself, during the voyage out, that Ike had a job—a big job—to finish; she would face it with him brightly, now that her health was restored.

This time the Eisenhowers settled in the newly opened air-conditioned wing of the Manila Hotel. Their suite, exotic as a movie set, was something of a shock to money-minded Mamie. She took one look at the lavish appointments and refused to unpack, saying that they could not possibly afford such elegance. Far better to swelter in their old apartment than live here and run into debt. But the manager of the government-owned hotel set her fears at rest: the new quarters varied not a peso from the rental of their former suite. Ike and Mamie would have preferred living with less formality, but nothing less elaborate was available in the new wing. Scanning the opulence, Mamie decided that since they weren't paying extra for the décor they might as well enjoy the regulated comfort of the air-conditioning. The large, high-ceilinged living room included a dining alcove and was flooded with brilliance from crystal chandeliers and wall sconces. French furniture upholstered in brocade, damask-paneled walls, glass picture-windows facing the bay, marquetry floors, gilt bands on lamps and occasional tables, created the illusion of a continental salon. The same décor held in the bedroom, adjoined by a bath paved in colored tile, with American fixtures. No other hotel in the Far East has ever offered such elegance. Plain, everyday Ike and Mamie, who by then had covered quite a portion of the world and had lived in good, bad, and indifferent quarters, thought back to their Paris apartment; they told each other that it was mighty strange to be living in the Philippines in a French environment with American plumbing.

In a few days John was off for Baguio and another school term; Ike had resumed a heavy work schedule, and Mamie, fiddle-fit now and merry, kept her room-boy and a hotel porter busy unpacking and arranging clothing, objects and furniture. Her special flair for blending colors and grouping objects transformed the formal salon into a friendly room. Morning bridge was back on Mrs. Eisenhower's engagement calendar. Either she set up a table or made the fourth for a game somewhere in the hotel. Later, when the weather modified, she broadened her social activities to include luncheons and teas. Her husband liked to wind up his day with golf or a bridge session with men; so she had the choice of sitting alone until eight o'clock or later, or passing the time at a "hen party." As likely as not, Ike would be with the husbands of her closest friends, and it was not unusual for the couples to join for dinner and more bridge. Marge Clay and her husband were down-the-hall neighbors. Lucius Clay was then a captain, attached to General MacArthur's staff. In the decade ahead, he was to become a lieutenant-general and establish the American military government in Germany after World War Two. Anne Nevins, married to Major Arthur S. Nevins, would one day see her husband promoted to brigadier-general.

Mildred Hodges, wife of Lieutenant-colonel Courtney H. Hodges, fourth member of this group, was also destined to see her husband rise to become general, in command of the First Army that played such a valiant part in defeating the Germans.

One evening in the winter of 1939 Lieutenant-colonel Eisenhower was involved in a prophecy which, viewed in the light of what came after, could give comfort to believers in the occult. One thing is certain; no one then took the incident seriously, and if a friend had not jotted down the prediction, it would be beyond recall.

Madame Hebibi, Manila's noted gypsy fortune teller, was on hand at the home of Mr. and Mrs. Maurice Kahn to read the future of bridge-playing guests as "a passing diversion." Scanning Lieutenant-colonel Eisenhower's cards, she said, "I see you will be president—in the lucky cycle of thirteen you will be president." Ike winked at Aimée Kahn and said he guessed that stacked him up to be the thirteenth president of some officers' club. Mrs. Kahn, who has made a hobby of recording all her parties, entered the "thirteen president business" in her entertainment log book.

Madame Hebibi made her prediction in 1939. Dwight D. Eisenhower was elected President of the United States in 1952. The author has seen Mrs. Kahn's diary, and knows that the episode is not a legend tailored to subsequent events.

If Madame Hebibi had predicted a White House future for Paul V. McNutt, United States High Commissioner to the Philippines in 1939, no one would have been surprised. At that time the bright star of Presidential destiny was more than a faint glimmer for Mr. McNutt. A likeable, genial man, with sharp business sense and legal training, politically astute, he seemed most likely to be the man picked by the Democratic party for president in 1940—if President Franklin D. Roosevelt adhered to the tradition of not seeking a third term. Normally ambitious, Mr. McNutt was determined that his appointment as High Commissioner would make history—and stateside headlines. He had many problems to solve, including distrust on the part of Filipino politicos of American capital and manpower in underwriting mining, sugar, copra, and hemp production and in the financing and operation of banks and mercantile firms. Bills designed to curb "foreign" economic intervention had been introduced into the Philippine Legislature by Filipino nationalists determined to drive Americans from entrenched economic positions. Mr. McNutt, knowing that his political future hinged on his executive determinations, had his hands full. He worked night and day trying to meet the explosive situation.

Mrs. Eisenhower does not remember being particularly aware of Mr. McNutt's political problems. She knew and liked his wife, Mary. Ike, in the course of many dealings with the High Commissioner's office, found Paul McNutt ready to cast his influence on the side of a strong defensive Philippine Army. Mr. McNutt's political ambitions have no place in Mrs. Eisenhower's story except to point the fact that in the Philippines at that time there was a public figure who was striving to be President of the United States. The brilliant hard-working Army officer who centered his aims and ambitions on helping to build a strong defense for the islands, for a war he believed inevitable, had no personal interest in the office of President. Dwight Eisenhower's sole ambition was to be worthy some day to become a general officer.

There is notable all-around silence on why Lieutenant-colonel Eisenhower asked, late in 1939, to be transferred back to the Zone of Interior. It has been intimated that the declaration of war against Germany by France and England on September 3 made him eager to return to regular duty in the United States and be available to command troops if the history of World War One was duplicated and the United States entered the conflict. It is more than likely that the European War was the pretext, rather than the reason, for his desire to transfer from General MacArthur's command in the Philippines. Whatever the cause, President Eisenhower and General MacArthur have recently healed any breach that may have existed.

The Filipinos hated to see Ike go. President Quezon officially expressed his nation's regrets and awarded Ike the Philippine Distinguished Service Medal in a public ceremony. Mamie was asked to pin the decoration on her husband's blouse, and did so under a battery of news cameras. It was the first time she was photographed as a public figure.

Chapter 10

FORT SAM HOUSTON, TEXAS
WASHINGTON, D. C.
1941–1947

On July 1, 1941, the dust-filmed "Katy Special" arrived punctually in San Antonio at 1:55 P.M. Hedged in the stuffy vestibule of one of the Pullmans ever since the train had slowed down in the outer yards, Mamie Eisenhower and her husband were exchanging murmured nonsense and laughing with holiday excitement. They were impatient to end their journey from Tacoma, Washington. The porter had no sooner cleared the last of the baggage from the car entrance than Colonel Eisenhower descended hurriedly to the station platform, spun around and reached up and grabbed his wife's forearm. He steadied her downward progress—Mamie's high heels were uncertain on the slick steel steps—and still holding her arm, steered toward the line-up of car baggage.

Mamie looked with happy surprise on the almost forgotten sights and sounds of the busy terminal. Her mind turned back to another July day—in 1916, when she and Ike, decked in honeymoon finery, had emerged from a Pullman in this very station into the arms of noisy, well-wishing friends. Warm-eyed, she looked up at Ike. He too had remembered that long ago arrival. Laughing, he squeezed his wife's arm and turned to gaze into her eyes.

Dwight and Mamie Eisenhower had good reason for sentimentality. After long years in far places, a quirk of fate had returned them to San Antonio on the twenty-fifth anniversary of their marriage. Once again they would start housekeeping at Fort Sam Houston; but now it would be a colonel's spacious house, not a lieutenant's two-room apartment. The years between counted as nothing; they were as eager and excited as they had been as newlyweds.

In contrast to their 1916 arrival, there were no familiar voices calling welcome; but the questing eyes of an Army lieutenant had singled them out while they were happily surveying the station's unchanging grime, racket and confusion. The young officer stepped forward and with proper formality presented his respects to the new chief of staff of the Third Army. Colonel Eisenhower snapped out of his abstraction, responded easily, kindly, and introduced the somewhat self-conscious youngster to Mamie, who beamed friendliness. Noticing two enlisted men, who had come to handle the baggage, Ike spoke pleasantly to the soldiers and began identifying grips, suitcases and hatboxes. Mamie's eyes danced, seeing her husband casually hand over claim-checks for the trunks. A quarter of a century before, Ike had "mothered" their baggage and agonized over the missing trunks; now he was shucking off all responsibility with calm indifference. A joke about their former "baggage blues" rose to her lips, but her husband, reading her mind, anticipated the sally with a flickering wink and an "okay" sign of his hand.

A staff car, with a soldier driving and the lieutenant sitting eyes-ahead, took them into midtown traffic. Gawky as tourists, Colonel and Mrs. Eisenhower peered for landmarks as they drove along the once-familiar streets. All had been "modernized." Gone were sun-baked adobe, wooden sidewalk awnings, loungers in narrow doorways. Blatant American commerce had supplanted easy-going Spanish trade; only a scattering of venerable mercantile names recalled the past. Instead of rocks, ruts and dust, an arterial highway stretched ribbon-smooth north to Fort Sam. It was bordered by chain groceries, quick-lunch diners, garages, automobile showrooms, neighborhood theatres, and local drug, tailor and variety stores. A few private dwellings, gaunt and tired with age, seemed as incongruous as tattered overalls at a banquet.

Mrs. Eisenhower and her husband wasted no time bewailing San Antonio's new face. Not that they wholly approved, but as Ike said, they, too, had changed in the more than two decades since they last bounced in and out of town in their Pullman runabout. Mention of their first automobile convulsed Mamie. It had been rugged transportation, yes—but what about the "coffee mill contraption" that had plunged, bucked and side-swiped pack-donkeys and horse-carts during the roaring ride from the station to Fort Sam on the morning of their bridal homecoming? Compare that bone-rattling journey, she said, to this smooth-running Army sedan that stopped and started effortlessly for traffic lights. Ike, pretending fretfulness, looked out the rear window in a fair imitation of his own bridegroom fear that their goods and chattels would be flung in the dust from the pell-mell truck. She warned him that the joke might backfire—their present load of baggage could become a traffic calamity.

Fort Sam's dun-colored rock quadrangle was as frowningly impressive as always, even if the sentries at the steel gates were only the toss of a baseball distant from stores across Grayson Avenue. Fancy, Government Hill with a bustling business district! Off to the right, the stone posts marking the beginning of Infantry Row seemed dwarfed by trees grown tall and spreading. There was no chance to glimpse their old quarters, in the seconds it took the car to swing left around the quad and head up toward General's Row back of the artillery post. At 179 New Braunfels Road, the driver pulled to the curb. The sober-faced lieutenant—Mrs. Eisenhower says he rode the whole way in silence—slipped from the front seat and opened the rear door, expecting that his passengers would want to make a quick trip through their new quarters. But Mamie sat quiet, staring at the wide-porched, many-windowed house. It was box-shaped, freshly painted white, with green trim, being in all other respects a counterpart of other quarters strung down the tree-shaded, curving thoroughfare. Why go in the empty house now? she said; anything that big would have plenty of problems. They could better be tackled later when the house-hold shipment arrived. Ike, who never questioned her house-keeping decisions, nodded agreement. They could go over and shake down in rooms at the Officers' Club.

Mamie hadn't expected to find the Officers' Club so elaborate. The rambling hacienda was complete with swimming pool and tennis courts, (shades of old Texas!) and the Army had kept alive the atmosphere of old Spain—with air-conditioning. In the lobby a larger, far noisier reception committee than the group which had stood outside their Pullman in 1916 took over. *Goodness,* where had everybody come from? It was like being back at every post they'd lived on through the years; every post, except Fort Sam. Ike and Mamie greeted the crowd of middle-aged officers and wives, hopefully expecting to see Fort Sam associates from the old days, but fate ruled otherwise.

In the whirl of welcome, as she hugged, kissed and held hands with long-time friends, Mrs. Eisenhower had only one regret— Johnnie wasn't around to share in the fun. Over and over, when asked, "Where's that boy of yours?" she replied proudly, "Getting ready for West Point." But deep inside she had an empty feel-ing; the cadet-to-be should have been at Fort Sam—if only for the day.

Early that morning, in the train compartment, she and Ike had agreed that Johnnie's insistence on going back to Washing-ton for pre-cadet studies was a necessary preliminary to the hard years he faced at the Academy—yet, goodness, how they missed him! When the porter brought Mamie's light breakfast from the diner, her husband had stepped to the door and fumbled an instant with the tray; he had then stepped back while the tray was placed on her knees. Abstractedly, her mind still in Wash-ington with Johnnie, Mamie had glanced down—fruit juice, toast, a pot of tea—and what's this! a small package. Tugging open the wrappings, her heart beating faster than the train's wheels ("I knew it was something wonderful; Ike's surprises are always wonderful"), she snapped open the lid of a jeweler's box. There it was! A platinum watch, with diamonds around a tiny dial! Ike, generous, devoted Ike, had outdone himself. She wanted to cry. He was a man in a million—no, in a hundred million. In a flash she realized how he must have pinched the weekly cigarette and petty-cash allowance which was all he ever wanted from his pay; how he must have hoarded his checks from technical articles—all to give her this. When he could have been buying golf clubs, a new hunting rifle or trout rods—

From that moment forward, Mrs. Eisenhower has worn the watch constantly, on her left wrist, above the hand on which flashes the large solitaire and diamond wedding band—Ike's gifts on her wedding day in Denver.

The next four months at Fort Sam Houston were a blur of house-settling and nervous tension for Mamie. She liked the big, five-bedroom quarters with one exception: the pass-pantry into the dining room had to go. She argued that the shelf and sliding-door arrangement broke up the only wall long enough to accommodate her sideboard. In a few days a captain was turning down her request; then a major. But Mamie was determined to have a solid wall. "It almost took an act of Congress—government property is supposed to remain intact until it falls apart—but I got my way," Mrs. Eisenhower says. "I think they gave in to shut me up, so other wives wouldn't get the same idea."

It was downright impossible to keep a house that size in order and cook three meals a day without help; but houseworkers weren't hiring out. The draft of men into the Army had begun; war plants had started paying big wages to women as well as men for unskilled work; hotels, laundries, and restaurants offered fat salaries for untrained hands; schoolgirls, grandmothers and housewives, glad to get away from household chores, were going out to work. Mamie's only hope was to locate some enlisted man who would be willing to clean and scrub in his off-duty time for extra pay. She had a notice posted in barracks asking for a "striker"—which is the Army term for such a helper. A young soldier named Michael McKeogh offered his services. A former bellboy in a New York hotel, Micky claimed to have learned housework at his mother's knee; he began as a "lick-and-a-promise" worker, but he quickly improved. His neatness was much appreciated except when he insisted on buttoning the Colonel's freshly laundered shirts and blouses just in from the cleaners. Rather than hear her husband's strong language when he lifted a buttoned-up garment out of his closet, Mamie took to undoing the striker's unwanted efforts. This worked fine, until Micky would discover her handiwork; then, sure as fate, he'd re-button every shirt and blouse.

This around-the-rosy game was of short duration, however. Micky McKeogh dedicated his Irish heart, nimble mind and capable hands to keeping the Eisenhower household running exactly right. Mamie's striker was soon a perfectionist and became indispensable. From part-time striker chores, Micky rode along on the tide of world events that made his colonel Supreme Commander of Allied Forces in Europe during World War Two. Night or day, on the ground or in the air, Staff sergeant Michael McKeogh gave loyal and devoted service as General Eisenhower's orderly.

Those were difficult days for everyone concerned; Ike was preparing "battle plans" for the projected Louisiana maneuvers—working long hours with his chief, Lieutenant-general Walter Krueger, head of the Third Army. Eisenhower was carrying a big responsibility. He had been transferred from Fort Lewis on the recommendation of Brigadier-general Mark W. Clark, who valued Ike's Philippine tactical record highly, as well as his superior work as chief of staff of the 3rd Division, to the same executive position with the Third Army during intensive training maneuvers of drafted and regular troops.

Home life and post life were so close a parallel to prewar 1917 that Mamie knew—how well she knew!—that the United States was on the point of engagement in another world conflict.

The German Army had driven into Russia. Prime Minister

Winston Churchill and President Franklin D. Roosevelt had joined together and signed the Atlantic Charter. United States Navy destroyers were guarding American-made war goods en route to Europe in convoys. The Army Air Corps was sending mass flights of its new B-17 Flying Fortresses across the Pacific. Tanks were again in production to supply the four divisions of the newly created Armored Force.

What spark would ignite this tinder? When—and how—would the aggressor nations force the issue? Every day was a whirlpool of conjecture. Mamie listened to the radio; listened to other Army wives, but only talked around the subject when her worked-out husband came home. Give him good meals; discuss Johnnie's letters and the latest news from Papa and Mama Doud; have Major Alfred M. Gruenther and his wife, Grace, in for bridge for a change—that was her job and her social life.

Ike went off to Louisiana, and again she was alone during long empty nights. Much worse than when she was a bride; much worse now. There was Johnnie, moving toward his father's soldier life. Because Mamie hated the echoing bigness of the house, Mrs. Florence Cowie, hostess at the Officers' Club, allowed her two high-school daughters to alternate as Eisenhower "house guests." They came after supper and used the upstairs single room. So long as someone was in the house; just to know that someone, even someone sleeping youth's heavy slumber, was near on the nights of vigil. A month—six weeks—and then Ike was back—jubilant. General Krueger's Third (Blue) Army had out-foxed, out-classed, out-maneuvered Lieutenant-General Ben Lear's Second (Red) Army, an outfit operating strong units of the newly-activated Armored Force. It had been heavy going, very heavy going, Ike said but the Third Army's counter-offensive plan worked.

All of Fort Sam was jubilant. "Well done" was passed down from Washington. The strain of maneuvers over, Ike settled down to a slightly less rigorous routine. On Sunday evenings he and Mamie held open-house. A buffet table laden with foods he had labored through the day to prepare—stew, an ambrosia of meat and vegetables; hot potato salad, sauerkraut and spare ribs; or just plain hamburgers, spiced and flavored with perfectionist skill. That was the sort of food Ike put out. It was great good fun. The gang came back for repeats at the buffet table; the gang raised voices in song, with Mamie banging out tunes on her rented piano. Those who wanted to, played cards, thought up riddles, or told jokes. A slightly zany atmosphere, but it eased the tension of the times.

Then Ike's promotion came through in September—a star! One of the biggest thrills of their lives, Mrs. Eisenhower is sure. Fort Sam held a review for Ike—for Brigadier-general Dwight D. Eisenhower—all shine, polish and precision. Mamie, just behind him in the reviewing stand, remembering the long-ago days when she had dreamed of her husband with a star on his shoulder, took grains of comfort. In the war that was bound to happen, Ike, as a general officer, would seldom be under fire. Johnnie, at West Point, had four years of classroom learning— then. Like every other wife and mother, she could only hope and pray.

October and November were torn from the calendar; then December started. It was Sunday. One o'clock dinner was over. Micky had washed the dishes and left; Ike was cat-napping in the bedroom, dragged-out with weariness. He had been up at dawn, in the office until noon, and was due back at three for another conference. Sunday had become a work day like the rest of the week, except for the long mid-day meal period. But relief was in sight. One more Sunday like this, then they would be off for two weeks' Christmas vacation with Johnnie at West Point.

Mamie settled beside the radio in the upstairs hall sitting-room and tuned in softly for a football broadcast. Working needles through a piece of knitting, she considered vacation plans. She listened with but half an ear to the announcer's voice barking the game's line-up. Then came what seemed to be a transmission break. The radio fell silent. Suddenly a new voice tumbled words: "Pearl Harbor—Japanese planes attacking!" Mamie twirled the knob for full volume. "Battleships in flames!" She leaped from her chair, crashing open the bedroom door as the bedside phone shrilled. Groggy with sleep, Ike rolled over and groped for the instrument. Stepping inside and pulling the door shut behind her, Mamie stood rigid. Her husband's eyes widened, then closed to slits as he caught the import of the swift words barking out of the receiver. He swung himself to a sitting position, then rose. His deep voice snapped "Right away"; then he lowered the receiver slowly into its cradle. "The Japs have hit us in Hawaii. That's it—that's war," he said. Not another word, not another glance, during the seconds it took to draw on and lace his shoes, knot his tie and shrug into his uniform blouse. Mamie went ahead down the stairs and helped him into his overcoat. She noted the pulsing neck cords below his ears, and knew he was grinding his teeth in anger. He jerked around, patted her arm, and went out of the door to his car.

Mamie hurried back to the radio and turned it still higher. It got to be sundown, and still the same dreadful news over and over; not only Pearl Harbor a smoking shambles, but the Philippines too. Nichols Air Field just outside Manila—gone! Clark Field, farther up country, also in flames. The Japanese were striking with deadly accuracy at America's Pacific outposts. Numb and outraged, as was the whole nation, Mamie wept for the dead, the maimed; the children left fatherless, and the wives and mothers who must now bear the crushing sorrow.

Grace Gruenther and other neighbors came in, women neighbors; the men had all rushed back to duty. What should they do —wait, or go over to the Officers' Club? A buffet supper had been scheduled; the food would be wasted unless part of the crowd turned up. Who cared about food? Well, just to sit around together would be better than sticking it out at home. To the club they went, in whatever clothes they happened to be wearing and without bothering to freshen their tear-stained faces. It was a sorrowing evening for everyone. A common desire not to be alone brought women into the club from all over the post. In the lounge, the dining room, the halls, the waiting women, spurning all but a token meal, moved restlessly from group to group, even more deeply disturbed by the news still sounding from radios. Schofield Barracks "strafed"; Hickam Field in flames; the whole island of Oahu under martial law—barbed wire going up on the beaches; Manila bombed; Jap landings on Northern Luzon.

Mamie cringed. This was that "danger from the north" which Ike and others had sought for years to overcome by building up the Philippine Army. What now? What friends had been trapped? Schofield, Hickam—friends there, too—dead or desperate. Mamie stayed on. She knew Ike would see dawn at his desk; here, among women who were suffering the same keen thrusts, the helplessness of inaction was less leaden for being shared.

"Only when my little boy Icky died did I suffer more—it was the next most terrible night of my life," says Mrs. Eisenhower.

By midnight a few husbands, hoarse of voice, dog-tired, began to wander in. Food? Food would taste like straw, they said. Talk, talk. The women wanted headquarters news. The men replied that frenzied War Department orders had started coming through within an hour after the attack. Heavy bodies of troops were already entraining for terrified West Coast cities where it was thought the Japs might strike. That, and much more. Industrial plants needed guards; Rio Grande border patrols were out to prevent incoming spies; protection for port areas required more troops. Mamie's quick mind had understood at once what a heavy burden this hastily required improvisation of Third Army defense laid on her husband. She edged over to a couple saying goodnight and asked if they would drop her off at her quarters.

Home, in bed, with a single light casting shadows, she waited; dozed; then bolted up. It was morning; she heard Ike's firm tread on the stairs. Sleep? No, he didn't want sleep, but a bath and change would help. Unhurried, locked in his thoughts, he moved around. While the shower swished, Mamie went to the kitchen and brewed coffee. She heard him come down, snap on the library radio. He stood a while, parade-neat, checking every sentence of further attack. No fresh news—only ghastly confirmation of the death toll. Ike put down his empty cup, turned off the radio and quietly told his wife the obvious. He would be busy, very busy. She must please not bother about his meals; he'd eat at his desk, and get home sometime for a little tide-over sleep. His quick ear heard his aide's footfall then, and before the doorbell rang, the General had reached his overcoat in the hall.

Four more days of this. Mid-morning on Friday, Mamie answered the phone. It was Ike. General George C. Marshall had requested Ike's immediate air departure for Washington—so would Mamie pack plenty of everything. It might be indefinite duty, lasting months, or only a few days of conference on Philippine strategy.

"I prayed for Ike's safety and peace of mind; I dreaded having him fly on such a stormy day. He had left hurried and unhappy, and I knew he was hoping the Washington duty would be temporary—Ike wanted to stay with troops, not take on another staff job."

General Eisenhower's plane out of Randolph Field was forced down by the heavy weather a short while after leaving San Antonio, landing uneventfully at a small base in northern Texas. He continued on by train to St. Louis, was picked up by another military plane, and arrived in Washington late Saturday. Next morning he reported to General Marshall and was assigned to assist Leonard T. Gerow, now a brigadier-general and chief of War Plans. From West Point, on through the early days at Fort Sam Houston and the tough months of study at Command and General Staff School at Fort Leavenworth, Leonard Gerow and Dwight Eisenhower had been friends. Each had profound insight into the other's thinking. Under the impact of war crises, their teamwork was notable.

Mrs. Eisenhower had Johnnie's companionship at West Point during the drab, broken days of Christmas week. Cadet training! Yardstick-straight and literally inches taller; his cap squared above wiser, sterner eyes (so like his father's); lithe, quick, graceful; positiveness in his deep voice—Goodness! Her boy was all soldier now. Ike got through to them once by phone. "Bless you, bless you both," he said.

Bound back to San Antonio—not through Chicago as she had come up—Mamie arrived at Washington in New Year's bite and cold. Milton Eisenhower and his wife Grace met her train and drove her to their brick and white-trimmed house in Falls Church, Virginia, over the river from the capital. Ike was living at his brother's home, but he never saw sun's up or down there. The nation's strength was being rallied and Ike, in War Plans, carried a towering responsibility. He said little about his work, other than to announce that there would be no more duty at Fort Sam. He asked his wife to go back to Texas, compress their belongings into crates, boxes and barrels, and get the shipment started north. Quarters at Fort Myer, on the Virginia side of the Potomac, were being allotted, but quarters without furniture would be useless. There was a wartime emergency "snafu" on freight and it might be months before they could settle. Mrs. Eisenhower took the prospect of one more uprooting calmly. In all her married life, just once—years later—was her husband around when there was packing and shipping to be done. Even when it came to moving into the White House, she sorted and packed all their personal effects.

"I could have made quite a career out of running a transfer business," she says with a twinkle. "Or maybe I overestimate my ability; our belongings just about pack themselves. I might have less luck with other people's 'untrained' possessions."

While waiting in San Antonio until a trucking company notified her that the household shipment was rolling north, Mrs. Eisenhower stayed with her sister "Mike", who had married George Gordon Moore and was living in a furnished house in Terrell Road. Recently commissioned an Army captain, Mamie's brother-in-law was in the Quartermaster Corps at Fort Sam.

By the time quarters at Fort Myer could be moved into, General Eisenhower had his second star. He had been promoted to the temporary rank of major-general and made chief of the newly created Operations Division of the War Department.

Until May, when Ike was ordered to fly to Great Britain for a ten days' evaluation of American Army headquarters in London, and camps and air bases in the provinces for United States personnel, Mrs. Eisenhower lived from day to day. She kept house with the help of Micky McKeogh, now wearing a corporal's stripes and very much the majordomo, who relieved her of all but the preparation of meals that had to be cooked in a jiffy for her late-coming husband.

The British Isles venture was Ike's first over-water flight, and his wife, who froze at the sight or sound of an airplane, didn't get her heart back where it belonged until he finished the tour. He had gone over with Major-general Mark Clark and Brigadier-general Thomas T. Handy, the latter a key assistant in operations, and they had explored carefully the proposal for making Great Britain the base of United States military operations, a matter thrown into bold relief a few weeks before when General Marshall and Harry L. Hopkins had been in England to consider the problem of logistical support.

On his return from his first round-trip flight via the North Atlantic air route, General Eisenhower was immersed deeper in planning than before, and was little more than a boarder in his own home. On June 11, his wife had no hint of what was impending, except that for several days he had been sparing of words during his brief hours of wakefulness at home. Wifely intuition made Mamie tense; she knew something had happened—or would happen. The words came slowly without personal elation, for Dwight Eisenhower knew he was in the hands of history. He told her he had been chosen by General Marshall, with the approval of the President, to be Commanding General of the European Theatre of Operations, as well as to exercise operational control over United States Navy forces in the theatre. Fantastic! Unbelievable! He agreed, but it was a fact—so they'd better face it. He must go to London. The separation would be hard, but she had been braced for it since Pearl Harbor Sunday. She knew he would be going away, but she had not dreamed he would go to such a pinnacle of honor and responsibility. A Commanding

General so soon! A year later, even six months hence, but now! Twenty-five years in the confines of Army rank and precedence hadn't conditioned her for such a promotion for her husband. A few blinks, while her husband talked quietly, and Mamie was calm again.

Great events followed thick and fast. Ike, her Ike, called at the White House to confer with President Roosevelt and Britain's Prime Minister Winston Churchill, a short-term visitor at the Executive Mansion. The conversations were reported as "informal chats," but informal or not, they were with leaders whose word would cast the final die of victory or defeat in the military struggle ahead. And they had listened to Ike; they had valued his plans and opinion; they had voted him their confidence in planning ways and means to beat the Axis. Mamie knew nothing of military strategy—she never has and she never will—and that goes for politics as well. Aside from being impressed then by what she read in the papers, she had no special knowledge of what was going on. Her husband had not changed appreciably. Perhaps he moved and spoke more rapidly but he gave no indication of pressure.

When arrangements were made to have Johnnie down for a week end late in June, she concluded that time was getting short. The week before, Marie Kahn, teen-age daughter of the Maurice Kahns who had been friends in Manila, stayed over on her way back from school in Virginia. The General enjoyed having Marie with them. Privately, he was concerned about the girl, for her father had been taken prisoner by the Japanese in the Philippines. He put up a great show of depriving her of the Sunday funny papers. Mamie felt comfortable watching her husband in a joshing mood. He might be a commanding general, but he still liked the funny papers; and as long as he could relax, even so fleetingly, she knew he was holding up under the intense strain of his new job.

It was another boost to the General's spirits to come home and find Johnnie in razor-creased sun-tans, soldierly and precise, ending his sentences with "Sir." The boy was shaping up just as Ike had hoped he would, and father and son were immediately in accord. His son's just-finished term as a plebe and how it compared with his own first year at West Point was a favorite topic of talk. All week end they lived, breathed and talked West Point. Precious hours, precious days, over too soon. Johnnie's final leave-taking from the bottom of the walk before he entered a cab was a wrench. Sober and straight as a reed, Johnnie saluted His father returned his son's mark of respect, and kept his proud bright eyes steady. Mrs. Eisenhower, watching them, realized poignantly her privilege in kissing her son good-bye.

June twenty-fourth, one of summer's longest days, and again a staff car waited at the curb. The General's aide was at the door Micky came out carrying luggage. Mamie held fast and smiled but, try as she could, her words would not come with usual punch and vigor. Her husband, harried too, asking this and that —and would she be in the yard when the plane went over for final good-bye? Of course—of course! Another closing door another scudding automobile, airport bound. She fled upstairs fighting not to give way to tears. But she did cry—and hard, if briefly. To clear her eyes, and her mind, she puttered out the hour; there were soiled clothes in the wash hamper; closet doors to be closed, fresh linen for the bathroom. Then it was time to go out in the garden's sun—and wait.

"I stood under the flagstaff in the front yard where I knew Ike would be sure to look. The plane roared in very low. I waved and tried to tell myself I saw Ike at a window waving—but I didn't. I was crying too hard."

With her husband on duty overseas, Mrs. Eisenhower was no longer entitled to occupy the Fort Myer quarters. Her parents wanted her out in Denver, away from the congestion and confusion of wartime Washington, but she declined. She was quite prepared to face discomforts and inconveniences in the nation' crowded capital, even if she wound up living in an over-sized broom closet. By staying on, she could preserve the closest possible ties with her husband and son. The General's air-mail special-delivery letters would reach her the same day they arrived at the National Airport. If she wanted to visit Johnnie, West Point was only a morning's train ride. When critical war news was officially released, she could get in touch immediately with War Department officers. Also, friends shuttling to and from London might be other links of communication with her husband.

Mrs. Eisenhower says the extra twist she gave her elephant hair ring worked wonders—or something did. Following up on a tip that a three-bedroom apartment in the Wardman Park Hotel was about to be vacated by a government family ordered abroad, she found the management willing to shuffle their waiting list so she could have immediate occupancy. Budget-minded as always, she reduced the rent by having her good friend Ruth Butcher move in with her. Mrs. Butcher was also waiting out the war. Her husband Harry, newly commissioned a Navy lieutenant-commander, was naval aide to General Eisenhower. She was glad to lease her big home and share kitchenette housekeeping in a residential hotel. Mrs. Eisenhower, forced to put all her belongings in storage, groaned over one more upset—plus having to pay rent for duplicate household effects.

Oppressed by the usual torrid summer climate of Washington, the two women preferred entertaining in their air-conditioned apartment to facing the outside humidity—foursome parties usually, for bridge or mah jongg—eight people at the most. The guests were other war-separated wives.

Never an early sleeper, Mrs. Eisenhower shortly found herself subject to night-long insomnia. Lonely, restless, bound up with apprehension, she began and ended her days with radio newscasts. None of the news was good, and the midnight roundup commentary always came over like a dirge. Perhaps if she had not listened she might have felt more conditioned for sleep. The few times she tried leaving the radio silent at bedtime, the greater was the flood of uneasiness. Far better to hear the worst than to wonder. What rest she got came between daylight and noon, unless a messenger arrived during the morning with one of her husband's letters. The penned pages—he wrote always in longhand—were about family matters, the weather and innocuous social items. There was nothing he could tell about his action-filled life to hearten her concerning the war. Where he went; what he saw; his conferences—all these were locked in security. No censor was ever more strict than the General. As the months turned into years, Mrs. Eisenhower learned more about her husband through regular news channels than in his letters. Once he wrote cryptically that he had received the new pictures of herself and Johnnie and was enjoying them "down here." Eventually, when news censorship was lifted, she discovered that "down here" had been his underground headquarters at Malta.

Mrs. Eisenhower began to slip downhill physically. She had next to no interest in food; she combined her breakfast with lunch, and ate half-hearted dinners. Her weight dropped to 112 pounds, but she kept going on nervous energy. She says that, for the first eighteen months of her solitude, she "lived after sorts, read mystery thrillers through the nights—and waited." During the first winter she was out of Washington for several months, visiting in San Antonio with her sister "Mike" and her mother and father. Mrs. Moore and her four children had been asked to move from their Terrell Street house. The owners, Army people, had to reoccupy the premises.

There were no houses for rent. "Mike's" husband was overseas and "Mike" shared Mamie's reluctance to move to Denver. Papa Doud, a generous facer of facts, sized up the San Antonio real estate market, found that several houses were offered for sale, and promptly bought a big place on Grandview Street, footing the bill for the furnishings as well. "Mike" and the children had to have a house—so he bought one. It was as simple as that. He and his wife moved into one of the spare bedrooms; Mamie had another. The family under one roof again. It was good, very good. Mamie was less despondent, having her namesake niece to bathe, cuddle and amuse, even though those months were the critical time of the North African invasion when General Eisenhower was first proving his genius for planning and command.

For part of the summer, Mr. and Mrs. Doud, who had returned to Washington with Mrs. Eisenhower, lived with her at the Wardman Park Hotel. A shift in living arrangements was made. Mrs. Butcher took an apartment across the hall and Mamie changed to a two-bedroom unit. Urged by her mother, who was not going to let her daughter wreck her health by too much introspection, Mamie bought a baby grand piano. It was her first truly "own" piano, and she has loved and treasured it ever since. Wartime had caused a shortage of pianos, but Mamie sat doggedly through an auction sale and bid in the fine mahogany instrument for $700. She had a bargain and a blessing.

Autumn's advent found her enrolled as a volunteer in the big canteen for servicemen located on The Mall near the Washington Monument. She had regular hours of duty there and enjoyed her work as waitress. Few people knew that she was the wife of the general whose every move was front page news. Not even Army wives working on shift with her had the faintest idea of her identity, unless they were personal friends. On the job to see that the boys in uniform were served promptly and made to feel at home, she proved an effective as well as a witty waitress.

One of her associates tells an amusing anecdote. An out-of-town friend of Mrs. Eisenhower who had a little time to kill while waiting for a train connection sought her out in the canteen. They had just greeted each other when the canteen supervisor tapped Mrs. Eisenhower on the shoulder and remarked freezingly that rules forbade waitresses having visitors. Mrs. Eisenhower attempted to explain, but was curtly ordered back to duty. And she went, winking broadly. The witness to this episode has often wondered if the supervisor, an officer's wife, ever learned that she had bawled out Mrs. Eisenhower.

Christmas. North Africa was securely in the hands of the Allies. Paratroop invasion of Sicily had been a sucessful prelude to the landings on the Italian mainland that forced Italy's surrender. President Roosevelt and Prime Minister Churchill, who had met in January at Casablanca in French Morocco, met again at Teheran early in December together with Premier Stalin. On the President's return an announcement came from the White House: General Dwight D. Eisenhower was appointed Supreme Commander of Allied Expeditionary Forces in Europe.

Mrs. Eisenhower was spending Christmas at West Point with her son. Supreme Command! What an honor and what a responsibility! But they were confident that neither the honor nor the responsibility would prove too great for their husband and father. His generalship would make history. They were sure of it. John spoke with classroom knowledge of military problems—of Germany, of France, the Rhine; his mother, with faraway eyes, could only express her concern for her husband's health under such pyramiding military obligations. All they could do was bless him; tell him so in letters—and wait.

Mid-week of the holiday season. The streets in Washington were sleety; icy trees arched the avenues; the Potomac was chunked with ice. Mrs. Eisenhower had returned, busy with letters when she wasn't working at the canteen. Then came some unbelievable news, from General Marshall, no less—her husband and the New Year would be arriving about the same time. Ike in Washington! Yes, but no one must know; press speculation on his visit could not be risked. No one must know? Not even Johnnie? No one, not even Johnnie.

Those were days to sit out, the days of the interim; days and endless nights. On New Year's Day, she heard that the General was en route from French Morocco. Commander Butcher was coming too! That set Ruth in a frenzy. Neither woman could sit still. They rattled away; they smoothed, dusted, rearranged flowers. Everything must be perfect. Security officers strolled in the corridor that night, a grim touch of realistic caution that kept Mamie flashing between alternate pride and worry. The hands of the clock crept on. Midnight. Half-past one, and a dropped handkerchief would have startled both women. Clang! That was the rear service elevator! Mamie pulled open the hall door. A big man, his head turtled into his overcoat collar and his cap peak halfway down his nose, almost bowled her over. The General was home!

The first embrace he gave his wife was awkward. A black nose poked out at her from the "V" of his coat, a pair of beady eyes blinked inquisitively and a shrill "ywhipe" came from a small pink mouth. The stowaway was a small Scottie pup. More excitement in the doorway then, as Harry Butcher barged in with another small Scottie. The room became noisy as a kennel at feeding-time. Once Sergeant Michael McKeogh had his arms free of baggage, he bedded the puppies in a bathroom. It was not to be a permanent arrangement, Ike explained; the Scotties, offspring of his dog Telek, were to be given away. One was for Milton Eisenhower's children; the other for the Butchers' daughter, Beverly.

Mrs. Eisenhower drank in her husband's presence. He was more serious, that was to be expected; his voice a shade more decisive, but he laughed the same old laugh, made the familiar expansive gestures. He had the same old appetite too; there he was, rooting around the kitchenette, biting into an onion as if it was an apple. Marrakech the day before—in a top-level policy conference with Prime Minister Churchill in the garden of the fabulous Mamounia Hotel; on the wing out of French Morocco long before dawn; and now absorbed totally in watching the coffee perk. It was as if he had never been away.

The hide-and-seek tactics forced on the General, during the top, top secret twelve days he was home, made his wife think she was the heroine of a mystery thriller. Up and down the freight elevator; in and out of limousines with drawn curtains; a private railroad car, accessible only on deserted sidings. Hush, hush, hush! Mrs. Eisenhower, while not in disguise, felt that someone should have given both the General and herself masks. It would have seemed appropriate. They used the private car to visit West Point, and it also carried them down to White Sulphur Springs for several days at General Marshall's Virginia home. He wasn't there, but he had insisted they use it for "a quiet time alone."

Mrs. Eisenhower gladly boarded the car for the West Point and Virginia trips, but she balked at becoming a passenger in a transport plane that flew her husband to Kansas for a short visit with his mother and brothers. She had never been off the ground; she devoutly hoped she never would be. That was that. Word that her mother and father were going to be at Milton's house in Manhattan, a short highway drive from the Army's air base at Fort Riley, in no way affected her decision. Airplanes were, well—airplanes. She was staying out of them. One day she had to "eat her words" but that was in the future.

The West Point trip was an epic of deception—for John. On order, he reported to the office of the Superintendent of the Academy, Major General Francis B. Wilby, an old friend of his father. "Local people" wanted six cadets for dinner, said General Wilby, never blinking an eye. He asked John to name the rest of the group. Cadet Eisenhower, already upset over the Superintendent's summons—you didn't get hauled on the carpet unless the news was really bad—was too blanked out; so the guest selection was left to the General. Actually General Wilby was sending a group to cover John's absence, which would otherwise have been noticed.

At the appointed hour, John and his friends presented themselves for the evening assignment. They were driven down the sheer palisades of the Hudson to the small railroad station and directed to follow a guard up the tracks to a Pullman car. Strange location for a dinner, the cadets snorted. Strange indeed. John climbed aboard first, and there was his father! *Goodness*, says Mamie, what an evening.

On the thirteenth of January, General Eisenhower flew back to England and his colossal task of shaping victory. Mrs. Eisenhower set off immediately for San Antonio and another stretch of living at her sister's house. Separation from her husband now seemed less distressing: she had gained new strength and awareness of her importance as a wife by talking through their mutual problems during the days she and the General were together. She had known that a towering task had been placed in his hands, but from face-to-face discussions, sometimes very fragmentary, there had dawned a widening realization of how he counted on her strong faith in his talents. She must be firm in his heart of hearts, and firm she became.

Returning to Washington in the spring, Mrs. Eisenhower had then to override her fears for her son's safety. John was graduating from West Point in June. A regimental assignment was bound to follow, undoubtedly with combat troops. John wanted it that way. He had picked the infantry, his father's branch of the service, remarking repeatedly on his "luck" in being a member of the Academy class that would graduate in three instead of four years of intensified training, so that the Army could absorb a greater pool of young officers.

Graduation was set for June 6. The day before, Mrs. Eisenhower, her mother and father, and Ruth Butcher went by train to Jersey City where they were met by General Wilby's car and driven to West Point. They registered at the Thayer Hotel, dined quietly upstairs and retired early. Ruth and Mamie shared a room. They plugged in a portable radio and, true to custom, listened to the midnight newscast. It mentioned "the static situation in Europe," and then reported the bitter island fighting in the Pacific. Bad news; marking-time news—the way it had been for months. No use listening any longer. They turned out the lights. Curiously enough, Mrs. Eisenhower went right to sleep.

Next morning at seven o'clock, the phone's shrilling brought two wobbly heads unceremoniously up off twin-bed pillows. The phone! It was D-Day, the start of the Normandy beach landings. The wife of the general who was directing the Allied offensive was learning of it from a reporter. Fully awake, fully alert, but dazed by the news, Mamie Eisenhower could only repeat "This is the first I've heard—I can't express an opinion—you know more than I do." She put up the phone and looked across at her friend. "I'd better go tell Papa and Mama," she said evenly, and reached for her dressing gown.

Breakfast was forgotten; dressing postponed until the last minute, so that no word coming out of the radio would be lost. The

assaults on Utah and Omaha Beaches were described in screaming commentaries against the actual background of roaring Navy
guns, small-arms fire and enemy artillery. General Marshall,
General Eisenhower, General Sir Bernard L. Montgomery, Prime
Minister Churchill, Admiral Ernest J. King, General Henry H.
Arnold—their names resounded against the pounding confusion
of the Battle of the Normandy Beachhead. Conflict was then
many hours old, but still indecisive. Mrs. Eisenhower learned
afterward that if she had not been so quick to snap off the radio
after the midnight report, she would have heard the first stark
announcement of the invasion that began at six A.M. European
time. Always philosophical, she says it was all for the best; at
least she slept well before what was to be one of the most difficult days of her life.

She was in double focus during the graduation ceremonies,
staring hard at her son so as to retain a "carbon-clear memory of
his every action" and mentally picturing his father in the crash
and clamor of conflict. It was only by the "narrowest of margins"
that she checked her tears and remained rigidly observant during
the ritualistic ceremony. She says it was as if "the drums of my
mind tattooed 'Ike in battle, Johnnie going toward battle.'

"For Ike's sake, I forced myself to keep my eyes and senses
clear. I knew one day he would ask for every detail," says Mrs.
Eisenhower. "Johnnie's graduation was to have been one of the
great personal moments of his life. Writing him about it would
help, but later he would expect to hear me describe everything,
so I had to keep alert."

After each uniformed member of the class had stepped forward and received a diploma, and the chaplain had spoken
solemn benediction, the crowded gymnasium dissolved into eddies of humanity. Mrs. Eisenhower found her son and they went
away to talk quietly. Up to then, she had every expectation that
he would spend his graduation leave with her; but he explained
that he had received sealed orders and would be leaving by night-
fall for an undisclosed destination. Sealed orders in wartime

meant combat, of that she was sure, but she appeared undisturbed.

Mrs. Doud remembers that time of parting very well. "Mamie kept the chuckle in her voice and the happy gleam in her eye; she even joshed Johnnie and got him to smile. He left us in a fine frame of mind, which was just what Mamie wanted."

After many anxious days, and then through a news dispatch, Mrs. Eisenhower learned that her son's sealed orders had been authorization from General Marshall to spend graduation leave at General Eisenhower's side in the battle area. John Eisenhower returned to the United States on July 1, to begin advanced infantry training. He had failed to convince his father that he should remain in France for a combat infantry assignment.

Johnnie's report on his father's well-being raised Mamie's spirits, but she continued to worry. Her husband, in spite of being Supreme Commander, might try to overreach his luck in some sortie to forward positions. Her anxiety was justified. Early in September, radio commentators speculating over the General's absence for several days from headquarters, guessed openly that he was suffering either a breakdown from overwork, or was injured. The latter proved to be true; a forced landing of the General's small observation plane on the beach not far from headquarters had left him with a badly wrenched knee. After this incident, Mrs. Eisenhower lived all winter and spring in hour-by-hour fear as the fierce Allied drive into Germany brought war's end closer.

Chapter 11

The sleepless night had ended. Mamie Eisenhower was gazing intently at the dawn sky, spreading rose tints over the placid coastal waters of Florida. Leaning against a window-frame in a bedroom at the Hollywood Beach Hotel, the wife of the Supreme Commander of Allied Forces in Europe was consciously recording in memory the quiet and peaceful loveliness of the new morning. The date was May 8, 1945. V-E Day was dawning, and with it new hope for peace and freedom among the shattered nations. War had ceased in Europe during the night, with the unconditional surrender of the German Army to the Allies.

General Eisenhower's wife was waiting to hear his voice. For three years her waking hours had been concentrated on news broadcasts and newspapers, in an effort to follow every move of the bitter struggle. From the June morning when her husband first left for overseas command, Mamie Eisenhower had lived a withdrawn existence. She had worried for the safety of her husband and her infantry officer son, and she had been crushed by the casualty lists. To the fullest degree she shared her husband's sense of responsibility, and the loss and maiming of other women's husbands and sons had seemed to her almost personal tragedy. Even now, with V-E Day at hand, she could not forget that brave men were bleeding and dying in the continuing war against Japan.

On the evening before, turning on her portable radio for the regular six o'clock newscast, she had heard the first flash of Germany's unconditional surrender, followed by SHAEF's official communiqué announcing the signing of surrender documents at 2:41 A.M. May 7, in a schoolhouse adjacent to General Eisenhower's headquarters in Rheims, France. The communiqué stated that the German Army immediately began carrying out the cease-fire provisions of the pact, and that now, at 11 P.M. European time, fighting had stopped on all fronts and Allied troops were preparing to occupy Berlin. In conclusion it was indicated that there would be no further official statements on the surrender until the following morning, when Allied leaders, including General Eisenhower, would speak to the world. The time of these broadcasts would be announced later, but the assumption was that they would begin at 10:00 A.M. European time, which would be five o'clock in the eastern time zone of the United States.

Not until long after midnight, when quiet settled over the hotel and a close woman friend who shared the apartment had fallen asleep from sheer exhaustion, had Mamie been able to listen to the broadcasts without interruption. The dinner-time surrender statement had been broken into when friends from nearby Fort Lauderdale and news and radio reporters started besieging her by telephone. Eventually Mrs. Eisenhower had been obliged to ask the hotel switchboard operator to black out all incoming calls except long-distance—she wanted the line kept free for family conversations and talks with Washington intimates. Next came constant rapping on the living-room door. Impressed as an impromptu secretary, her apartment companion turned away would-be callers, many of whom were total strangers; only bellboys delivering telegrams and phone messages and waiters bearing food were admitted. Shut into her bedroom, Mrs. Eisenhower could hear the rumble of many voices in the hall, as a growing crowd tried to gain admittance to the apartment. The fact that the clamor was high-spirited—something in the nature of a triple-strength New Year's Eve outburst—did not lessen the strain on her nerves. The noise ended abruptly when the hotel management sent for police, who cleared the corridors and stationed a cordon in the lobby to turn back curiosity-seekers.

This was Mrs. Eisenhower's first experience with spontaneous public acclaim. It startled and frightened her. All through the war, as her husband's fame mounted, she had kept herself out of the public eye. Now more than ever, she was determined to remain in seclusion. She held to this resolution until 1952, when she made her first platform appearance with General Eisenhower at Convention Hall in Chicago, a few hours after he had won the Republican nomination for President of the United States. Her adjustment to a new situation was natural and genuine. From that evening on, throughout the campaign and now in the White House, she has revealed herself as a poised and friendly person with an endearing genius for doing and saying unpremeditated things.

All night the airwaves crackled with overseas broadcasts by radio correspondents who had witnessed the formalities of surrender, including Field Marshal Jodl's departure from the schoolhouse to General Eisenhower's office for a face-to-face interrogation by the Allies' Supreme Commander. Mrs. Eisenhower hung on every word, trying to fashion a mental picture of the dramatic events surrounding her husband in the high hour of victory.

The V-E Day overseas broadcasts started coming in at five o'clock, only a few minutes after Mrs. Eisenhower had turned from the beauty of the sunrise.

Clear, controlled, with deep overtones of disciplined emotion, General Eisenhower delivered his "Victory Order of the Day." He thanked Allied military forces and the people at home for their unfailing support of the common cause of liberty, and paid reverent tribute to "each honored grave."

"Cry?" says Mrs. Eisenhower. "Of course I cried. I think most people did when they heard the sad awareness in Ike's voice; his words brought home victory's dreadful cost in human lives, and in bombed and blasted home-lands."

Mamie Eisenhower had gone to Florida in the final month of the war, hoping that a complete rest would rebuild her strength and increase her weight. The wartime pitch of Washington tension had aggravated her lack of appetite and her inability to sleep. Her weight had dropped dangerously to 102 pounds—34 pounds below the present reading of her scales—and her emaciated state hampered recovery from a stubborn spring cold.

V-E Day brought the beginning of better health, with an upturn of her spirits that started long before breakfast when her husband's cable arrived. That was Ike all over, putting her first on the busiest day of his life. She hoped that her message, sent the night before, was in his hands; she hoped too that they would soon be talking by transatlantic telephone. She dared not speculate when he would be coming home. Not for months—not with the big work-load of the occupation ahead of him.

The morning hours sped by like minutes; there were more wires, more phone messages sent up from the switchboard, more long-distance calls. She was unwilling to miss a single word of the broadcasts. All the great leaders of the free world were speaking, and none omitted paying tribute to General Eisenhower. With the smile of devotion that always lights her eyes when she speaks of her husband, Mrs. Eisenhower says, "Imagine how I felt, hearing presidents, prime ministers, kings, and generals praising Ike to the whole wide world. I was so happy I could hardly breathe."

One broadcast produced astonishment. An announcer began: "Here is Mrs. Dwight D. Eisenhower's V-E Day expression of gratitude for the end of fighting in Europe." He then read "her" victory statement, concluding with a sign-off from the government's Office of War Information. So that was what the OWI writer was up to—asking last night on the long-distance phone for permission to prepare a victory statement! Mrs. Eisenhower didn't know whether to be flattered or annoyed; she had rigorously avoided radio interviews, and she would have preferred writing her own statement, but the thing was over and done.

The broadcast produced an avalanche of responses. For days the stacks of letters, post-cards, wires and phone messages grew, to alarming proportions. If she could have afforded it, Mamie would have used secretarial help; instead she methodically attacked the correspondence, answering every last communication in longhand. Never had she dreamed that her firm principle, "A letter received is a letter answered," would be put to such a test. Yet she quickly found her penmanship a blessing in disguise. The colossal task quieted her nerves, restored her appetite, and sent her to bed for sound sleep.

The vigilance of the hotel management and the police in preserving Mrs. Eisenhower's privacy was not without its humorous surprises, at least so far as Colonel and Mrs. Sam White were concerned. Arriving from vacation leave on an off-shore Florida island on V-E Day, the Whites followed through on a prior agreement to let Mamie know when they reached Hollywood Beach. Mrs. White telephoned from a midtown hotel. Upon being told that Mrs. Eisenhower was not accepting calls, she put up an argument. It got her exactly nowhere; she had to leave her name, like everybody else.

Debating whether to forget the whole thing and head on north, or drive out to Mamie's hotel and send up cards, the Whites dallied over lunch. They were eating dessert when a bellboy approached and announced in awed tones that Mrs. Eisenhower was on the phone. "Bootsie" jumped up and raced toward the lobby. A deferential clerk—she swears he bowed himself double handing her the counter phone—stood transfixed while she talked. "Sure, sure," she told Mamie. "Sam will find the way." What was that? Get a cop? Honest? Were birth certificates and passports also required? Laughing, the Colonel's wife hung up, summoned her dignity, and asked the clerk how to go about locating a motorcycle policeman—Mrs. Eisenhower had said that an officer would have to vouch for their identity, otherwise the Colonel would not be able to drive into the hotel grounds. The clerk promised to have a representative of the law on hand by the time she finished lunch.

Hollywood Beach believed in doing things right. Two motorcycle officers—and the chief of police, accompanied by a detective —drove up with a flourish. Mrs. White rode with the chief; her husband trailed close behind in their trusty Ford. With the sirens wide open on the motorcycles, they had the right-of-way and streaked toward the beach as if to a fire. "Nothing too good for friends of General and Mrs. Eisenhower," declared the chief. "Greatest man alive. His wife's a fine lady." Why, only that morning, all excited over V-E Day and everything, she had made him stop and have coffee when he was making a routine check to be sure she wasn't being bothered by nosey outsiders. "A famous woman—putting herself out like—"

"A famous woman . . ." Mrs. White took a quick breath. She wondered if she and Sam were intruding—Mamie probably wanted to be by herself—well, they'd make it a quick visit. But Mrs. Eisenhower kept them with her for hours. She calls Sam and "Bootsie" White two of her "very, very special people." Hadn't they been together Pearl Harbor Sunday at Fort Sam Houston; hadn't "Bootsie" dug in and helped her pack after Ike had gone to Washington? And long ago before that, hadn't Sam and "Bootsie" called every day when she was hospitalized in the Philippines, bringing silly presents, making her laugh? On V-E Day their gay companionship was just what she needed.

In one of his letters to his wife soon after V-E Day, General Eisenhower revealed a secret plan which he hoped to launch early in June. While it concerned the military, the idea could not be classified as a military secret. It would be a private, sentimental pilgrimage for the General and twenty of his West Point classmates to the Academy, to celebrate the thirtieth anniversary of their graduation. As he visualized the journey, it must be operation "hush hush," involving only three days' absence from European duty. The other officers, all of whom were in the European theatre, would assemble at his headquarters for the overnight transatlantic flight; they would have a day and a night at West Point for the graduation exercises; then back to Europe. All wives were to be secretly alerted to meet at West Point. The Superintendent of the Academy would also have advance notice, but until the group was in flight back to Germany, the fewer people who knew about the project the better. The reunion would be no fun if newspapers and radio networks got wind of it and turned loose a battery of photographers and interviewers.

The news caused Mrs. Eisenhower double delight. She was thrilled by the prospect of seeing her husband for even so short a time, and she was relieved at his boyish eagerness to contrive the reunion as a secret mission for himself and war-weary classmates. Until now she had been worried over the effect of post-surrender perplexities on his health. Here was proof that he was in top form.

The reunion idea had to be shelved abruptly, however, on word from Washington that the War Department expected General Eisenhower to head a large group of combat officers and enlisted men who would be official guests at home-front victory celebrations. If he went to West Point at all, it would be long after graduation day. He arrived in the capital in mid-June, and was greeted with military honors due his five-star rank. Standing with General Marshall in front of other high-ranking officers waiting to pay their respects to the Supreme Commander of Allied Forces in Europe, Mrs. Eisenhower shifted uneasily as the "Sunflower," the General's four-motored transport, set down on an outer runway and reduced its landing speed to a standstill. She still feared and distrusted all airplanes, especially this one, for her son John was aboard with his father.

The big plane swung around and taxied to the reception enclosure. General Eisenhower was first out the door. A second's pause, and he stepped briskly to the ramp and started past the honor guard, standing stiffly at attention. A swift, wordless embrace for his wife; a salute and handclasp exchanged with General Marshall; a few happy phrases; eye-to-eye laughter. Behind the barriers, the packed-in spectators screamed and yelled; the band played, but the reception committee stood like ramrods. Then General Eisenhower started down the line, saluting, shaking hands, speaking nicknames and grinning.

With her gaze on the men filing out of the plane, Mrs. Eisenhower saw the lean length of her son ducking carefully out the low door. She wanted to call out, but the band and the shouting crowd made a solid wall of sound. Never mind, he saw her! It was only a few short months since they had said good-bye—but how good to feel his quick hug, to catch a suppressed twinkle in his eyes. Then, correctly conscious of his junior rank, John sought anonymity with a group of young officers.

The formalities of arrival concluded, a tidal wave of photographers, reporters, and radio men swirled from behind guards. Microphones were set up; cameramen asked for arrival pictures. Would the General start down the landing stairs again, would he shake hands with General Marshall?

To avoid being photographed and interviewed, Mrs. Eisenhower beckoned to her son and they melted from sight. She had no wish to intrude on the military aspect of the homecoming, and she mistrusted her contacts with reporters. Early in the war, horrified to read what seemed a distortion of straightforward answers she had given a reporter, she vowed to stay out of print and off the airwaves. Except for a few magazine articles, she avoided public statements of every sort until she held her first press conference during the Republican Convention in Chicago. After that there were cordial associations with reporters, and today she is on very friendly terms with the news men and women who cover the Executive Mansion.

The air terminal reception was a foretaste of the uproar and excitement ahead. General Eisenhower spent most of his waking hours waving, smiling, shaking hands, and keeping up with the crowded timetable of his two weeks of official engagements. A man of lesser stamina and enthusiasm could not have stood the pace; but he throve on it. He called first at the White House for an exchange of courtesies with President Truman, then addressed a joint session of Congress in the Capitol. Next he rode in a big military parade. Schools were closed; government offices and mercantile firms shut up during parade hours; spectators came to Washington from as far as Philadelphia and Richmond. The home front was out, all right; a sea of people jammed every inch of foot-space along the route of march. "General Ike" they screamed, happy to see him standing tall and straight in the back of a jeep. The jeep was a big surprise; the crowd had expected to cheer a General mantled with the austerity of rank, seated in an over-sized open car. Here was a friendly, informal man who grinned and waved and called out "Thanks!"

New York worked itself up to near madness on June 19th, when General Eisenhower got the traditional ticker-tape snowstorm on lower Broadway and stopped off at the City Hall before heading up Fifth Avenue. Cheering millions yelled "Ike!" as if he were one of the boys up the block, just returned from war. That was just how he wanted people to feel. Never was a man more happy or humble. He knew—how well he knew!—that he was but a symbol—the channel through which the public expressed its gratitude to the millions of Allied fighting men whose strength and courage had won the battle on land and sea and in the air. Mrs. Eisenhower has said that under the tremendous ovations the General was "proud, awed, and completely selfless."

The General could see but little of his family. Mrs. Eisenhower stayed completely in the background, leaving her apartment in the Wardman Park Hotel only for a few evening functions where service guests predominated. The parties were fun; she was seeing old friends, enjoying social life with her husband for the first time since Pearl Harbor Sunday. It seemed like a dream.

She might have gone along for a side-line seat at the New York celebration if the General had not been scheduled to fly up and back in the "Sunflower." He tried to persuade her to take the big step and fly with him; her mother and father favored the idea; John added his plea. The more they talked, the more determined she was to stay on firm ground. Mrs. Doud, who had become converted to flying during the war, when she got into the habit of boarding commercial transports for Denver, San Antonio and Washington, did not press the argument about the New York trip.

On another morning, however, when the General and John were eating an early pre-flight breakfast—the day's schedule called for a trip at long last to West Point for a wreath-laying ceremony—Mrs. Doud excused herself from the table and disappeared into her daughter's bedroom. She found Mamie in a state of indecision over what to wear for the day. Half teasingly, Mrs. Doud suggested "a flying outfit." The black look she received in response quickly turned to "wiggly nose and tongue-tip between teeth"—Mamie's old childhood trick when she was willing to yield a little ground. Keeping to banter, Mamie's mother said that her refusal to look over the housekeeping arrangements in the "Sunflower" showed lack of wifely concern for the General's "Air Home." How did she know the window curtains weren't fading, the carpet showing signs of wear, and the stove in need of scouring? There might even be broken seat-springs, something Mamie wouldn't tolerate an instant in her own home. To be sure, the plane's crew was providing all the comforts of home, but Mamie ought to put her eagle eye to work—that didn't involve flying to West Point—and if nothing else, she ought to try out the seats.

Mrs. Eisenhower went on dressing in silence, though she was thinking hard. Her mother's teasing was taking effect, and she was beginning to feel herself a stubborn hold-out. The "Sunflower" was of course a paragon of neatness and comfort—imagine a General's personal plane being anything else!—but her refusal even to go aboard might be hurting her husband's feelings. As she clasped her pearls, she said, "I'll go have a look, but I'm *not* flying," and Mrs. Doud gave her daughter a squeeze. On their way out of the room, Mrs. Doud paused and picked up Mamie's small over-night case, which was always packed and ready. With a wink she said, "This had better go along—you changed your mind once this morning." Mrs. Eisenhower grabbed the bag, but did not put it back on the luggage rack. With a touch of complacency, she carried the bag into the living room and handed it to the General's aide.

The "Sunflower" was as compact as a Pullman car. In the rear section, partitions on each side of the center aisle provided seclusion for work-tables and typewriter-desks; forward, pairs of regulation adjustable airliner seats extended to the bulkhead of the crew compartment. Berths that let down at night were above the work-area windows. The pantry, just forward of the tail section, contained a small refrigerator and a gleaming electric galley for heating food. Mrs. Eisenhower took in every detail, beginning with the pantry and on up to the bunks in the crew compartment. The array of dashboard dials, floor and overhead levers, knobs and switches hemming in the pilot and co-pilot's chairs looked hopelessly complex, and she backed away. No use wasting the pilot's time in futile explanations—she hadn't the foggiest idea of any machine more complicated than an eggbeater.

The passenger seats looked inviting, and she dropped into one —briefly, mind you, just to get the "feel." An unfathomable urge caused her to settle back. The General smiled down at her, remarking that it was take-off time. When she made no attempt to rise, he said, in an "easy-does-it" voice, "Shall I tell them to close the doors?" Her answer was a jerky nod, and her husband's thumb and first finger gave the "okay" sign. As he moved aft, Johnnie leaned down and silently buckled his mother's safety belt, then took a seat across the aisle. The General returned and sat beside his wife. Quietly, as the "Sunflower" taxied down the strip, he explained pre-flight operations. In the vibration and thunder of the final run-up of the motors, Mrs. Eisenhower, like every first-flight passenger, stiffened in momentary panic. She strained against her belt, trying to rise, but was calmed by the reassuring pressure of her husband's hand on her arm. Louder roared the motors; there was a slight forward heave, the asphalt runway became a grey blur outside the window. In seconds, the grey turned to blue sky and puff-ball clouds, with green tree-tops below and a spread of toy-sized houses. Mrs. Eisenhower snuggled in her seat and began telling herself that *this* was flying, that *she* was flying; the bogie that had plagued all her adult years was finally routed. Against the heavy drone of the climbing motors, the clink of seat belts being unfastened was a reassuring sound. Smiling, she accepted a newspaper from a sergeant.

The flight was smooth, the set-down at West Point perfect, but in the landing Mrs. Eisenhower's earlier confidence ebbed. The best she could muster was a rueful smile as she rose to leave the plane. Next day she took the train back to Washington and informed her mother that no one was going to argue her into another flight. Once, thank you, would do for a lifetime. Undiluted nonsense, said Mrs. Doud. This was the air age, hadn't Mamie heard? Soon passengers would be regular air commuters, riding over oceans, mountains and jungles with no more reluctance than if they were in a baby buggy or on an automobile outing. She begged her daughter to keep an open mind; sure as fate the day was coming when she and Mamie would have no hesitancy spanning even the Atlantic by plane.

Six years later, fate fulfilled this prophecy; mother and daughter flew home from France in sorrowful companionship when Mr. Doud died unexpectedly in Denver.

On his return to Europe, General Eisenhower was due for another round of turbulent victory celebrations in Allied capitals. Before starting out from Berlin he broadcast a message of thanks and good-bye to Allied troops and officers who had served with him during the years he was Supreme Commander of SHAEF. After July 14, when SHAEF was to go out of existence, he would command only American forces in Europe. As an official guest, visiting London, Paris, Brussels, The Hague, and Prague, he was thunderously welcomed by great crowds; monarchs and heads of state conferred high decorations and praised his achievement. It was clear that General Eisenhower stood forth as the world's first citizen. Even more amazed than he had been during America's acclaim he went back to Berlin still wrapped in wonderment, still without any personal sense of exaltation, and plunged at once into the details of providing suitable accommodation for the impending "Big Three" conference at Potsdam. President Truman, Prime Minister Churchill and Premier Stalin were to come together in the Berlin suburb on July 17 and work out joint agreements for post-war cooperation in the occupied areas of Europe. General Eisenhower's military status barred him from taking part in these negotiations conducted at diplomatic level, but he sat in private consultation with the President, Secretary of State James F. Byrnes, and Secretary of War Henry P. Stimson.

Mrs. Eisenhower kept abreast of these happenings via radio, newsreels, magazines, and newspapers, and she shared her husband's wonderment. Again, here were kings, queens, presidents, and prime ministers attesting their admiration of the man who had carried the final burden of the war's responsibility. And there he was, the same as always, smiling but serious; nothing ever could or ever would change her Ike. Never one to collect clippings systematically, she was delighted to discover her mother filling scrap-books. Before long, the bulging cartons of scissored stories and pictures became overwhelming and Mrs. Doud decided to give up trying to save every item and to concentrate instead on one big story and picture layout of each event.

On August 6, Mrs. Eisenhower, like everyone else in the world who could read or had access to a radio, learned the unbelievable. A single atomic bomb, dropped from a U.S. Air Force bomber, had killed and injured over 160,000 persons in the Japanese city of Hiroshima. Four days later, after a second atomic blast almost disintegrated Nagasaki, Japan accepted the ultimatum calling for unconditional surrender which had been issued July 26 by the "Big Three" conference in Potsdam.

After the Japanese surrender, Mrs. Eisenhower learned from her husband's letters that he had not known until the leaders at Potsdam had released the ultimatum, that a prior agreement had been reached at the conference table to resort to atomic warfare if Japan ignored the surrender demand. Secretary of War Stimson also informed him that cabled information reporting the success of the first test explosion of the top-secret bomb in New Mexico demonstrated the effectiveness of the weapon and removed it from the realm of scientific experiment. General Eisenhower's immediate reaction was to hope that Japan would accept the ultimatum, making it unnecessary for the United States to introduce such a fearful weapon of war. He foresaw that once atomic warfare began, and other nations learned the secrets of nuclear fission, civilization would be under threat of extinction. After the bombing of Hiroshima, it was made clear to his wife that General Eisenhower was wondering if this horrifying proof of the transcendent destructiveness of atomic weapons might not make all nations realize the futility of competitive force. It was his hope that an international body of scientists could be set up, to work together for the conversion of nuclear power to peaceful improvement of industry and agriculture. The long-range effect of such a program, he believed, would be an improvement of living and health standards throughout the world, and a lessening of fear, suspicion, animosity and aggression. He realized that this bold plan was already crystalizing in the minds of many people; he was sure that it would succeed if and when public opinion understood and endorsed the new underlying moral and spiritual precepts.

The General said that he could think of no more fruitful way to spend his years after retirement from military service than in helping to make people understand how atomic war had altered previous concepts of national security. Youth was his special concern; he wanted a part in sharpening the awareness of today's youth to the responsibilities of leadership and of the decisions facing them as adults in the atomic age.

Mrs. Eisenhower had long known that her husband would seek a constructive outlet for his energy and intelligence after he laid aside his uniform. They had talked for many years of buying a small country house when he left the service, and had agreed that it should be far enough from a city for peaceful living, but not so isolated that their friends could not come for week ends. Now she wondered if the dream house would be compatible with the General's plans for the future. She so wanted a home of her own! Never again to pack and unpack, to store and re-store the possessions she had started collecting twenty-nine years before as a bride at Fort Sam Houston. There wasn't much left from that first tiny apartment, just the red Khiva rug and a few pictures; but she lived for the day when these bridal treasures and everything else that had survived her many moves would be given permanent place in a permanent home. There was no use speculating now on where and how she would live; whatever Ike wanted was all right with her. Retirement was still a long way off; the General was in line to serve four years in Washington as Army Chief of Staff, beginning some time after the first of the year. When that happened they would move back to Fort Myer, probably into the very quarters they had occupied until he went overseas in 1942.

For the time being, the General was in Berlin, absorbed in a wide range of postwar problems, many of which stemmed from the division of Germany into four zones of separate Allied occupation. In an effort to achieve a coordinated and harmonious administration of the zones, an Allied Council had been set up. It was headed by commanders of the British, French and Russian Armies and by General Eisenhower, commander of American forces. The council began its life on July 10 in a fine spirit of cooperation. Each Allied commander had a large staff of assistants, including a political adviser. Marshal Gregori K. Zhukov, Russia's representative, was advised on political matters by Andrei Vishinsky, and there was nothing in the attitude of either man— or, for that matter, of the entire Russian advisory staff—to impair the cordial relations with all council members, including the Americans. Marshal Zhukov himself was friendliness personified, both in Berlin and when he became host during General Eisenhower's official visit to Russia.

This trip, made on the formal invitation of Premier Joseph Stalin, had been postponed from early June because of General Eisenhower's absence in the United States. Eventually Generalissimo Stalin had set a date which permitted his guest to be in Moscow on August 12 for the mammoth National Sports Parade. Mrs. Eisenhower knew, from conversations with her husband before he returned to Europe, that the Moscow invitation, carrying as it did the implication of Stalin's willingness to develop friendly contacts with the United States, was of the utmost importance. She knew also of the General's hope that this first visit to Russia would afford him deeper insight into the post-war convictions and aims of the Soviets.

When she learned, just before the Moscow take-off, that John was going along as temporary aide to his father, Mrs. Eisenhower braced herself for another "grit-and-bear" period of waiting out another long flight. To have the General airborne over the wide wastes of Poland and Russia was bad enough, but to have John in the same plane seemed an overweighting of fate's scales, even though John, like the rest of the small staff, considered himself one of the luckiest of men to be chosen for the important mission. The only other members of the group were General Lucius Clay, Brigadier-general T. J. Davis—both of them old and trusted friends of General Eisenhower—and Master sergeant Leonard Dry, who had been personal driver for the Supreme Commander of SHAEF all through the war.

The Moscow visit rated top headlines, even though it began on August 11, the day after a second atomic bomb was dropped from a U. S. Air Force plane. The target was Nagasaki, and so great was the devastation of the port city that Japan's Premier Suzuki lost no time in proposing his country's surrender, on the condition that Emperor Hirohito retain his throne. While the Western Allies weighed the terms, General Eisenhower arrived in Moscow and was shown every courtesy by Premier Stalin, and every event of the visit was chronicled in news and radio stories. From the smooth landing of the "Sunflower" under the capable handling of Air Force Major Larry Hansen, to a visit to the Kremlin Museum, attendance at a football game, a state banquet within the grey stone walls of the Kremlin, and a review of the National Sports Parade, all social aspects of General Eisenhower's sojourn were covered in detail. It was evident that foreign news correspondents, as well as Soviet newsmen, fully cognizant that the United States and Russia were emerging from World War Two as the world's strongest military powers, were working overtime to satisfy global interest in General Eisenhower's visit to the Soviet capital.

The political significance of the General's stay in Moscow and subsequent tour of Leningrad was well understood by Mrs. Eisenhower, who read and heard all press and radio dispatches. When she learned that General Eisenhower had stood for five hours with Premier Stalin and other Soviet dignitaries on a parapet of Lenin's tomb overlooking Red Square, in a start-to-finish review of the National Sports Parade, despite his unfailing smile in the news pictures of the event she was all wifely concern for him—the concern of one who describes herself as "a poor walker and a worse stander." In that year of 1945 she little realized that she herself would become so conditioned that she too would be able to stand and smile and really enjoy a five-hour parade—the endurance test which she met on the afternoon of the Inaugural.

Early in November of 1945, General Eisenhower was called back to Washington. The first meeting of the Council of Foreign Ministers in London had ended early in October with a sharp show of cleavage between the United States and Russia, thereby setting the military occupation problems in Europe on a course that led to the outbreak of the cold war early in 1946. Mrs. Eisenhower arranged to go to Boston to meet her husband, who was flying over to take part in a special Armistice Day program. She arrived when gale-driven sleet was knifing the city already shrouded with fog. Marrow-chilled, she waited for the overdue plane; then, on word that it was coming in on instruments at Squantum Naval Air Station, she drove to the installation panicked by the fear of the blind landing. Once the plane came out of the overcast and its wheels touched the runway, she roused herself to give her husband a bright welcome.

After Boston had staged a great celebration, the Eisenhowers left for Boone, Iowa, Mrs. Eisenhower's birthplace, for special homecoming festivities. Worn by the excitement of Boston's ovation in bitter winter weather, the General and his wife arrived in the Midwest suffering from colds. Overnight Mrs. Eisenhower was showing symptoms of dread pneumonia, but her husband was sufficiently improved to supervise her medical care. As quickly as possible, he had her stretcher-borne aboard a train for Washington, where she could receive convalescent care from Army doctors at the Army's Walter Reed Hospital.

It was weeks before she pulled back from a respiratory attack that threatened to be fatal. Through this desperate period, the General's troubled figure was a familiar sight in the hospital corridors as he went to and from her bedside, often with Mrs. Doud on his arm. His stalwart mother-in-law, who had helped her daughter over other physical crises, spoke always the right word of assurance to give Mamie new fighting courage and ease her husband's fears. When the black nip-and-tuck days ended, there were weeks of watchful care while Mrs. Eisenhower won back her vigor in the Wardman Park Hotel apartment. The rooms, so long her lonely home of anxious waiting, now rang with the hearty laughter of her husband and mother. Best of all, there was to be no more separation. The War Department had decided that the General would not return to Berlin for the brief period that would elapse before he took over the office of Army Chief of Staff in the Pentagon.

When Mrs. Eisenhower began examining green paint samples for redecorating her bedroom in the quarters they would soon reoccupy at Fort Myer, there was no longer any doubt about the completeness of her recovery. On moving day she had all her old vivacity as she counted off the familiar and beloved pieces of furniture—dust-coated from long storage—and watched the movers put them back exactly where they had stood nearly four years earlier. Same house, same furniture, same flagpole—Mrs. Eisenhower took a long look at the white staff. As a soldier's wife the flying colors spoke to her of the heartache and sacrifice of millions of men and women in the war years, and moved her to a renewal of her wifely resolve to help her husband meet his responsibility. She phrases her resolve very simply, with the little gasps in her speech that are characteristic of her when she is driving home a point:

"I knew Ike had a big peacetime job ahead that would require all his energy and concentration. The smoother things moved at home, the better he could do his job—so I worked fast and got our Fort Myer quarters in shape so he could really relax in his off hours."

Chapter 12

WASHINGTON, NEW YORK, PARIS

1946–1952

A man wearing a floppy straw hat, rumpled trousers, and an open-neck shirt sat leaning comfortably against a tree just below the kitchen entrance to General Eisenhower's quarters at Fort Myer, Virginia. He was shelling peas abstractedly, his keen blue eyes roaming up and down the neat rows of a vegetable patch in the rear of the yard. It was a Saturday afternoon in early summer, brightly humid with a mild rift of breeze; a perfect atmosphere for this lazy but purposeful undertaking. As the peas fell from the split pods to *plunk* into a pot that he gripped between his braced knees, the happy gardener appraised a row of knobby cabbages, reflecting that it would soon be time to hack off some of the crisp heads and take them to the basement for preparation in a secret brew.

It had been a long time—a very long time—since General Eisenhower had made his own special brand of sauerkraut, much less cooked a heap of the well-pickled leaves with spare ribs. Another week and the cabbages would be ready to harvest. He was about to whistle his satisfaction when Marie Hall, a neighbor, and wife of General Charles P. Hall, one of his long-time Army associates, hove in sight. Before he could rise, she dropped beside him and they discussed the progress of the cabbages, the succulence of pork done to a turn in sauerkraut, and why homegrown vegetables—pickled or otherwise—make a family dinner table enticing.

Mrs. Hall remembers that sunny summer scene affectionately. A lifelong Army wife—her husband passed away in 1953—she had lived on several posts with the Eisenhowers, as well as in Manila. As young wives, Mamie and she shared household and child-raising problems while their husbands performed the day-in and day-out routine of Army service. She had been left as Mamie was left, to wait out the war. Now the families were neighbors once more, visiting back and forth, playing bridge, sharing the letters of their grown-up children and recalling the fun and frustrations of the "old days."

It had been an intimate association, and Mrs. Hall took special satisfaction in contemplating General Eisenhower in the role of backyard gardener. "Only a great man like Ike could put his responsibilites aside and hunch against a tree, shell peas, and speculate on his cabbage crop," she says. She had eaten Eisenhower sauerkraut and spare ribs, and she felt anticipation rising as they regarded the cabbages. It was some time before the cabbages emerged as sauerkraut, but she recalls the dinner when it did come as being "super-Eisenhower."

Mamie Eisenhower has often said: "Ike cooks anything better than anybody—that's why I hate to work hard over a meal." His cooking is straightforward and business-like in all respects, except for his already-noted antipathy toward potholders. His insistence on using kitchen towels when handling hot pots, skillets, and roasting pans has resulted in many a seared towel to outrage his wife's thriftiness.

As a gardener, General Eisenhower is no amateur, either. The first pennies he earned as a small boy in Abilene, Kansas, came from selling vegetables and fruit which he and his brothers raised on the small acreage surrounding the simple frame dwelling of his parents. Money was scarce; even so, the Eisenhower boys were allowed to keep a small percentage from their sales of garden truck and fruit, and there was healthy rivalry among them to see who could raise and sell the most. Ida Eisenhower, their mother, had her boys help her during the canning and preserving season. She also taught them to cook—everything from bread, through soup and meat and vegetables, to pie and cake. The situation might have been different if there had been even one girl in the family. As it was, Ike Eisenhower and his five brothers never thought twice about pitching in and preparing a meal.

Until they moved back to Fort Myer after the war, the Eisenhowers had never been able to have a competent full-time staff in their home. During the stringent beginning years of their marriage, Mrs. Eisenhower stretched the budget and managed to keep a cleaning woman. In Panama, she had a native cook and houseboys who weren't too dependable. In Paris, there had been a cook of sorts; but during the next six years in Washington—on a major's pay—Mrs. Eisenhower did all her own work except the heavy cleaning. Later, after hotel-living in the Philippines, when Ike's advancement in rank made it financially possible to hire a cook a further difficulty appeared—all good cooks sought employment off Army posts.

When General Eisenhower became Chief of Staff, he retained Sergeant John Moaney as his orderly. Moaney's wife, Dolores, left her wartime job as cook with a Maryland family and took over the kitchen of the Fort Myer home. Then Rose Wood, only a few years over from Ireland, became upstairs maid, and General and Mrs. Eisenhower's household worries were at an end. The Moaneys and Rose Wood have rendered the most devoted and unselfish service from that day forward. Moaney is now the President's valet. Dolores helps care for the family living quarters on the second floor of the White House. Rose Wood, in addition to her regular maid's work, cares for Mrs. Eisenhower's clothes.

Home life at Fort Myer, during 1946 and into the following year, continued to be peaceful and relaxing for the Eisenhowers. The General had plenty of out-size headaches during the course of his busy days in the Pentagon, but he is gifted with the ability to snap the door of his mind on burdens that no amount of pondering and worry could solve away from his desk, and he enjoyed the easy-going pattern of secluded living on the post.

During the summer he induced his wife to accompany him by air to Great Britain and Europe while he made a quick inspection trip. She took the transocean flights very well, boasting to John, who joined them in England, that she was fast catching up on his air mileage. While in the British Isles, the Eisenhowers spent a week end at Balmoral Castle as guests of King George VI and Queen Elizabeth. Princess Elizabeth, now England's Queen, and her sister Princess Margaret were also at the ancient royal estate of Scotland. John Eisenhower, on short European leave, was with his parents.

The Eisenhowers arrived at tea-time and joined the royal family in a small drawing-room. It was a lived-in, comfortable room, brightly touched with color. The fine furniture showed evidence of long use. The Queen and her daughters wore country clothes. The King's jacket and vest were tweed but kilts and knee-length socks bespoke his Scottish sovereignty. Other guests came, dressed with similar informality but punctilious in their manner toward their royal hosts.

Queen Elizabeth and Princess Elizabeth poured at opposite ends of a long table. Conversation was sprightly, but there was a studied avoidance of all topics that could possibly be construed as "matters of state." As is almost inevitable when English and Americans gather in a big British house, the lack of central heating was discussed. The Queen observed to Mrs. Eisenhower that stone-walled Balmoral, on the wind-swept moors of Aberdeenshire, never completely lost a winter's chill; she thought that the General's wife might wish to borrow a hot-water bottle. On hearing that Mrs. Eisenhower always traveled with a pair of them, her Majesty laughingly admitted taking the same precaution.

After a formal dinner, the evening was spent at a ball unforgettable for its splendor and charm. The King's frail health forced him to withdraw early, accompanied by the Queen; and

Princess Elizabeth, in the absence of her husband the Duke of Edinburgh who was serving at sea with the British fleet, did not seem as gay as her sister and the other dancers who whirled through the happy night. Fires roared on massive hearths; tartan-clad pipers skirled; feet slipped like running water over the satiny dance floor.

Mrs. Eisenhower danced long and late—so late she found it difficult next morning to dress in time for church. The General and John walked with other guests down a winding road to the chapel of rugged stone. Not so his wife. She drove with the royal family, inwardly thankful that tradition required them to ride to worship.

The Eisenhowers were also received by Queen-Mother Mary in London, an afternoon that Mrs. Eisenhower treasures in memory. She considers Queen Mary the most remarkable woman she has ever met. Her Majesty's richly human qualities deeply touched her American guest, who had expected an austere figure of regal remoteness. "Queen Mary revealed herself almost instantly as a great, unselfish mother who valued family love above all else. She was queenly to look at, but her mother's heart made her ring true."

As she and the General were ushered into the sitting-room at Marlborough House, Mrs. Eisenhower saw the Queen-Mother erect and smiling in a chair. A robe lay across her knees and she had just put aside a newspaper. Unable to rise, Queen Mary extended a hand to the General and spoke in a full, rounded voice. As soon as she had clasped Mrs. Eisenhower's hand, the Queen-Mother looked searchingly behind her guests, and then expressed disappointment that their son had not come. She remembered John from the war years in London with his father; she had looked forward to seeing the family together. On learning that a sudden indisposition had kept John abed, she spoke with much motherly solicitude of the matter.

As the Queen-Mother spoke, her expressive hands moved slowly with infinite grace. They were unlined, flexible, petal-soft and pink; the hands of a young and mettlesome woman.

Here, more than in her high-held head, bright eyes and rapid speech, was the strongest evidence of her unquestionable spirit. It was hard to think of her as a woman well past eighty. Except for finding it tiring to stand or walk, she seemed to have triumphed over the infirmities of age.

An absorbing interest for General Eisenhower in his final months as Army Chief of Staff in 1947 was his heavy writing stint in the preparation of his war memoirs for book publication as "Crusade in Europe."

The checking and re-checking of documents and dates for accuracy was turned over to retired General Arthur Nevins and Lieutenant-colonel Kevin McCann and Lieutenant-colonel Robert L. Schultz, but General Eisenhower produced his own book paragraph by paragraph. When reflecting on personal experiences and opinions, he wrote in longhand; but he dictated excerpts from letters or written pronouncements. It was a long, tough grind that had to be done in the intervals of his heavy daily schedule. He did much of this work at night, but without any sense of undue pressure. Unhurried, precise, sure of the direction of his military saga, the General put his historic book together with an easy mind.

After a few vain attempts at dining in Washington hotels, the Eisenhowers were forced to confine their social life to their own home, or at most to visit friends. The public refused to let the General eat in peace. After one experience, when a crush of insistent autographer-seekers would not disperse until the hotel manager climbed on the bandstand and made a little speech about letting the General finish his dinner, Mrs. Eisenhower begged to go home. Except for invitation banquets, she does not recall having dined again in a hotel or restaurant with her famous husband. Private theatre-going also became taboo—and Mrs. Eisenhower loves musical shows.

In view of these restrictions on amusements, less than ten days before the General's inauguration Mamie remarked that living behind the iron fence at the White House would not be as sharp a change as most people would think.

"I have been forced to limit my going and coming for quite a few years," she said. "Actually, I expect to meet more people with much less sense of restriction in the White House. It will be our home while my husband is President and I like nothing better than entertaining at home."

When the Eisenhowers entertained at Fort Myer, the room set aside for the General's military decorations and gifts always dazzled the guests. These priceless historic possessions were displayed in glass-enclosed cases, as in a museum. Mrs. Eisenhower, proud of everything concerning her husband's achievements, never failed to feel a tightening in her throat when she gazed on the glittering and colorful objects. She told one old friend that the sight always filled her with a full sense of the General's imperishable place in history. Later, after General Eisenhower's old home in Abilene became a historic shrine, a considerable part of the display was transferred there; and many of the cases of decorations are now kept in the President's study in the White House. They will be removed with other personal belongings when he is no longer Chief Executive, and placed in the house on the Gettysburg property, which the Eisenhowers are reconditioning.

The first Christmas the Eisenhowers were at Fort Myer the house glowed with lights, and there was a tree; but with John absent on duty in Austria, and with Mrs. Moore—Mamie's sister "Mike"—living in Panama where Colonel Moore was on duty, it was impossible to stage a full-scale family reunion. Mr. and Mrs. Doud had exchanged the snows of Colorado for Washington's unpredictable winter weather and were house guests on the post; so the tradition of family singing of Christmas Eve carols to Mamie's piano accompaniment was resumed as gaily as possible by the incomplete circle.

Though they did not know it at the time, John was about to embark on a serious courtship. The young woman of his affections was Barbara Thompson, daughter of Colonel and Mrs. Percy Thompson. Her father was on duty in Austria. It may have been their mutual shyness that brought them together; at any rate they became involved quickly in serious romance. When writing home, John said nothing of his interest in Barbara, until one day his mother received a cable from him asking if she would order and ship a miniature of his West Point class ring. Bursting with curiosity, and quick to divine that Johnnie was still romantically "on the fence" or he would have let his parents know the girl's identity, Mrs. Eisenhower and the General decided to rush the order to Bailey, Banks & Biddle in Philadelphia. They figured that the quicker the ring reached Austria, the sooner John would make known his intentions. The transaction filled them both with sentiment. The same firm that had duplicated young Ike Eisenhower's class ring for his Mamie was now asked to fill John's order.

Weeks went by; and then Johnnie's voice on the transatlantic phone connection. He was on the road to matrimony all right. Gaily he put his fiancée on the line. Their happiness was obvious and contagious. After many repetitions of "fine," "wonderful," "we'll write," "see you soon," and "let's have pictures," the call terminated.

Barbara, who admits to having been scared out of ten years' growth when the call began, hung up the phone happy and confident. "They accepted me sight unseen; they were wonderful," she said.

The General and his wife were enchanted by the low-pitched voice of the girl who had agreed to marry their Johnnie. "Barby's voice won us instantly," declares Mrs. Eisenhower. "We knew she was fussed—so were we—but she had a downrightness in spite of being excited." Letters, pictures—and plans—followed. Johnnie's foreign service would be over in the spring, and they wanted to be married before his new assignment.

At first there was talk of a wedding abroad, but the young couple were persuaded to come home and have the ceremony at Fort Monroe, Virginia. Barbara Thompson bade her parents good-bye and journeyed through Italy to board the same military transport that was carrying her future husband back to the States. It was a choppy springtime voyage, through the Straits of Gibraltar and across the Atlantic in lashing winds. On a wet, chill May morning, they arrived in New York, cleared customs, and hurried across town to catch a noon train for Washington. They felt that they had set something of a record in their dash through baggage examinations and dock congestion. Fast as they were, the news wire-photo service was faster. Long before the four-hour run of their express train ended in Washington's Union Station, General and Mrs. Eisenhower were passing judgment on an arrival picture in an afternoon paper. It was windblown, to say the least.

But when the train arrived, and Mrs. Eisenhower took one look at the tall, slender, hatless girl, wrapped in a polo coat, who swung gracefully from the steep steps, she warmed instantly. "Beautiful! Beautiful!! *Really* beautiful!" said her heart.

Shy almost to the point of diffidence, Barbara edged around behind John. The General announced, "Barbara, you're not a bit rain-soaked like the girl they photographed this morning." Then they all laughed, and after that there weren't four happier people in all the world.

"Ike and I loved Barby on sight, and she loved us—it was as simple as that—and every day we love each other more," said Mrs. Eisenhower, a good five years after her son's marriage.

The wedding was simple. Lieutenant John Eisenhower and his bride might have been any of the countless young service couples who have exchanged vows in the plain pine interior of the Fort Monroe chapel. There was no bevy of bridesmaids, no profusion of flowers, no yards of satin ribbon, no platoon of ushers. Barbara, in traditional satin and lace, a white orchid on her prayer book, and John in a summer tan uniform, his left breast bright with service ribbons, stood alone and spoke their pledges. The only special feature was the participation of the Fort Monroe choir, whose fine voices gratified the senior Eisenhowers' love of choral singing, and the only exceptional occur-

253

rence was a mishap to Mrs. Doud. When she turned aside in the crush of guests at the reception in the Officer's Club, a step-down was hidden from her and she fell, snapping her wrist.

During the autumn and early months of winter, General and Mrs. Eisenhower had something more to occupy their minds. John and Barbara, home-making in a small walk-up apartment at West Point where he was instructing in English, were expecting an addition to their family. On the last day of March, a new Dwight David Eisenhower emitted his first cry, and Mamie Eisenhower moved over into what she called the "grandmother department." She showed noble restraint by staying in Washington the first two days of the young man's life, "so his mother could regain her strength before relatives swooped in." Newsmen were permitted to take a bedside family portrait. Well-swaddled David was not revealed then as being without question a third generation Eisenhower, complete with grin and bright blue eyes. His Grandmother Mimi (Mamie had become Mimi to Barbara; she says she chose the diminutive because it reflects the light spirit and youthful quality of her mother-in-law) left a small tissue-wrapped package for David. Inside was a christening dress and slip, garments she had stitched with care for her first-born son, "Icky."

The photographic record of David's infancy always produces family chuckles, especially from "Nana," his great-grandmother. Mrs. Doud never laughed more than during the 1952 campaign, when pictures of round-faced, bald-headed babies appeared in magazines and newspapers with captions claiming that this or that infant was a double for General Eisenhower. She granted that many babies vaguely resembled the General, but the dead-ringer of them all continued to be David, then a sage four-year-old with crew-cut hair who was his grandfather all over again, feature for feature, even to gait and thrust of shoulders. Baby David's wide grin and steady gaze made him an amusing small edition of the General; today, the child is a serious and interesting counterpart of his grandfather, evincing the same sharp, decisive mind, the same quick temper mastered by self-restraint.

Mrs. Eisenhower is convinced that David's mannerisms are the unconscious result of mimicry. She points out that John Eisenhower grows to be more and more like his father; consequently, David has plenty of opportunity, even when not within eye-shot of his grandfather, to pattern himself after the General.

As she praises Barbara Eisenhower for being "a mother of surpassing wisdom and infinite patience" in having brought David along as an unspoiled, obedient child who shows loving consideration for his two younger sisters, Mrs. Eisenhower says she still doesn't know how her daughter-in-law managed to keep a tight rein on David during the year-and-a-half his father was in Korea.

Except for six weeks in 1949, a period when his mother was in New York for the birth of his younger sister, David's visits with General and Mrs. Eisenhower have been of short duration, though frequent. At summer's end in 1953, all three children stayed at the White House and were "good as gold" while their parents shifted household belongings from Highland Falls, New York, to Fort Benning, Georgia. Major Eisenhower, then just back from Korean duty, agreed that the children would be better off romping around the White House during the excitement of moving. There was also the matter of security. The President's grandchildren are guarded by the Secret Service, and the upset would have left too many opportunities for unidentified strangers to gain access to the New York premises.

Vigilantly protective of her grandchildren, Mrs. Eisenhower says that her mind was eased for the first time in six months when the Secret Service began guarding David, Barbara Anne and Susan on Inauguration Day. Throughout the campaign and after the election, she had been fearful about Barbara and the children, living alone in the small Highland Falls house with only Julia, their black Scotty dog, for protection. But Barbara, calm and unruffled, lasted it out. In spite of a constant procession of doorbell-ringers and a telephone that was never still, she managed to keep her house in order, cook for her three hungry youngsters, and keep them happy and amused without any outside assistance.

Mrs. Eisenhower and the General resolved to make their Christmas gift to Barbara that year one which would reflect their abiding love and respect. Mrs. Eisenhower shopped the New York fur stores, finally selecting an all-enveloping beaver coat. "No mother was ever more entitled to a fur coat than Barbara," she said. "I've never heard her complain once about being tired, or raise her voice to the children, yet from dawn into the night she almost never had time to sit down. Her house was always spotless, she even waxed the floors herself; and she had time for gardening. She is dedicated to her family—do you wonder I worship her!"

All this is far ahead of the story. General Eisenhower had reached a momentous decision concerning his future in the course of a visit to West Point in 1947. During his day-long tour he met with the trustees of New York's Columbia University and agreed to retire from active military service, in order to become president of the University early in 1948.

Laconically, the General told his wife that there hadn't been much to talk about, since the trustees took his acceptance for granted. For weeks before, he and she had weighed the future carefully and felt that his identification with a great institution of learning would afford him the best chance to develop his ideal. The presidency of Columbia he evaluated as the logical place to carry out his firm intention to serve America and humanity through the education of youth. The University's international roster of students and its location in the metropolis that would soon be headquarters for the United Nations, were factors that helped harden his conviction. He expected to spend many active years at Columbia, exerting leadership in a field he believed would benefit from his experience of military negotiations with world powers. He went to Columbia to work for enduring world peace and for clarified understanding and confidence between nations. It was on this high note of hope that the General and his wife bade good-bye to Army life.

As early as March 1948, when the General and his wife had moved into their new home, a hue and cry began all over the country to draft the General for the Republican Presidential nomination at the Republican National Convention scheduled in June in Philadelphia. Strong in his friendship for Governor Thomas E. Dewey of New York, who was considered the most likely contender for the nomination, General Eisenhower was firm in his rejection of political pressure that sought to place his name in nomination. The General was not insensible of the surge of confidence in his ability to head the nation; it was primarily because he felt Governor Dewey's political experience and achievements would make for better leadership, that he withheld himself. He told his wife this repeatedly.

Far from being saddened by severance from a lifetime of military routine, the Eisenhowers entered the new cycle in a spirit of fresh adventure. There was only one drawback—and that was domestic; Columbia's president lived in a four-story, completely furnished dwelling. Mrs. Eisenhower thought the big stone house at 60 Morningside Drive delightful. There was every comfort, including an elevator. Antiques abounded in the large formal rooms; the upstairs quarters were arranged in suites, and the penthouse afforded a dramatic view of the city. If it could only have been empty, or even partially equipped, so that she could live with her own belongings! All she was able to take to their new abode was her piano, her paintings and pictures, a few small tables, and the General's glass-cased decorations.

Mrs. Eisenhower entertained many famous and prominent people in the Morningside Drive house, but she did so without any of the formality of her predecessor, Mrs. Nicholas Murray Butler. At Mrs. Butler's receptions, always a thousand or more strong, the term "white-kid gloves" was to be taken literally by her guests. Her dinners ran to many courses—perfect food, prepared and served to her exacting requirements. Mrs. Butler's luncheons and teas were tailored to the same scale; she was a hostess of the old school who did things magnificently.

Mrs. Eisenhower discontinued the big receptions, substituting small dinners or informal buffet-supper parties, where there would be a chance for the General and herself to mingle and talk with all guests. She dressed, as always, with exquisite taste, usually wearing wide-skirted gowns of exceptional elegance, but her easy, lively personality far overshadowed her clothes. Royalty from abroad, the Far East as well as Europe, and many civil figures of international importance dined with the Eisenhowers in an atmosphere of proper protocol, for Mamie Eisenhower's Army training kept her sensitive to such matters; but she dispensed hospitality without rigid self-consciousness. The great, the near-great and just plain people, all went away feeling that she and the General were genuinely glad to extend hospitality.

It is the same now at the White House. At state dinners and receptions, the President and Mrs. Eisenhower take a lively interest in every guest. After a recent reception, when over fifteen hundred persons passed down the receiving line, Mrs. Eisenhower later described in detail a pair of earrings worn by one woman guest and called her by name.

From the time General Eisenhower became Chief of Staff of the Army, he was asked repeatedly by artists to sit for portraits. He did not mind posing briefly for photographs, but felt he could not spare the time for the many sittings required to complete a portrait. At Columbia, on his wife's urging—she particularly wanted John to have a good portrait of his father as a family heirloom—the General gave in and agreed to sit for Thomas E. Stevens. From the start he enjoyed the experience. Tommy Stevens was taken in promptly as a friend, and from the preliminary sketches on through to the final phases, the portrait was executed under the best possible circumstances of intimate association. Mr. Stevens insisted on doing a companion portrait of Mrs. Eisenhower, thereby setting in motion a chain of events that prompted the General to take what he called "a flyer at painting."

During his close association with Winston Churchill, the General had been impressed by the British statesman's absorption in painting as a means of relaxing from official cares. He envied Sir Winston's talent, but had never thought there was a spark of creativeness within himself. Mrs. Eisenhower believes that the idea to try painting first occurred to the General during the sittings for Tommy Stevens. She remembers that he inquired into the technicalities of composition and line and the application of color; but at the time she presumed he was just making conversation agreeable to the artist's interest. It never entered her mind that her husband aspired to paint. If he had taken up tatting she couldn't have been more surprised, so daring was this departure from his regular hobbies of outdoor sports, bridge, and reading. Somehow, she has never thought of cooking as a hobby with the General, possibly because of the long years when he literally out-cooked her at preparing everyday family meals.

His actual resolution to paint came abruptly, at the conclusion of his wife's final sitting for her portrait. The General had been lounging in a chair, watching attentively while Tommy Stevens retouched expression lines around the eyes. The work was being done at Mrs. Eisenhower's bedside. She was laid up again with a bronchial disturbance; but, wanting her picture finished in time for a Christmas gift—along with the General's portrait—to John and Barbara, she tied up her hair with a ribbon and did her best to sparkle as a subject. After the last brush stroke, Mr. Stevens began to collect his paraphernalia. As he prepared to scrape the blobs of pigment from his palette, however, the General put out an arresting hand, remarking quietly that it seemed a shame to waste good paint. If the paint was going to be thrown away, General Eisenhower wondered if he could have it for— well, experimentation. Tommy Stevens glowed with pleasure and started immediately to transfer the oils to a scrap of cardboard. He said he was tickled—really tickled—and would leave the residue paint, some extra tubes, a bottle of thinner, and several brushes with one proviso—the General must promise to exchange his first finished work for the equipment. Laughing heartily, they shook hands on the deal.

The incident seemed all surface fun, except for a purposeful gleam in the General's eyes. His wife reads him like a book, and she knew this wasn't a bantering exchange. He was in dead earnest. Sergeant Moaney, the General's orderly, was sent to borrow a smock and easel from the art department of Columbia.

Mrs. Eisenhower becomes engagingly serious today—six years and many pictures later—when the subject of the General's hobby of painting is introduced.

"Ike paints well, awfully well," she declares. "I was struck dumb when I saw his first artistic effort; it was a portrait of me, done from a photograph—and it really looked like me. I hated to give it up, but it was promised to Tommy Stevens, who calls it the 'first treasure' of his studio."

When the General produced the portrait—he had done it in solitude—his wife knew he would be painting through the rest of his life. No man could be that good and not work at it. Valentine's Day was in the offing—the day she and the General always celebrated with gifts. Hadn't he shyly slipped an engagement ring on her finger on a Valentine's Day? So she consulted with Tommy Stevens and arranged to get all the material an artist working in oils would need. These she gave her husband on February 14, saying she hoped his "new love" would prove as enduring as herself.

"If Ike had stopped with just one picture, I would never have been the same," she says. "I knew he had found an unexpected and wonderful outlet for his store of creative energy."

In their own quarters in the White House, many fine pictures and portraits (including Mr. Stevens' latest of Mrs. Eisenhower, which she has chosen as frontispiece for this book) hang in the wide traverse upper hall; in the President's study and bedroom; in Mrs. Eisenhower's sitting room, and in the room at the northwest corner used by Mrs. Doud. But it is notable that the President's own pictures are conspicuous by their absence. His sister-in-law, "Mike" Moore, has a Colorado snow scene over the living room mantel of her home in Klingle Drive; a new portrait of grandson David is a feature of the upstairs sitting room of the "retreat house" at Augusta, Georgia; the Bobby Jones portrait hangs in the nearby clubhouse of the Augusta National Golf Club; but in the main, the President's pictures are not on display. Not that they aren't good enough. It is simply that in most cases he has presented his canvases, asking with typical modesty that they be considered "as personal as a snapshot."

Mrs. Eisenhower says she never knew her husband to be in better spirits than during this period. She was amazed at the amount of time he could spare for leisurely meals at the house, or in the homes of friends, and for relaxing hours at bridge. He always walked home at noon from his office in Columbia's Law Library; and then sauntered back for an afternoon of executive tasks.

For the first time in their married life, the Eisenhowers were free of a scrimping budget; the General's retirement pay, plus his Columbia salary, was adequate for saving and spending; and the prospects of royalties from the sale of the book assured a handsome nest-egg.

A sidelight may reveal much of the stringency of their 1948 finances, when the General left the Army after thirty-three years of serving in uniform. He was standing in a recess by one of the tall windows of the second-floor drawing room of the Morningside Drive house, gazing down pridefully at a large limousine at the curb. Turning to a close friend he said: "There you see all of the assets of the Eisenhower family on four wheels." He explained the remark by saying that when the Columbia job came up, he realized he would have to buy an automobile. The Army was allotting him Sergeant Dry as a driver, but there would be no car. He said he talked things over with Mamie, and they decided they would have to purchase a "good closed car that wouldn't crowd the chauffeur." He asked her if they could afford such a vehicle. Wait a minute, she said; she would look at the family check-book. There was just enough of a balance to swing the purchase.

As the friend who related this anecdote said: "I looked at the automobile and thought, 'Here we are, the richest of nations; yet the man whose military genius has kept our country intact had nothing more than an automobile to show for his lifetime savings.'"

One thing was sure—the car was paid for in cash. Mrs. Eisenhower has always steered away from the shadows of debt. She has never dressed beyond her means; the food bills are always kept in line; and even in the White House she still buys cautiously. She still is mistress of the family check-book. A few weeks ago, a certain Washington shop received a return envelope sent out with its monthly bills. In one corner in small script was "Eisenhower, 1600 Pennsylvania Avenue." Inside was a non-personalized check for the amount of the current statement drawn on a local bank in Mrs. Eisenhower's handwriting. It was amazing to the shopkeeper to realize that the First Lady literally pays her own bills, right down to sealing the envelopes.

"Think of the time she must give to settling her accounts— she must have dozens of monthly bills," said the recipient of the check. "How does she have the energy to bother with bills and keep up her heavy official schedule?"

Mrs. Eisenhower's sound money-sense has had a great deal to do with her family's solidarity. She has always been responsible for her husband's pay-check and she won't change now. "Family independence," she says, "is based on not owing anyone anything."

The first major investment made by General and Mrs. Eisenhower was the purchase of their Gettysburg place—a 189-acre farm and eight-room house overlooking Cemetery Ridge, the battleground where Lincoln delivered his immortal Gettysburg Address. The purchase was the result of an impulsive decision, the outgrowth of a coincidence. If they had not caught a certain train out of Kansas City for New York in 1950, and if their friends, Mr. and Mrs. George E. Allen, had not been aboard, Mrs. Eisenhower feels that she and the General would never have taken the step.

Aboard the train but a few moments, they were discovered by the Allens who occupied an adjoining compartment. A talkative Pullman porter had spread the news of General Eisenhower's presence. On through the dinner hour the two couples did a lot of "catching-up." The Allens revealed themselves pridefully as "Pennsylvania farmers," and raved about their Gettysburg place. "Simple country life—a place to wear old clothes and loaf," they said. Mamie and the General nodded, remembering well the green reaches of hills and fields, as well as the friendly folk of Gettysburg town, from their World War One duty at nearby Camp Colt. A nostalgic feeling overcame them. A farm in Gettysburg! A retreat from the helter-skelter of city living; a logical place to spend their sunset years.

When they separated from the Allens in Chicago, it was with the understanding that they'd drive up on the first free week end and see what farms were for sale. Meanwhile Mary Allen would find out quietly what farms were on the market. They agreed it would be senseless to prime local real-estate values by letting anyone know that General Eisenhower might become a settler.

The Gettysburg excursion was successful, and enlivened by comic undertones. In an attempt to keep the General's identity a secret, so that his wife could maintain her bargaining position if she saw a likely farm, they put up at a motor court outside Gettysburg, and then phoned the Allens, warning them not to mention names. Like conspirators, the couples hatched their plan in the cabin. The husbands would drift into town, while the wives drove off in the Allen car to look over the Raphael Redding farm on Cemetery Ridge, which seemed to be the best buy among local listings. The Allens recommended it as worth at least a quick once-over.

The wives arrived at the Redding farm just as the family were sitting down to an early supper, but the owner was glad to show them through the century-old brick house. It was most unprepossessing at first sight; a house that had been lived in hard, and a "carpenter and stone mason house" at that. The three-story structure was devoid of any architectural theme or line, but it was as solid and dependable as the generations of farm families it had sheltered. Mrs. Eisenhower quickly sensed the possibilities for remodeling, and she liked the sweep of countryside beyond the windows. She reviewed mentally the possibilities of a house-high wing on either side of the first floor parlor, dining-room and kitchen; that would allow ample downstairs living space, and would also permit expansion of the five bedrooms and one bath upstairs. The big kitchen actually "sold her" on the house; it could be reconstructed into a real "farm kitchen" with a fireplace and a dining area at one end. There would be plenty of working space for modern appliances, too, with which the General, when the spirit moved him, could prepare a meal.

She took in these impressions in a flash, knowing that it was her opinion of the house only that would count; her farm-wise husband would be the one to evaluate the report on the acreage that George Allen was prepared to make. The asking price was reasonable, and she felt confident about modernizing the farm homestead, if only the fields and pasture land would prove sufficiently productive to make the property self-supporting. A herd of twenty-two, pure-bred, Holstein dairy cows were offered with the property, along with over 500 laying hens, and farm machinery for cultivation of the wheat, corn and alfalfa land. Five cats were included. They lived mostly in the big red silver-roofed barn.

As the women drove back to rejoin their husbands for dinner in a small roadside diner, Mrs. Eisenhower was buoyant with lively plans. She was now busy envisioning a guest house for John and Barbara and the children. In another woman, this would have been hasty judgment; but her sharp scrutiny had taken in all the possibilities. If Ike approved, and the price was right, she was ready to go ahead with her plans.

264

The men reported that their Gettysburg sortie into several stores had resulted in recognition of the General and a sensation up and down the main street. They had fled by car to the diner and had been killing time feeding nickels to the juke-box from the privacy of a booth. Dinner was hurried. Anything to get away from the polite curiosity of the waitress, the counterman, the cook and cashier, and avoid the evening rush of customers. The Allen house on Emmetsburg Pike was still undergoing repairs, but the modernization of the old whitewashed stone homestead was far enough advanced for Mrs. Eisenhower to make note of all improvements. The more she saw, the more eager she was to get to work on a house of her own. The men talked land values and farming prospects. The General was of the opinion that the dairy herd might be increased for large-scale commercial milk production under the supervision of a capable tenant farmer. Time flew by in such exciting conversation, and the Eisenhowers were not back in their motel cabin until well after midnight.

As they were fumbling at their door in the dark, the beam of a flashlight fell on them. It was the manager. He peered closely into their startled faces, and then asked suspiciously if they were *really* General and Mrs. Eisenhower. For the life of him he hadn't been able to make out the scrawled signature on the register, but word had come out from town that the General had been seen in a drugstore. It was an absurd situation, carried off with great soberness by the General, who removed his felt turned-down hat and revealed himself without a word.

They did not revisit the Redding farm in the morning, but drove back to New York and consummated the sale through an attorney. They paid $24,000 for the land and buildings and $16,000 for the machinery and livestock. The deed was registered in Mrs. Eisenhower's name, the General maintaining that only the family's financial "wizard" could manage her budget so as to create the home of her dreams—the home that had taken thirty-three years to materialize.

Relying on his wife's judgment throughout the entire transaction, the General waited until several weeks after the farm's transfer before first setting foot on the property. It was then November. Mrs. Eisenhower was at the point of consulting an architect and the General was gathering information on dairy cattle. Happily they were looking forward to spring week ends in their home, when fate once more intervened. Russian aggressiveness had Europe fearful. Washington was waiting for the United States Senate to ratify American participation in the North Atlantic Treaty Organization, but cohesive military leadership of NATO countries would have to be developed. Only one man seemed right for the job.

NATO's Council of Foreign Ministers in agreement chose General Eisenhower to be Supreme Commander of Allied Powers in Europe. From headquarters to be located in a suburb of Paris, he would range out over free Europe. It would be a long and difficult assignment, in many respects as racking to mind and body as the war years. At least, this time, he would not be separated from his wife. NATO was prepared to provide a spacious furnished house for General and Mrs. Eisenhower, either in Paris or a suburb.

One more house—still not her own. Life seemed to be always one more strange house. Philosophically, Mrs. Eisenhower reflected that only clothes and knickknacks must be packed for this move. The real wrench would be years of separation from John, Barbara and the children; there was precious little chance that an Army transfer would uproot her son and his family from Fort Benning for another European assignment—unless his father went through channels. But that was something he'd never do. John was on his own, and he was as insistent as the General on a "hands-off" policy.

Sailing on a February midnight in the liner *Queen Elizabeth*, General and Mrs. Eisenhower could barely move about in their suite for the piles of *bon voyage* gifts. It had been a big and noisy send-off, so far as friends and family were concerned, but SHAPE's Supreme Commander was in a serious mood. As he commented to reporters on the dispatch of four Army divisions to Europe (which he called "a modest measure"), the General said emphatically: "The United States has no aggressive purposes and everybody knows it." He added that he, like the divisions, was returning abroad in "the hope that our job will be done soon and we can return."

The Eisenhowers stepped on French soil at Cherbourg after a cutter raced them through the harbor from the *Queen Elizabeth*. Formalities of welcome over, they flew to Orly Field, outside Paris, in a United States Air Force plane. The routine 225-mile hop found Mrs. Eisenhower in control of her nerves; and for good reason. This was her third flight within a month. A few weeks earlier, she had put up no argument when her mother backed the General's suggestion that an air trip to Puerto Rico for a few days' loafing in the sun would do them all a lot of good. In addition to the gay, five-day vacation in the pleasant seclusion of Ramey Air Force Base, the 2400-mile flight over Caribbean waters gave Mrs. Eisenhower a veteran's confidence in aircraft.

"I made up my mind then, I'd fly whenever Ike wanted me to," she says, adding, however, that she balked at going by air to France because of uncertain winter weather. Too many vivid stories of iced-up wings and air turbulence had come her way, and she wished to avoid air sickness. Berth-bound during most of the *Queen Elizabeth's* crossing, she said she guessed there was no way to win against winter elements on the Atlantic.

Huddling over an electric heater in the splendor of her six-room suite at the Trianon Palace Hotel in Versailles, Mrs. Eisenhower reflected on northern Europe's March and April wetness. She blamed her discomfort on being a "steam-heated American; we can't adjust to a room where the thermometer doesn't register up in the 70's unless we wear woolen underthings."

Her selection of Chateau Villeneuve l'Etang in the small 13th-century village of Marnesse la Coquette, halfway between Paris and Versailles, had not brought immediate occupancy of the picturesque two-storied country house that curved around a small artificial lake set in acres of quiet park. The French Government, anxious to transform the old chateau, used as a residence by Napoleon the Third and occupied later by Louis Pasteur, had loosed fourteen of the nation's leading decorators on it, to bring the many-windowed, wide rooms up-to-date.

The decorators had trouble coming to an agreement; one faction demanded modern impressionism throughout the house, the other side insisted on traditional tapestry, brocade and gold. While the argument was raging, Mrs. Eisenhower (who had very positive ideas of her own that were neither impressionistic nor traditional) remained neutral. The experts compromised at last; the rooms would combine the traditional and the modern. Speaking through an interpreter, Mrs. Eisenhower explained tactfully that so long as her wishes were followed in her bedroom, the decorators could have *carte blanche* for the rest of the house. She requested green walls with a faint overtone of blue; gladiolus-pink draperies; a slipper chair covered with gold-hued fabric; and lighter pink hangings in the bathroom. So that there would be no mistaking the keynote colors, she produced a piece of plywood, postcard size, painted the shade of green to be matched; also she showed them several pink-and-gold swatches of drapery material. The color guide was battered and cracked from long use; it had been her "traveling companion" many years, brought out for comparison whenever a new bedroom was to be decorated.

Mrs. Eisenhower made only one major change after the chateau was furnished; a long wall in her bedroom was covered with mirrors. This was done to create the illusion of greater space and light.

"A cozy, closed-in bedroom depresses me," she says. "I like to awaken and feel surrounded by sky and trees, with the sun pouring in."

Official and personal invitations bulked up her mail, but she and the General sent regrets to all but a handful. "We were not in France for social life," she explained. "Ike couldn't possibly have worked so hard, and gone out evenings." Often they had SHAPE people in for dinner family style and cards afterward, with an occasional formal affair for diplomatic and military figures. Mrs. Eisenhower might not have been in France so far as the French public was concerned. She did no shopping in Paris, attended no big functions such as an opera gala, or exhibition openings, nor was she an honor guest at luncheons or teas. But her days were anything but empty. There was always a stack of mail to be answered, and household accounts required tallying, along with the run-of-the-mill work like menu-planning and food-ordering. Dolores and Sergeant Moaney, and Rose Wood were the mainstays of her staff, but they had difficulties, chiefly in the use of the French language.

Mrs. Eisenhower was not content to be surrounded entirely by impersonal belongings, for she had every expectation of living several years in the chateau. She bought a few fine small tables —they were traditional; filled the library shelves with new American publications; replaced pictures with canvases chosen by the General and herself; and added many more lamps and flower vases.

Her friends felt that she improved the character of the imposing rooms. Margaret Thompson Biddle, who grew up in Paris and now has a gem-like house in the Rue las Cases, was of the opinion at first sight that Mrs. Eisenhower rescued the chateau from "exaggerated décor" and gave the rooms "exactly the right, lived-in feeling." On later visits she saw even greater evidence of what she termed "Mrs. Eisenhower's talented sense of rightness."

The luncheon at which the house was viewed was an all-American party, except for Madame Jacqueline Patenotre, chic and beautiful French senator, with a Philadelphia grandmother. Mrs. Eisenhower's mother, just in from the States with her daughter Mrs. Moore, and Caroline Walker, wife of General Walton Walker, were staying at the chateau. General Gruenther's wife Grace (he was deputy to General Eisenhower at SHAPE), and Marion Norstad, wife of Air Force General Lauris Norstad, the officer responsible for American air participation in NATO, completed the circle of intimates.

Instead of playing bridge, the eight women quit the large dining room with its angular modern furniture (the single hark-back to tradition being a priceless Savonnerie carpet underfoot) and went exploring through the upstairs rooms. Mrs. Eisenhower's enormous pink-covered bed—she prefers an oversize bed, so she can spread out her "office" on the wide expanse when working mornings on her mail—dominated the room. Other sleeping rooms were in blue, rose or yellow. All had at least one deep lounge chair, and a well-placed reading-lamp. An abundance of drawer and wardrobe space was concealed in the beautifully crafted furniture. Some pieces were mahogany; others dull-rubbed walnut, or beige enamel with gold. Only one room, used by the General as a study and studio and already filled with reference books, painting gear and family photographs, was in rich deep tones of masculine heartiness and a contrast to the other chambers.

The view of the lake and rolling lawns from the salon was picture-perfect through the large windows, bordered by sun-yellow draperies. Purplish-maroon covering—"eggplant" more clearly defines the color—was used on a sofa and several chairs. Other upholstered pieces, arranged in conversation groups, were tapestried, or showed modest accents of dull yellow, blue, lavender or pink. The white plaster walls made the pieces of burnished wood stand out in sharp relief. In Mrs. Biddle's words, the stylized room, without relaxation for mind or body, was saved by the cozy-corner feeling of the card-room library, invitingly evident through double doors at the rear of the salon. Outside, behind a side terrace, a barbecue pit, set in a rocky depression, was available for the General when he felt cooking-minded and had time to grill steaks.

In his firm-handed attempt to rebuild the defense of Europe through NATO, General Eisenhower traveled over the Continent, and to Great Britain many times, by air. His new plane, a Constellation named "Columbine" for Colorado's state flower, was "comfortable as a big parlor" in the opinion of Mrs. Doud, who was more than ever an ardent advocate of flying. When a flight was in prospect for Frankfort, Amsterdam and Stockholm, Mrs. Eisenhower agreed to go, provided her mother and sister made the trip. "Mama was the first one packed," said Mrs. Moore. "Mama is always packed ahead of everyone else when there's a trip to be made; she'd rather travel than eat."

The Frankfort stopover brought reunion with a very old friend, General Thomas T. Handy, and the women of the party had a flurry of shopping in the Army Post Exchange. Mrs. Eisenhower lingered at the magazine counter, while her mother and sister priced cuckoo clocks. Aside from reading matter, their purchases were nail-polish, plastic kitchen gadgets, paper napkins and other small notions not readily obtainable in France. It was more the fun of looking over the stocks of American merchandise and German souvenirs, than of buying, that took them from counter to counter.

The "Columbine" put down at Amsterdam's Schipol Airport by prearrangement, so that the Netherlands Army could welcome General Eisenhower officially. The state dinner was anything but an ordeal. Mrs. Eisenhower, who had entertained Prince Bernhard, Queen Juliana's consort, in New York, and liked his stimulating wit and unpretentious manner, found him just as delightful in the palace surroundings. The Queen joined in her husband's hearty welcome. After dinner, when the women gathered for coffee, the Queen, as knowledgeable about contemporary America as if she had just returned from a visit, discussed the variation in rules for canasta.

Mrs. Doud's Swedish heritage—she was born Elvira Carlson, not many years after her father settled in Boone, Iowa—asserted itself during a lively musical interlude that followed a royal dinner in Stockholm. Seated at a small table, with a daughter on each side, Mrs. Doud yielded to General Eisenhower's urging and started singing Swedish folk-songs. Before Mamie and "Mike" quite knew what was happening, they were singing too. While the applause was still ringing, Queen Ingrid moved to the table. With shining eyes, she held out her hands, telling them over and over how good it was to know that Swedish blood literally sang in their veins.

Within a few weeks, Mrs. Eisenhower and her mother

boarded a commercial plane at Orly Field for New York. Too sad that night to be conscious of the black Atlantic far below, the General's wife reclined in an extended seat beside her mother, watchful and tense. Papa was gone. Papa had died, pen in hand, at his desk in his small workroom at the top of the stairs in his Denver home. Working to the end; living his creed, "today's work today"—that was John Doud. Though he must have sensed the numbering of his days when doctors barred the exertion of travel, he never slackened.

"Papa died as he lived, keeping his affairs in order," says Mrs. Moore. "Papa was supremely self-sufficient. No one ever shouldered his responsibilities. Not many men of eighty have shown such stubborn faithfulness to duty, but Papa's strong mind drove his strong body."

It was a great blow to Mrs. Doud not to have been within sound of his voice on his last day of life. She had gone to France certain that he was hale and well. Scorning to be tragic in grief, Mrs. Doud turned instead to comforting her daughter, and her fortitude made easier the adjustment to death. Nor did she waver even when the day came to draw the blinds and turn the keys of her home over to a caretaker. It was needful to her peace of mind to close away those memory-crowded rooms and return to France with Mamie. A woman of sense as well as sentiment, Mrs. Doud knew that the healing effects of time would be swifter if she and her daughter stayed close.

By early autumn of 1951, the growing "Eisenhower for President" boom was reflected in stacks of letters from the United States that were delivered daily with Mrs. Eisenhower's breakfast tray. The mail reached deluge proportions after the General returned on November 7 from a three-day official visit to Washington on NATO problems. He had failed to give newsmen the faintest clew as to his political intentions. Strangers as well as friends wrote to his wife, begging her to use her influence and persuade him to announce his availability as a Presidential candidate. Touched by the confidence in her husband's greatness and the admiration expressed, Mrs. Eisenhower's pen raced through chatty, conversational notes of appreciation, which stated frankly that now, as in all matters affecting his career, the General would make his own decision. Until he decided what course to pursue, she was in the dark like everybody else.

"While Ike was making up his mind, he talked a lot about the sincere support of people who wanted him to be a candidate; but until he convinced himself it was the right thing to do, he never once so much as hinted he might run," says Mrs. Eisenhower.

As Mrs. Eisenhower describes it, her husband sat in the night's quiet and told her he would seek the nomination because he saw clearly that to withhold himself in a time of national crisis—and the next election would most certainly be a critical turning point in American history—would be to fail in his duty to humanity. Looking straight into her eyes, he said this; his deep voice strong, his powerful fingers curled tensely. She, who knew better than anyone the depth and sincerity of his convictions, was carried outside herself in the realization of the travail he had gone through to reach this decision. A man long used to the heavy load of command authority, he had fully evaluated the all-consuming responsibilities of the office of President. Some men might seek the power and prestige of the Presidency for the very human desire of establishing a place in history, but enduring fame and great honors were already the General's portion.

He spoke of the difficulties ahead. Political life was a public life, arduous and without privacy; sometimes it was exasperating; always it was a relentless drive, night into day, day into night, working with people, for people. It would be hard, very hard. Disappointments would be bound to come, but if they took all this on as a team they would be twice as strong as if he tried it alone. The General said that he was entering the race to win. It was going to be a tough fight. He had been in tough fights before, but in this one they would both have to learn a new set of signals. He guessed no two people knew less about politics

273

than themselves, but if they kept their minds fixed on winning, he had no doubt of the outcome. The best was going to be required of them, the best they could give.

The General told Mamie that he knew he was asking a lot in expecting her to put aside her lifelong disinclination to be seen and heard beyond the confines of their home. This was essential, however; if she stood beside him—literally, on stages and platforms—he couldn't help but do his best. Before her lips could shape a reply—she was about to say "Of course, I'll do anything you want"—her husband revealed the reason behind his political determination. If for no other reason, he said, he should regard the task as a service to be rendered their own grandchildren, to say nothing of hundreds of millions of other little ones, born and yet unborn. In the world's condition of danger to peace and freedom because of Soviet aggression with its threatened enslavement of minds and bodies, adult persons had a duty to secure for all children a legacy of reasonable trust and understanding among all peoples.

"Right then and there I knew that Ike's abiding love for all children had been the force that influenced him to seek political leadership," says Mrs. Eisenhower. "I was so proud he wanted my help. I knew it would be hard to change from a home-body, but I was perfectly willing to alter my life if and when he received the nomination."

On January 6, Senator Lodge of Massachusetts, one of the original "Eisenhower for President" backers, called a press conference in a Washington hotel and told a roomful of reporters that General Eisenhower's name would be entered in the Republican Presidential primaries in New Hampshire. There would be no campaigning by the General, since he was forbidden from active political affiliations by military regulations, Senator Lodge said. Later, if nominated at the Republican National Convention, the General could be expected to resign from NATO and return home and campaign as a civilian. Next day, reporters in France interviewed General Eisenhower and learned that he approved the placing of his name on New

Hampshire ballots. He also revealed that he belonged to the Republican party, thereby setting at rest the old rumors that he was an opposition Democrat.

In March, General Eisenhower won the New Hampshire primaries. His roster of convention delegates grew steadily as party voters in other states followed the example of New Hampshire.

Mrs. Eisenhower began to note signs of restiveness in her husband. He ate mechanically, talked little and then with rapid intensity, and was without laughter. Not by any means as calm as her behavior indicated, his wife knew they shared the same irritation. Professional politicians at home were out to give the General a lacing. They were calling him a "ghost candidate" who had no real interest in running for office. Furious over the false allegations gaining ground at home, the General's anger began building. This was his first taste of political insinuation, and he raged that anyone doubted his given word. He knew, without his backers warning him, that the only way he could offset his opponents' tactics was to get out of uniform and go home and start campaigning. After several days of transatlantic phone calls to people whose advice he valued, plus sit-downs with a group of his supporters who had flown over to review the situation, the General did an abrupt about-face. He scrapped his original plan to remain aloof from pre-convention politics, and wrote the Secretary of Defense on April 11 that he wished to resign at once. He would return to the United States immediately upon the arrival of his replacement at SHAPE. Next day he announced these intentions to newsmen. That night he ate with relish, and spiced his dinner conversation with his customary humor.

Appointment of his successor, General Matthew B. Ridgway, then Far Eastern Commander with headquarters in Tokyo, came within two weeks. A month later, General Ridgway was in Paris, ready to take over.

During the period of waiting, none of the days had enough hours for Mrs. Eisenhower. When she thought back to other hectic times in her life, she realized she had never really known what it was to be busy. Now she was up early and to bed late, and was thriving on the heightened tempo. As usual, her mail, though a molehill compared to her husband's mountain, was her first concern. Besides letters to be answered, there were many gifts to acknowledge. Total strangers, supporting the General's candidacy, were sending everything from "Ike" buttons to bedspreads. In her fine, slanting script she expressed a bubbling appreciation for every remembrance. The words came straight from her heart. Behind every kind letter, every gift, she recognized that someone who esteemed her husband wanted her for a friend. From Park Avenue apartments to Texas ranches, trailer camps to mansions, mountain cabins to suburban dwellings or farmhouses—why, here was all America before her, kind strangers who knew next to nothing about her, reaching out, saying "Mamie, we trust and believe in the man you married."

Mail was only one part of her life. Hardly a meal now without guests, and that meant extra planning. The farewell parties had started and there was—perish the thought—another job of packing to be undertaken. Things were left in place as long as possible, however, so that the chateau would measure up to the expectations of the many visitors who came tendering congratulations. The annual spring tourist rush was on; it seemed every American in Paris—or just passing through—clamored to meet the Eisenhowers. Only friends or those armed with letters of introduction got past the gate; even so the salon sometimes resembled a bargain-day rush.

As one correspondent put it, "to leave Paris without seeing the Eisenhowers was worse than missing the Arc de Triomphe."

The numerous going-away parties, from small women's luncheons to gala affairs given by the diplomatic and military staffs of member countries of NATO, had Mrs. Eisenhower changing costumes two and three times a day. No woman could be more clothes-conscious or careful of her appearance, but there were times when Mrs. Eisenhower laughingly envied the General his inevitable "brown ensemble." Uniform was Uniform—no stopping to pick the right hat, debate the color of purse and gloves, or worry about a neckline. It wouldn't be that easy for him much longer. At home, in civilian clothes, he'd have his daily necktie problem. The General is very fond of splashy neckties, although now he restrains himself to more subdued neckwear. His wife, who has ordered his civilian garb through most of their married life (she has her say, too, when his tailor comes around with suiting samples) passes up the noisy neckties, knowing from past experience that he'll be given plenty of the vivid variety for Christmas, Easter, and his birthday.

Far different from the gay social affairs that climaxed their residence in France was a solemn ceremony honoring General and Mrs. Eisenhower which took place on May 20, four days before they took the plane for Washington. In a small room in the Invalides, with less than thirty people present, they were invested with the highest awards of the Sovereign Military Order of Malta. This was an exceptional distinction. Not more than 5000 men and 500 women now living wear these orders, given for unselfish, dedicated service to mankind. Since the time of the Crusades, when the order was founded, membership has honored those persons who were motivated by high religious principles to liberate and unite nations in an accord of spiritual brotherhood.

General Eisenhower, on receiving the Grand Cross of the Order of Malta, the highest decoration of the order, was cited by Count Robert de Billy, principal Knight of Malta in France, as: "The famous soldier who saved civilization from servitude, restored to man his sense of values and rights, and brought to the liberated territories that which is better than military glory: freedom."

When Mrs. Eisenhower was invested with the Cross of Merit with Crown, Count de Billy said: "In France we could not possibly forget all you have personally added with your exquisite good will, delicate charm and intelligent kindness to the mission of the Commander-in-Chief of the Allied Forces."

In conclusion, the Count declared: "The Cross of Malta has

always been worn by women of remarkable nobility, not only of blood, but of heart. No one better than yourself could wear this cross, which it pleases us to regard as the emblem of your noble soul and generous heart."

Too overcome to speak, Mrs. Eisenhower reached for her husband's hand. The General looked into her eyes and smiled his concurrence and devotion. Instantly she regained her composure and turned a shining face to Count de Billy. Margaret Biddle, present during the ceremony, recalls that the glad humbleness of both General and Mrs. Eisenhower brought tears to the eyes of everyone.

"We knew we were seeing into the souls of two very great people who have always been joined by high and sacred ideals of duty to each other and the world," she says.

All Mrs. Eisenhower would say about her honors as a Dame of Malta, was: "It was more wonderful than anything I expected or deserved; I came away from France with new strength of purpose."

Chapter 13

THE UNITED STATES
1952

Air-conditioning was only partially responsible for the chill in the large gold and white private dining room in the Blackstone Hotel in Chicago. The frigid atmosphere intensified as the room filled slowly with women delegates and wives of delegates arriving from the opening session of the Republican National Convention, held that morning in a massive auditorium out near the stockyards.

The one o'clock luncheon, arranged in honor of the wives of men seeking the Presidential nomination at the convention, was held up almost an hour by congested street traffic. It was ordinarily a twenty-minute ride from the auditorium to the Blackstone, but most of the guests sat three times that long in cabs and buses, stopping and starting under the blazing sun. Trickling in by two's and three's, weary, wilted, wrathful and hungry, the women were much too upset to be selective about tables. Plumping into the first vacant chairs in their path, they started crunching bread and butter and uptilting water tumblers. Thirst slaked and immediate hunger appeased, they began taking stock of the candidate affiliations of their table-mates. Friends or enemies were quickly identified by the buttons and badges pinned on every breast. From narrow ribbon streamers to saucer-sized buttons, each guests was touting a favorite contender.

If the table-seating had been by opposing camps, the room might have conveyed less of the pantomime effect of an armed camp. Allies seated next to each other conversed *sotto voce*. Cross-table communication between matching badge and button-wearers was a matter of raised eyebrows, sniffs, open smirks, and eye-rolling in the direction of the "enemy."

At this point, the story of Mrs. Eisenhower becomes personal to the author. I was one of those who watched and waited. We newspaper women sitting at the press table had come to Chicago expecting battles on the convention floor and during committee caucuses, but we weren't prepared for this display of partisanship, of outright daggerishness, at an invitational social gathering. We speculated on what sort of reception awaited the candidates' wives. In a situation like this, silence would be truly a golden, precious thing. The audience, on the other hand, looked capable of engaging in hissing and bellowing.

The atmosphere thawed momentarily under a spatter of applause as the honor guests finally filed toward the speaker's table. The only candidate's wife in the line-up of congresswomen, senators' wives and national committee-women was Mrs. Eisenhower. She drew prolonged hand-clapping from those bedecked with "We Like Ike" buttons. In a black suit and white hat, with pearls at her throat, she looked incredibly young and carefree for a woman facing her first political audience. And what an audience! Her "never-miss-a-thing" eyes roved the tables. Seeing a familiar face, she gave a quick flip of her right hand in "hello." After being seated she reached around a table bouquet and shook hands with several women who rushed forward with greetings. Far from being impressed with her graciousness, the women who opposed General Eisenhower's candidacy turned glacial faces in the direction of plate-bearing waiters. As the meal progressed, except for sprightly conversation at the speaker's table the large room was voiceless. The clinking of silver on crockery showed that the audience was at least finding satisfaction in food.

Introduction of the distinguished guests was timed for dessert and coffee. Mamie Eisenhower was last to rise. She made a bobbing bow and was about to resume her chair when a voice rang out "Speech!" With a full-throated laugh that conveyed her amusement at anyone's thinking her capable of a speech, she leaned forward, turned a hand toward one of the congresswomen, and nodded, as if to say, "There's someone who knows her public speaking."

Her naturalness was captivating. The glowering opposition came to life and suddenly was openly curious about the happy, good-looking woman with the infectious laugh. There was a chip-chirping of surprise, and amid a general ignoring of campaign buttons women were asking and answering questions. "What's her name!" "Mamie." "Where's she from?" "Iowa—good solid stock." One matron asserted, "I thought she'd be tall and dowdy and taken with herself—most Generals' wives are."

Hedda Hopper, Hollywood columnist, was a speaker. As a preface to her remarks, the former actress, noted for wearing extraordinary hats, stepped around the head table and brought up the sides of her skirt like a fan so that the audience could read, in large red letters stamped on the green yardage, the name of her choice for the nomination. It was not General Eisenhower. She got a big hand and lusty cheers. Wise in stage ways, Miss Hopper waited for quiet, then went back to her place at the speaker's table. In a well-trained voice she began to lower the boom on all candidates competing with her favorite. With each quip about candidate Eisenhower, she ducked her head in Mamie's direction and met laughing, joking eyes. Everyone else at the head table was the picture of mortification.

Whispered betting started around our press table as to which would end up the better actress. Mamie Eisenhower, for a political amateur, was certainly absorbing the punches like a veteran.

At the end of the Hopper heckling the luncheon broke up in confusion as the audience crushed toward the front table to shake Mamie's hand or get a close-up look at this stranger to politics. She and Miss Hopper now seemed to be having a great joke that wound up on Mamie's, "Let's get together sometime."

Later, in one of the corridors, Miss Hopper said, "That Mamie's quite a woman. I thought I'd make her sore, but instead she asked my pardon for laughing and told me how she loved the long-stemmed rose on my hat, even if it did bob up and down every time I nodded my head."

So much for the preliminaries. Mrs. Eisenhower was scheduled for a main event at five o'clock: the "Citizens for Eisenhower Committee" was giving her a press reception.

The party, planned to give Mrs. Eisenhower a chance to meet and chat off-the-record with some seventy-five local and national news women covering the convention, got out of bounds when over half the women scribes showed up with photographers. The unexpected guests were flustering but not really displeasing to the reception committee, who were glad of this first opportunity to get their candidate's wife in close range of so many news cameras. Their problem was how to fend off the elbow-to-elbow crowd in the small Blackstone parlor without hurting any feelings, so that the photographers could get camera range. While the committee debated what to do, word reached reporters waiting around in the fifth-floor Eisenhower campaign headquarters that it looked as if Mrs. Eisenhower's first press conference was about to take place downstairs. Not wishing to be beaten by the women on such an assignment, most of the newsmen decided to investigate. Then the in-fighting began. The more combative women demanded that the men go back where they belonged. With lordly indifference the interlopers ignored the testiness and shouldered past the women to see what was brewing on the refreshment table. The committee, refusing to be referees, disappeared with a couple of cameramen.

Fifteen minutes passed, with no signs of an armed truce. Then, over the babel, a woman, standing alone and unnoticed in the doorway, said, "Sorry to be late." Like a subway crowd at the rush hour, the stampede began. Far from being discomfited, Mrs.

Eisenhower spoke up, saying good-naturedly that she wanted to meet everybody—so wouldn't it be a good idea if they spread out so that she could mingle? With everything under control, she was wedging her way from one group to another when a tall, grey-suited man, holding high an elephant plastered with red roses, yelled, "Hi! Mamie—look what I've got!" He worked his way from the door to where she was standing close to a mirrored wall, and they joined hands. Mrs. Eisenhower instantly satisfied inquiring eyes by introducing Governor Dan Thornton of Colorado. Cameramen yelled, tugged and shoved in a vain attempt to dislodge reporters. Here was the best shot of the afternoon—candidate's wife, elephant symbolic of the Republican party, Governor from her home state. Great picture, if only the reporters would stay out of camera range for five minutes. But the reporters wouldn't—no telling what pearl of news the Governor might drop.

Tempers rose with the temperature, for the air-conditioning was incapable of providing bodily comfort for the packed-in humanity. Mrs. Eisenhower was the only cool person in the room. As crisply fresh as when she arrived, she ignored the brawling and talked in a light vein with the Governor. A solution to the impasse came when a committee member reappeared with the good news that an adjoining room had been set up for pictures. The photographers scrambled out, followed by Mrs. Eisenhower. Governor Thornton, for his part, looked as if he had had enough press relations for one day.

Some twenty of the quicker-thinking and more muscular reporters darted down the hall and got into the picture parlor before the door was closed. They stood flattened against the walls, well out of camera range. Posed on a sofa, under blinding and very hot lights, Mrs. Eisenhower seemed to be taking her adventure without a trace of timidity. When the lights snapped off, questioning began. Reporters wanted answers on everything, from whether the General whistled when he shaved to how often she "baby-sat" with her grandchildren. It might be her first press conference—and an impromptu one at that—but she was not caught off guard. With a veteran's deftness she turned her replies away from personal ground. Whip-quick, too—and in quotable phrases. The news men and women, finding her a gold-mine of copy, were loath to let her go. A reporter's speculation that Mrs. Eisenhower, as an Army wife, wouldn't mind too much having her son Major John Eisenhower leave shortly for combat duty in Korea, brought a look of disavowal to Mrs. Eisenhower's face.

"I am an Army wife and mother, that is true," she replied. "Like the mother of every other veteran in that dreadful war, I will be anguished every minute he is gone. No woman, no matter how many times she has waited for a loved one at war, becomes used to the empty uncertainty."

In a following question, she was asked how she felt about the General's chances of winning the nomination. Quietly, with great force and honesty she declared, "I know that whatever happens will be for the best."

At last a Washington correspondent signaled the break-up of the conference with a polite, "Thank you, Mrs. Eisenhower." Rapidly, but with no effect of haste, the small, blue-gowned woman rose from the sofa, said that it had been nice to make so many new friends, and then observed that she had better be getting back to say good-bye to the many people waiting in the reception parlor.

So much for Monday. Through Thursday, Mrs. Eisenhower stayed in the big, cool corner suite located at the far end of the hall from fifth-floor campaign headquarters. Her mother was with her constantly; others of her family and relatives would come in for luncheon or dinner or for a few hours before the big television set in the living room. She saw little of her husband. When he was not occupied by campaign strategy meetings in his office, he was shaking the hands of the well-wishers who congregated throughout the day and far into the night in an improvised foyer in front of the elevators.

The uncertainty of the days of waiting sapped Mrs. Eisenhower's vitality. Television reported intimately everything that was happening in the convention hall, and the aggressive antagonism of those opposing her husband's candidacy struck deep at her sensitive nature. Right will prevail, right must prevail, she told herself while she watched and listened to the hard fight put up by the General's defenders. He, too, was shocked by the mounting fury of the personal attacks on his character and ability, but his crowded hours held little time to see the televised scenes of tumult at the convention hall that were so upsetting to his wife.

John Eisenhower and his wife and children were staying with the younger Mrs. Eisenhower's family at nearby Fort Sheridan. John was in and out of the hotel, trying to raise his mother's spirits. The General's five brothers were also in town, and Mamie's sister "Mike." All of them tried to mask their cold fury over the attacks with a lightness that fooled neither the General nor his wife.

After Thursday's night television viewing of the wind-up convention session before the start of balloting next morning, Mrs. Eisenhower dragged herself to bed too spent to join the family in a midnight snack. Her head was poker-hot; she felt log-heavy and wounded to the heart. Everything had been said, everything had been done against her husband in what news commentators called "the bitterest political convention in generations." But she was not without hope; Ike had made a clean-cut fight, steadily picking up support among the 1206 delegates who would vote the next day. It was still a big gamble, but she put her trust in the fair-mindedness of the men and women to be polled.

Friday, July 11, was a day of glaring heat, but it was cool and dark in the bedroom where Mrs. Eisenhower lay, almost insensible with pain from a stabbing headache. The General, up early as usual, was in a philosophical frame of mind, carrying no apparent grudge after the week-long assaults of his political enemies. Objective always in his outlook, he was ready to meet destiny without rancor, with a renewed peace of mind. Knowing that his wife's illness was the result of suspense and would only be aggravated by words, he considerately left her alone.

When Rose Wood took in a bedside tray, Mrs. Doud went in

to see her daughter. With a minimum of conversation she settled down by a half-raised blind and began reading newspapers. Mrs. Eisenhower tossed for a while, then dozed off. At eleven-thirty, whirs and duck-quackings from the next room announced the focusing of the television set on a channel carrying the opening of the convention, and broke her rest. The living-room viewing had been set up like a stag party; she could hear her husband and his five brothers indulging in—of all things!—a good-natured ribbing of each other. Agreeing with her mother that if the door were opened a crack it would be less harrowing to hear clearly word-for-word than to guess at the muffled television sounds, Mrs. Eisenhower backed herself with pillows and prepared to listen. Mrs. Doud spread a tally sheet from one of the newspapers and sat ready to tabulate the state-by-state voting.

Beginning with Alabama, polling of the delegations from forty-eight states proceeded in alphabetical order; Alaska, Hawaii, and the District of Columbia, Puerto Rico, and the Virgin Islands were at the bottom of the list. Tediously, often with maddening interruptions from the floor when someone demanded individual polling of a delegation, the state roll-call dragged on. After an hour, simple arithmetic showed a swing, but no landslide, toward the General's nomination. Two hours passed, another ten minutes, and still the Eisenhower count was nine votes short of victory after the Virgin Island delegation spoke out. For an eternity of seconds the television set hummed on; there was no sound from any of the Eisenhower men; Mrs. Doud and Mamie were scarcely breathing. Then *whack,* like a giant's fist on fate's door, came the pounding of the convention gavel as the chairman called for order, and bawled out, "The chair recognizes Minnesota." A ringing voice shouted, "Minnesota wishes to change its poll, giving Harold Stassen's 19 votes to General Eisenhower." The crash of sound that followed drowned all transmitted voices—there was only the thwacking gavel vainly calling the convention to order.

Now the Eisenhower brothers spoke over the noise of the broadcast, shedding their pent-up anxiety in brusque phrases.

Mrs. Doud beamed at her daughter; Mamie's eyes were suddenly as blue as the bow on her hair band. The door swung back. General Eisenhower, soldier-straight, smiling but grave of eye, looked questioningly at his wife and asked if she had heard Minnesota's shift. Mamie managed a nod. Mrs. Doud stood quickly, gave her son-in-law a squeeze, murmured that watching was better than listening to television, and stepped into the living room, closing the door behind her.

Before the final tabulation for the nomination, many states followed Minnesota, recalling original polls and giving their votes to General Eisenhower. The official total announced by the convention chairman was 845 victory votes, and a roaring cataract of human jubilation ensued that no amount of gavel-pounding could bring to order. Finally, on a signal from the platform, the band loosed a brassy deluge. It sufficiently quieted the howling crowd and enabled the chairman's voice, greatly magnified over the loud speaker, to be heard calling for a recess until half-past four.

Mrs. Doud, practical always, was first to speak after the television set was snapped off. She glanced at her watch and suggested that since it was nearly two o'clock it might be a good idea if lunch was ordered. Everybody should be fortified for what looked like a big afternoon and evening. The General, who had been drinking coffee all morning, left for his office. His brothers also begged to be excused. Mrs. Eisenhower called goodbye from the bedroom. She was reviving by the minute, she said, and would soon be up.

By late afternoon, when the convention reconvened and went quickly into the business of nominating Senator Richard M. Nixon of California to run as vice president on the Republican ticket, Mrs. Eisenhower was up and dressed and in front of the television set. She was groomed with utmost care. A blue taffeta dress, full-skirted and snugly bodiced, set off her fair skin and glinting grey hair. A white hat, with matching purse and gloves, were in the bedroom, to complete her costume when the General should return and be ready to leave. Ahead was a big test for the wife of the just-named Presidential candidate. She was to accompany her husband to the convention hall and appear on the platform while he formally accepted his nomination. A woman who had never been on a stage would shortly be facing 15,000 victory celebrants. All her life she had avoided crowds; even sitting in a theatre made her uneasy, through an aversion held over from childhood agony when her beloved kindergarten teacher's life had been snuffed out in the Iroquois Theatre fire, in Chicago.

Absorbed in watching the screening of the convention session, Mrs. Eisenhower did not relive the past, nor fear the future. "I knew going out to the convention hall was the beginning of my new duties as a candidate's wife," she says. "I was easy of mind and determined to do what Ike and everyone who believed in him expected of me."

The appearance of General and Mrs. Eisenhower in the massive hall had all the dignity of a great ceremonial. Slowly they walked down the center aisle; Mrs. Eisenhower, on the General's arm, was cradling a sheaf of cerise "Eisenhower roses." Under the wild acclaim that greeted her husband she was church-solemn, a gentle smile on her face, her blue eyes fixed on the platform far ahead. Once on the platform, she stood back with a group of convention dignitaries and watched the General. He moved forward, arms upraised in his familiar good-will gesture when facing crowds. He was flushed and happy, but sober-eyed; sincere gratitude and not high exultation was evident in his manner. At the height of the howling ovation he dropped his arms, swung around and reached for his wife's hand, pulling her gently into the brilliant pool of the spotlight. She bowed in a half-curtsy, repeated it several times, then withdrew until she was again merged with the background spectators.

Without a prepared text, General Eisenhower spoke briefly. There was more thunderous applause. Again he brought his wife forward and she repeated her deep bows. The band struck up, and, a shade less serious now, they retraced the center aisle and entered their car. As the limousine inched away from the curb between rows of blue-shirted policemen, General Eisenhower sat well forward, so that he could speak through the open windows of the rear doors. Turning from side to side, his right hand in half salute, he said pleasantly, "Good night, gentlemen."

As one officer said afterward, discussing the surprise effect of the farewell, "I've been lined up in front of big shots hundreds of times, but none of them ever gave me the time of day before; and none of them had half as much on their minds. That guy's got something, being polite to us fellows."

To Mrs. Eisenhower it was the most natural thing in the world for the General to bid farewell to men on guard. "Ike's done that all his life," she said. "As an officer it was his first duty to be considerate of his men, so of course he wouldn't overlook the policemen."

In no more time than it took to drive back from the convention hall, a small group of the General's close associates were being shown into the hotel sitting-room of the newly nominated candidate, for the first round of congratulations. There was no special excitement in the General's voice; he seemed so everyday they couldn't believe their ears. Mrs. Eisenhower was also calm; a hostess always, she suggested "high tea" to tide everyone over until the late dinner hour. Over protests that she should "not trouble at this big moment," Mrs. Eisenhower quietly ordered cold soup and sandwiches, reminding her guests that the General had also missed out on a "proper" lunch. Once the salient events of the morning's vote and the roar and thunder of the platform appearance of the General and his wife had been reviewed, he switched the conversation to food. Weren't his guests as hungry as he was? When they admitted eating "hot-dogs" he grunted. A well broiled steak—that's what they needed. He stressed "*well broiled*," saying that only a barbecue fire did justice to fine beef, and one of the men, who shared the General's hobby of cooking, asserted that the best steak could be ruined by bad seasoning. True, true, replied the Republican nominee for President, and for a good five minutes he discoursed competently on his steak-seasoning procedure.

One of his guests said afterward: "There sat the man who had just accepted his party's highest political honor conversing easily and happily about his hobby. It gave us deep insight into his character; he knows how to relax and restore his balance after a hard fight."

On Sunday at mid-day the Republican candidate, his wife and mother-in-law flew to Denver. The chartered commercial plane also carried political advisers and aides who would help set up advance campaign headquarters in the Brown Palace Hotel. A suite had been set aside there for the Eisenhowers, but they decided that living at home with Mrs. Doud would give them greater privacy and the comfort of familiar and loved surroundings.

A week later, the Democrats swarmed into Chicago and prepared to nominate a Presidential candidate. Their convention was mild compared to the bitter Republican battle, but it still had its moments of name-calling. Recalcitrant factions fell into line when President Truman arrived Thursday for the backstage maneuvering that resulted in the nomination by acclamation next day of Governor Adlai Stevenson of Illinois.

The hundreds of news men and women who had covered the conclaves packed up and went back to their home offices, to resume regular editorial duties or to be reassigned to one of the candidates' temporary headquarters (Governor Stevenson was working from his office in Springfield) to file stories on campaign preliminaries. I was sent by the New York *Herald Tribune* to Denver to do a series on Mrs. Eisenhower. Outside of a few inconclusive magazine articles, little was known about her personality and background. My newspaper felt that its readers should have full details about the wife of the Republican candidate. As the first paper in the country to sponsor General Eisenhower's candidacy for the nomination (this was back in October, 1951 at the closing session of the *Herald Tribune's* annual Forum, when Helen Rogers Reid, the paper's president, read the announcement that appeared next morning as a front-page editorial) my publication naturally wanted as many facts as possible on Mamie Eisenhower. And it was equally natural that Mrs. Eisenhower was glad to give as much time as possible to a *Herald Tribune* reporter who was also a friend.

In cool, mile-high Denver it was hard to believe that the Mrs. Eisenhower who sat stretched in a comfortable lounge-chair on the front porch of her mother's home was the same woman who a month earlier had appeared so solemn in the convention hall. Her feet were propped on an ottoman; she was wearing a blue-and-white-striped cotton sun-back dress, white sandals, and a ribbon around her head—the personification of an average American home-maker taking a morning respite from household chores. She was full of fun, full of reminiscence all the way back to her days as a bride, moving on then to witty observation of dozens of incidents shared over the years with her husband. Mrs. Eisenhower's animated face and lively gestures, the flawless perfection of her skin, her low rippling voice, were those of a woman youthfully alive with happy eagerness. It was impossible to believe that in a matter of months she would be fifty-six. Entirely without make-up except for lipstick, she could easily have cheated the calendar by two decades.

Conversation was not all in a light vein that morning. Looking beyond the porch rail at traffic-free Lafayette Street, she spoke softly of the recent leave-taking of her son John at the Denver airport when he departed for Korea, touching on this sad memory to illustrate the degree to which the General's entrance into politics had made their every move in public of noteworthy interest.

"Ike and I said good-bye to Johnnie surrounded by dozens of reporters and camera men," she said. "It was just as much a strain on him as it was on me—maybe more so; he knew at first-hand the awfulness of war. All the three of us could do was stand and stare until it was time for me to kiss Johnnie. Anything we might have said would have been news, the reporters all had their notebooks open. Even after Johnnie boarded the plane and Ike and I choked back our feelings while waiting for the take-off, flash bulbs went off. I don't blame the photographers, or reporters, they had jobs to do; it was just that we would have liked to keep our private grief to ourselves."

On successive mornings of interviewing (she liked starting at nine—"My mind's freshest when I first come downstairs") she gave me a complete word picture of her life and feelings. Though neither of us sensed it at the time, she was laying the foundation for this book. There were constant interruptions. She would be called to the telephone; mail had to be checked with her secretary, Mary Jane McCaffree—letters were coming in at 500 a day; there were conversations with unexpected callers and even housekeeping decisions. Should this or that go to the dry-cleaner, should a gift crate of fruit be opened?—these were typical details. Never saying "Where was I before that happened?" she always resumed narration from her last sentence.

One unexpected message, relayed by Mrs. McCaffree, said that the General hoped his wife would be at the hotel for lunch with a committee of women. Mrs. Eisenhower weighed the matter and remarked, "Goodness, that's a business luncheon—all politics. I think I'd only be in the way, so please say I'd rather not."

The secretary returned to the phone, then reappeared with word that the General had stressed its importance. If she could make it, he would be grateful.

"Oh, in that case Ike must have a good reason for wanting me. Of course I'll go," said Mrs. Eisenhower. With a look of pleasant bemusement she added "That's spur-of-the-moment Ike for you. He could just as well have warned me at breakfast—and not give me only thirty minutes to dress and get downtown." But in thirty minutes to the second, smartly turned out in a black-and-white cotton suit and white hat, Mrs. Eisenhower stepped out of the elevator on the second floor of the Brown Palace Hotel and walked to her husband's office.

There was an opportunity in Denver to see her surrounded by many of her 1914 classmates from Miss Wollcott's School. A picnic lunch beside the swimming pool on the estate of one of the Wollcott alumna was to be the scene of the reunion. Mrs.

Eisenhower arrived on the dot of twelve, promptness being one of her cardinal virtues. Baffled to find the house closed, she hurried to the rear and, leaning over a rail, called down "Here's Mamie!" to several women fussing over a buffet table in the lower garden. Setting her black high-heeled shoes carefully on each step, she descended slowly. Eleanor Wickenbaugh, her hostess, started to shake hands, but was promptly hugged instead. Ducking under an awning, Mrs. Eisenhower repeated this greeting after first calling each old friend by name. Afterward she admitted that she was terrified all afternoon lest she fail instantly to recognize her former classmates, many of whom she had scarcely seen since girlhood. But she never faltered. Her clues were the tone of a voice, an expression in the eyes, or some small gesture.

"Most people can remember if they try hard enough; I wanted very much to show that in spite of thirty-eight years I had not forgotten a single face, so I concentrated. If I didn't know at first glance, I would say, 'Don't tell me, let me guess,' and sure enough I'd catch some small characteristic that clicked in my memory," says Mrs. Eisenhower.

On the morning when Sergeant Moaney was due to leave the house for a few hours concerned with the all-important business of becoming separated from the Army, Mrs. Eisenhower called, "Moaney, come back here!" as she saw his khaki-clad figure flash down the driveway. The tall, slender colored man crossed the lawn and bounded up the porch steps.

"Now when you get all those papers signed and are a civilian, you go out and buy a good blue suit, like you promised," said Mrs. Eisenhower, with warm concern. The Sergeant renewed his promise, adding that he would bring the suit back on approval. After he left it was explained that his devotion to the General was causing John Moaney to leave the Army so that he could continue his eleven years' supervision of the General's belongings. The Sergeant was forgoing the accrued benefits of his many years of enlisted service rather than be reassigned to other duty, now that the General had resigned from the Army.

That, Mrs. Eisenhower said, was an example of loyalty you didn't come across very often. She and her husband had begged the young man to think twice before casting aside the perquisites and security of a sergeant's stripes, but they got nowhere. Sergeant Moaney was sticking by the General.

General Eisenhower's resignation from the Army had been a foregone conclusion if he won the nomination, Mrs. Eisenhower said. They had talked it over in Paris and agreed that he must cut all military ties if his name was on the November ballot for President. As a General of the Army, he was entitled to $19,541 a year inactive pay, a personal staff of five officers and enlisted men, and numerous other benefits. Upon resignation he assumed the status of any other non-disabled veteran; he was entitled to medical care and hospitalization and nothing more.

According to his wife, few things have affected the General as much as the farewell ceremony at the Pentagon on the day he resigned. He flew to Washington expecting to sign a few papers, shake hands with old friends, and slip away. Instead, his comrades through the years had arranged a formal review.

"I have never seen Ike look worse, or be more deeply moved, than he was the night he got back after the ceremony," recalled Mrs. Eisenhower. "He said that if he had suspected what was planned he would have had me along—our being together would have made it easier. As it was, standing in uniform and saluting for the last time the honor guard flanking his five-star flag brought such a rush of memories that Ike had to fight back tears."

She recreated the scene vividly: the General, his eyes fixed on rows of ruler-straight, marching troops; then his hand at his cap visor honoring the five-star ensign, his proud emblem earned during thirty-seven years in the service of his country. "Looking at the immeasurable sadness written on Ike's face when he described the farewell ceremony I made up my mind that there would be nothing he asked during the campaign I would not do," said his wife.

On August 24—it was a Sunday—the Eisenhower campaign

entourage, including press representatives, met shortly after breakfast on a little-used asphalt apron beyond the repair hangars at the Denver Airport. Two four-motored United Air Line transports were parked, waiting to take the party aboard for chartered flights to New York. Governor Thornton and other prominent Colorado Republicans, Denver news people, and some of Mrs. Doud's neighbors were buzzing around. There was plenty of handshaking and hand-waving for news pictures; then Mrs. Eisenhower, her mother and campaign staff filed into one of the transports. The General was last aboard, stopping at the door to wave and yell good-bye. As soon as the press plane filled up, both aircraft taxied out to a landing strip. The General's plane was first to be airborne.

The through flight to Chicago was uneventful and very fast in excellent flying weather above the 10,000-foot puff-ball clouds. The press plane let down first about four o'clock, coming to rest far down the field from the passenger terminal. It emptied quickly so that its occupants could line up and watch the companion plane come in. In less than ten minutes, the second transport touched down, rolled across the field, and swung into place beside its mate. As soon as the propellers stopped and men started pushing out the landing stairs, a four-year-old boy wriggled through an opening in the fence. He strode confidently across the concrete, just so far and not too far, then pulled up, arms akimbo, and waited. The plane door opened, and General Eisenhower appeared. The little boy whooped and made a bee-line for the stairs. They met at the bottom step. The big man scooped up his grandson David in a smothering hug, then pivoted so that the child could reach out and kiss his grandmother, who had followed closely. David's mother, carrying one-year-old Susan and watchful of three-year-old Barbara Anne galloping ahead, hurried toward the steps. There were more kisses, more hugs, in a happy mix-up of big and little arms.

Photographers closed in for the first news pictures of the Republican candidate and his wife with their grandchildren and daughter-in-law. One camera man called to David to kiss the General. He complied eagerly and was rewarded with an extra squeeze from his grandfather. Mrs. Eisenhower, snuggling baby Susan and bending down to talk to Barbara Anne, was all excited affection. During the half hour required for refueling she sat in a field office while the two little girls bounced and climbed all over her smart rose-and-black print dress.

David, walking around outside with the General, drew much comment. In features, in build and mannerisms—especially when walking—he was his grandfather in miniature. This was to be no brief interlude of hail and farewell between grandfather and grandson, for the children and their mother were also to make the air journey to New York.

Through the early weeks of September, the Eisenhowers lived in the reopened President's residence at Columbia. On most mornings the General was up with the sun and at his desk in his Commodore Hotel headquarters while mid-town Manhattan office-workers were still eating breakfast at home. His staff, nearly all of them volunteer workers, also kept long hours. Soon it would be time for their candidate to start cross-country campaigning, and preparation for the arduous tour was a complicated matter of planning details right down to the last whistlestop.

Mrs. Eisenhower was also loaded with work. Besides her secretary, three typists helped with the mail. While it was impossible to read and answer personally the average of 5000 letters arriving every week, Mrs. Eisenhower kept up the remarkable pace of dictating over seventy-five letters a day and of never going to sleep before she had signed all the day's mail, including letters written by her secretaries. As organized as any business executive but less formal, she dictated while in bed, often stopping to answer one of two telephones on her night table.

"I get up with letters, I go to bed with letters, I guess I'm what you'd call a well-lettered woman," remarked Mrs. Eisenhower, with bouncy humor.

She was also confronted with the problem of choosing a becoming and useful wardrobe for campaign travel. That was anything but easy; she needed many changes, and space aboard the campaign train would be cramped. She bought a few hats but no new dresses. The tight "pencil silhouette" was being introduced for fall, a style she considered unbecoming to her medium stature and most impractical for campaign travel, when she would be constantly in and out of trains, planes, and automobiles. Besides, everything she owned was perfectly good; after the election would be time enough to start buying new clothes for the winter season.

When the campaign clothing had been set aside, she reserved final decision until her husband looked over the collection. His interest in her clothes centered more on color than style. He has always been partial to all shades of blue, but detests red, a color she has obviously avoided. Her small bonnet and pill-box hats have rarely evoked his comment, but her fur jackets and coats have never been bought without his approval.

The rear car of the nineteen Pullmans, diners and club cars of the campaign special was for the exclusive use of General and Mrs. Eisenhower. It was there they lived and dined, greeted thousands of people, gave press interviews, and worked with their secretaries. A more compressed existence for two extroverts could not be imagined, unless it was the life in the cars ahead where several hundred news correspondents and photographers worked. Each day was geared to: Where are we going, how long do we stop? Rest, work and eating had to be fitted around the schedule. Five minutes gained or lost wasn't too bad; but let an hour's delay occur and the trainmen, press and campaign workers began to go slowly mad. The General's right-hand political strategists and corps of assistants led a similar life in their Pullmans, meeting up in the diners and lounge sections to trade woes.

The Eisenhowers' private quarters were no less cheek-by-jowl than those in the other Pullmans, the only difference being that their car had its own lounge, dining area, and the train's one shower bath. An observation platform opening off the lounge was often used when the General made impromptu speeches at whistle-stops, the rural stations or cluster of isolated country store and houses where people sometimes from a hundred miles around would gather to see the man who wanted to be President.

Five staterooms opened off the corridor connecting the lounge and dining room, every one such a space-saver that Mrs. Eisenhower dubbed hers "Mamie's Bird's Nest." Except for pictures of her son John and his family and a "good-luck" horseshoe swung from a light fixture, she had no place for personal belongings except in suitcases. The General's room was of the same meager proportions as his wife's green and brown quarters, and was next to the connecting shower bath. Mrs. Doud's room, on the other side of her daughter's, also had a connecting door.

Rose Wood slept next down the line, alongside the last compartment, which was her work room. It was fitted up with a pressing board and small iron, so that the clothes squeezed on the high rod over an unused berth could be made wrinkle-proof before each wearing. Stacks of hat boxes, drying lingerie and numerous pairs of shoes took up what little space remained. At least once a day John Moaney edged in as Rose edged out, so that he could press one of the General's suits.

For all these handicaps, life was merry. Though Mrs. Eisenhower stayed in the rear car, except for visits in cities and towns, she managed to project her fine spirits the length of the train. Always a systematic housekeeper, she promptly set up a routine in her own bailiwick. Train schedule in hand, she planned each day's food with the chef. Meals had to be served between stops. Dinner was sometimes as late as nine o'clock, and lunch was always cold buffet for everyone except the General. His wife insisted he would become run-down if he didn't have a hearty hot meal at noon. It did him no good to rebel; she always won the argument. But she was forced to retire in defeat when mouth-watering regional foods were sent in as gifts. Leaving Cumberland, Maryland, he spooned up big helpings of apple pan-dowdy; he made inroads in a two-foot pumpkin pie presented in West Virginia. All over the country it was that way: baked beans in Boston, fried chicken in Virginia, tamales in New Mexico, and smoked salmon in Seattle.

Only once was she pleased at seeing him eat a gift of food. In San Antonio, on the evening of his birthday, many of their retired Army friends now living within whistling distance of Fort Sam Houston climbed aboard, and "Bootsie" White produced a home-baked chocolate cake, with one big candle.

Gifts of fruits, flowers and candy would have reached astronomic proportions if they had been allowed to accumulate. Mrs. Eisenhower saw that a big "snatch" bowl was replenished daily from the baskets and crates of fruit sent to her and the General. She encouraged campaign workers and news people to help themselves in passing, asserting that plenty of fruit was health insurance. Boxes of candy were sent up through the cars and were handed out to children at wayside stops. All flowers not used on tables in the lounge and dining room were dispatched promptly, with parcels of excess fruit, to hospitals and to old-people's-homes at the next stop up the line. The General received many Bibles, but his wife was rarely given presents of a religious nature. Jewelry, perfume and hand-made articles were showered on her. A white crocheted sweater decorated with many emblems, including the American flag, was handed up to her on the observation platform by a California woman at a stop between Santa Barbara and Los Angeles. She replaced her suit jacket with the sweater, drawing whistles and yells from the crowd.

Crowds had been whistling and yelling for weeks at Mamie Eisenhower. Her most important role as campaign wife was her personal appearances with the General, not the "housekeeping" aboard the train. Her breezy way, her talent for personalizing people, created spontaneous informality the instant she was introduced—usually the General said from the platform, "I want you to meet my Mamie!"—and sent the greeters wild.

Silent before crowds, she talked readily to individuals or small groups. Hundreds of people filed through the train for handshaking every day; receptions, luncheons and banquets in big cities brought her into contact with thousands. During press and television interviews, local news people were fascinated with her grasp of regional affairs. As in her first press conference in Chicago, her comments were pithy and quotable. She averaged ten interviews a day, some in the train lounge, others in hotels or broadcasting stations, and never repeated herself.

She was also the delight of photographers, posing easily, not averse to "gag" shots as long as they were dignified. The over-sized four-leaf clover, engraved with "Ike," that she wore suspended from a thick chain around her right wrist was in focus in a great many pictures. She wanted it that way, remarking, "The luck of the Irish is no joking matter."

There was no sense of drive in anything Mrs. Eisenhower said or did, and she was in good health every minute of the trip. A sore instep caused by a tight new shoe was her only "ailment."

"I slept like a top, except on nights when Ike flew off on side trips. The bigger the crowds, the more people I met, the happier I became. Seeing thousands and thousands of people adoring Ike, believing in his leadership, kept me cloud-high all the time. Honestly I was never tired or worried, unless I thought about Johnnie in Korea," says Mrs. Eisenhower.

Did she anticipate victory for the General?

"Ike and I worked to win, but we counted on nothing. I never thought ahead until election day."

November fifth, the eve of the election, witnessed a thunderous final Eisenhower rally in Boston. Fred Waring, besides being master of ceremonies, directed his band and choir in stirring musical numbers. George Murphy, the motion picture star, was another celebrity who contributed talent during the evening. All of them were asked to ride back to New York on the wind-up trip of the campaign train.

It was well past midnight before the special pulled out of Boston. In the lounge in the rear car every chair was occupied, and high-strung conversation clittered and clattered above train noises. Mrs. Eisenhower caught the tension; everybody was like so many over-stretched rubber bands, worn out but wide awake and talking to eat up the minutes. That wasn't good. She took Fred Waring aside and asked if the four soloists from his choir would provide a little music—or was it expecting too much after the big evening? He replied that nothing was too much, not at a time like this. Easily, softly, the four trained voices broke into "I've Been Working on the Railroad," then wove in and out of dozens of songs, tender, humorous, sentimental. The minutes really took wings. It was very late when the last number, Stephen Foster's immortal "Swanee River," reached into the hearts of the now relaxed and drowsy men and women.

Next morning at seven, no one was exactly bright-eyed and sparkling, trudging up a ramp at Grand Central Station to face the day of days. General and Mrs. Eisenhower and Mrs. Doud went directly to the Morningside Drive house. One thought was uppermost in their minds, a hot bath. Well scrubbed and in comfortable clothes, they ate breakfast off trays in Mrs. Eisenhower's upstairs sitting-room. A quick run-through of the newspapers, and it was time for the candidate and his wife to dress and go out and vote. Mrs. Eisenhower was anxious to reach their polling place early. Briefed on the operation of a voting machine, she was still uneasy. During the migrations of post-to-post Army life, she had been either too early or too late to qualify as a resident voter. This would be her first experience in a voting booth.

Voting accomplished, the General left his wife at the house and drove downtown to campaign headquarters. Mrs. Eisenhower says that she marked time until he returned for dinner. She talked to no one, kept radio and television set silent, discarded newspapers; she found it impossible to concentrate on anything. Too tense to sleep, too weary to sit up, she went from bed to chair many times. Lunch tasted like straw. She did her nails, always an absorbing task for a woman, but that didn't take much time. Choice of an evening dress was also swift: pink taffeta overlaid with black lace, a gay garment for what she prayed would be a gay and victorious midnight.

She threw off depression and uncertainty when at last the elevator door slammed and her husband called her name. Instantly matching her mood to his, she was energy and gladness. They had dinner in the sitting-room, without benefit of radio or television—what good would newscasts do, it was still too early to discover the trend—and talked until the clock moved toward eight. It was time now to dress and be off to the Commodore Hotel to wait out the hours for the deciding election returns.

As she was fastening her pearls, Mrs. Eisenhower saw her husband, well turned out in evening clothes, reflected in the long dressing-room mirror. Now he was unsmiling, almost grim, and she turned quickly. He took her hands and said with spirit that she must remember, no matter what happened later in the evening, they had done their best and—he thanked her. They clung together wordlessly; then he turned away quickly to locate her mother and Caroline Walker for the drive to headquarters.

Early returns were an accurate weathervane for victory, but until Adlai Stevenson, the Democratic contestant, conceded defeat in the small hours of the morning, General and Mrs. Eisenhower refused to budge outside the small made-over bedroom they occupied on the sixth floor of the Commodore Hotel. Surrounded by thirty-odd people whom they held in close affection, in a room dimmed for television, they watched and waited. Mrs. Eisenhower had one of the few chairs; the beds had been pillowstuffed to serve as sofas, with the overflow of screen-watchers sitting on the floor. People with messages fumbled in and bumbled around unnoticed amid the cheers and racketing accompanying the rising tabulations in favor of the General.

After midnight there was no question who would be the next President of the United States: Dwight D. Eisenhower wasn't being elected by a whisker, he was winning by a mounting majority. At last came a flash of Adlai Stevenson's overdue statement, a signal for official celebration. In the hall, photographers blocked the Eisenhowers' departure for the ballroom "shindig." Pictures they asked for and pictures they got; then into an elevator hurried the President-elect and his wife, followed by two unobtrusive, lean young men who stood facing the door as the cage zipped down. The Secret Service was beginning its eternal vigilance.

The ballroom party had been building elation all evening; after twenty years of defeat, the Republicans really put their hearts into bellowing, screaming, and thumping. Once on the stage, General Eisenhower let the deafening noise roar unchecked, as he and his wife threw up their hands in greeting. Then he spoke his thanks, and Mrs. Eisenhower cut the high-tiered Victory Cake. It was a blinding experience of light, sound, and movement. Nobody quite knew what was happening, so great was the exaltation, and while the cake was being distributed the next President of the United States and his wife vanished from the dais.

The heavy glass-and-iron door of the Morningside Drive house swung open under the vigilant hand of John Moaney. Mrs. Eisenhower walked into the warm, familiar hall, then paused and turned to see what was delaying her husband. On the top step, he was saying "Thank you, gentlemen," to the lean, unobtrusive young men of the Secret Service.

Seventy-five days is a lot of days—unless you're planning to move into the White House. The crowded days of November slipped by almost unnoticed by Mrs. Eisenhower. She couldn't be blamed for this unawareness; she was buried most of the time under a blizzard of mail. A thousand letters a day—not a week—was the average as soon as the General was elected President.

"I answered what I could and signed the rest," she declared.

Impossible? You don't know Mamie Eisenhower.

In December, the nearness of Christmas slackened the mail and she had time to settle on costumes for the Inauguration: a grey suit for the swearing-in ceremony; a gown of pale pink, spilled over with brilliants, for the festive balls. Time also was available to make out holiday shopping lists and even to slip away for store-buying.

Christmas Eve would have been perfect, if only Johnnie had not been in snow-fast Korea. His wife was under their roof, his children called gladly through the halls, were kissed, cuddled and adored; the big tree's many lights sparkled on the mounds of packages on the living room floor; all was right, all was bright —for the children.

At mid-evening, the high, clear voices of carolers reached the house. Memories of her childhood, when she had made the rounds of neighborhood doorsteps on Christmas Eve, came flooding in, and Mrs. Eisenhower slipped into a fur coat and ventured out into the piercing cold. Clinging to her husband's arm, she listened to the young voices. What mattered the tearing wind? Overhead the stars shone clear, the same stars that spangled the heavens of Korea, she told herself.

Many gifts were given and received next day, but for Mrs. Eisenhower none was more wonderful than the General's remembrance, a gold bracelet with three heart bangles inscribed "David," "Barbara Anne," and "Susan." Her thoughts went back to his first Christmas gift thirty-seven years ago, the silver heart-shaped box, lined with green velvet and scrolled with her initials; it held her jewelry on her upstairs dressing table right now.

On Christmas Day the good health which had sustained Mrs. Eisenhower through the campaign deserted her. Sitting at dinner while the General carved the turkey, she began feeling ill. Hoping that it was nothing more than a headache induced by holiday excitement, she said nothing. By bedtime her feverish condition was obvious, and stabbing chest pains had begun. Immediate sulfa injections headed off serious trouble, but she was in bed for days, too weak even to hold a newspaper.

The last time I talked to Mrs. Eisenhower alone was less than a week before the Inauguration. She was still house-bound, and was drawing on her slender reserve of strength no more than necessary. In a pink, quilted dressing-gown cut Chinese fashion, she laughed and talked with her usual verve, explaining that she had begun to feel like a new woman the instant she heard the wonderful news that Johnnie was flying back for ten days' leave. While discussing with me his reluctance to leave his regiment (he had not felt he was entitled to any special privilege, but had been ordered back by the kindness of President Truman) Mrs. Eisenhower was told San Francisco was calling. She flashed out of her chair saying, "That's Johnnie!" and took the call in her bedroom. Ten minutes passed, and back she came, bright and vital. Johnnie had just arrived at Travis Air Base and was expecting to be eastbound in a few hours. He had called her first, asking if she would notify Barbara and say that he would phone his wife as soon as he had a confirmed reservation. So now Barbara had had the good news and was standing by, and would relay the information. With a chuckle, Mrs. Eisenhower said, "Johnnie certainly figured out how to make two calls do the work of three. Barby and I had a good laugh over his 'economy'."

On January eighteenth, two days before General Eisenhower became President, Mrs. Eisenhower had a final look around the Morningside Drive house, wondering if anything had been forgotten. It had been very difficult to remember, right down to the last book and water-tumbler, what was or was not University property. Earlier, when she had been in the midst of separating her possessions, Mrs. Eisenhower declared she had learned a big lesson and was labeling all articles to be shipped to the White House with a large "E."

"I'm not going through this mix-up again. When it comes time for us to leave the White House, I'll know exactly what belongs to us," she said.

The Eisenhowers, sitting in the first of several automobiles carrying family, friends, and aide, drove unnoticed to Pennsylvania Station. It was Sunday morning, and they used a side entrance to reach their special train on a lower level platform that was shut off from the public. Four hours later, on arriving in Washington, they were wildly cheered by people massed around an outer reserved vehicle enclosure. The motorcycle escort to the Statler Hotel cleared traffic so that the line of limousines could streak rapidly to the inside, always used when important guests arrive and depart. Ready access to the elevator just inside one of the doors made it possible for the Eisenhower party to avoid the jammed lobby.

305

All Monday Mrs. Eisenhower stayed in the big suite, checking the last details of the morrow's program. Rested now, and keyed with excitement, she had rousing fun entertaining relatives and friends at a progressive buffet luncheon that extended well into the afternoon. Her mind was at ease in all respects, except for a few nightmarish apprehensions concerned with the delivery of her pink ball gown. The elaborate garment had been hung in a tall wardrobe and placed in one of the motor trucks that was transporting personal baggage down from New York. It had been arranged that as soon as President and Mrs. Truman started the drive to the Capitol with General and Mrs. Eisenhower, the baggage truck and other vans carrying the "E"-labeled household effects from the Morningside Drive house would pull up at a White House delivery entrance and begin unloading. So long as the baggage truck wasn't side-swiped on the highway, or delayed by motor trouble, all would be well. Although to entertain such fears was to dread what was practically impossible, Mrs. Eisenhower was now regretting the size of the gown's container. She would have preferred keeping the dress in sight in a garment bag on the train. But this would have had elements of danger, such as crushing the gown from too much handling and from jostling it in and out of motor cars. The black suit to be worn to early morning church services on Inauguration Day, and the grey costume in which Mrs. Eisenhower would appear during the swearing-in ceremony, had traveled with her, safe in garment bags.

Wishing to be well rested for the demands of the next day, General and Mrs. Eisenhower secluded themselves early, ate a light supper off trays, and retired shortly after nine o'clock.

Long before the noon ceremony that would make Dwight D. Eisenhower President of the United States, the vast plaza on the eastern side of the Capitol was literally a sea of humanity. From the press section directly under the temporary columned portico where the oath of office would be administered, spreading back several hundred feet, all seats were occupied by eleven o'clock.

The bleacher-like seats fanning out on each side were also entirely occupied. Only the tiers behind the inaugural platform, reserved for members of Congress, for high government officials and the diplomatic corps, were still admitting guests almost up to the time of the ceremony. Mrs. Eisenhower and Mrs. Truman, walking together, were escorted last of all to front-row chairs close to the rostrum. Both wives shook hands with their near neighbors, then sat staring ahead.

The color guard marched in from one side; the band struck up "Hail to the Chief," and President Truman and General Eisenhower came down the steep center aisle. They had been delayed twenty minutes, and the anxious crowd had grown nervous.

History was swift. Chief Justice Fred M. Vinson spoke the clear, sober words of the oath; General Eisenhower responded faultlessly. As his deep voice ended, Mrs. Eisenhower, who had been battling successfully against tears, began to sink into her chair. Abruptly, President Eisenhower took the few steps that separated them. Grasping his wife firmly by each shoulder, he bent and kissed her cheek. She gasped with surprise, flashed him the briefest of smiles, and regained her composure. The tens of thousands of spectators who saw this unprecedented action buzzed excitedly; no President had ever publicly kissed his wife after taking the oath of office. In a flash of movement, President Eisenhower was back at the raised desk, ready to break another precedent. Instead of beginning his inaugural address, his first words as Chief Executive were a prayer to Almighty God.